Shaping the City

Shaping the City: Studies in History, Theory and Urban Design takes on important themes and debates in urban design and the critical ideas that have driven them in the context of particular cities, at important moments in their development.

This is a wide-ranging collection of case studies featuring a variety of perspectives in the field, with different styles and methods of inquiry. Included are studies of Chicago, Los Angeles, Detroit, Philadelphia, San Francisco, Brasilia and Atlanta and discussions of such themes as the Cybercity, the Asian Megacity and the New Urbanism.

The book should be of interest to students, scholars, or professionals who engage the city as both an idea and a design project. This is a new genre of textbook that relinquishes the traditional survey format in favor of in-depth studies of important issues in urban form, design, and theory. Each case study has been written by an author – a scholar, architect, and/or urban designer – who has demonstrated a depth of knowledge about the city and period under discussion. The various approaches to the different cities provide rich insights into the manifold processes that shape the city, and an introduction to the critical methods and tools used in describing and theorizing complex urban environments.

Edward Robbins is Professor II Urbanisme, Oslo School of Architecture, Oslo. **Rodolphe El-Khoury** is Chair of the Department of Architecture, Californian College of Arts and Crafts, San Francisco.

Contributors: M. Christine Boyer, Joan Busquets, Farés el-Dahdah, Rem Koolhaas, Richard Marshall, Edward Robbins, Mitchell Schwarzer, Paulette Singley, Richard Sommer, Charles Waldheim, Sarah Whiting.

Shaping the City

Studies in History, Theory and Urban Design

Edited by Edward Robbins
and Rodolphe El-Khoury

NEW YORK AND LONDON

First published 2004
by Routledge
29 West 35th Street, New York, NY 10001

Simultaneously published in the UK
by Routledge
11 New Fetter Lane, London EC4P 4EE

Routledge is an imprint of the Taylor & Francis Group

Typeset in Univers Light by Wearset Ltd, Boldon, Tyne and Wear
Printed and bound in Great Britain by TJ International Ltd, Padstow, Cornwall

British Library Cataloguing in Publication Data
A catalogue record for this book is available from the British Library

Library of Congress Cataloging in Publication Data
Shaping the city : studies in history, theory and urban design / edited by Rodolphe El-Khoury and Edward Robbins.
p. cm.
Includes bibliographical references and index.
1. City planning—Case studies. 2. Metropolitan areas—Case studies. 3. Cities and towns—History—20th century—Case studies. 4. Cities and towns—History—21st century—Case studies. 5. Sociology, Urban. I. El-Khoury, Rodolphe. II. Robbins, Edward, 1944–
HT166 .S399 2003
307 .1′216—dc21

2002156108

ISBN 0-415-26188-0 (hardcover, alk. paper)
ISBN 0-415-26189-9 (pbk., alk. paper)

Contents

Contributors

M. Christine Boyer is William R. Kenan Jr. Professor in Architecture, Urbanism, Princeton University

Joan Busquets is Architect Barcelona, Martin Bucksbaum Professor in Practice in Urban Planning and Design at the Harvard Design School

Farés el-Dahdah is Assistant Professor and Director of Graduate Studies at Rice University

Rodolphe el-Khoury is chair of the Department of Architecture, California College of Arts and Crafts

Rem Koolhaas is founder of the Office for Metropolitan Architecture

Richard Marshall is Associate Professor of Urban Design and Director of Urban Design at the Harvard Design School

Edward Robbins is Professor II in Urbanisme at the Oslo School of Architecture

Mitchell Schwarzer is a Professor at CCAC

Paulette Singley is an associate professor at Woodbury University

Richard M. Sommer is an associate professor at the Harvard Design School

Charles Waldheim is an associate professor and director of the Landscape Architecture Program, Faculty of Architecture, Landscape and Design, University of Toronto

Sarah Whiting is an associate professor at the Harvard Design School

Acknowledgments

The editors would first and foremost like to thank all the authors who contributed to this volume.

The editors and publishers also gratefully acknowledge the following for their permission to reproduce material in the book.

Rem Koolhaas, "Atlanta" © 1995, Rem Koolhaas and The Monacelli Press, Inc, was first published in S, M, L, XL, by Rem Koolhaas and Bruce Mau, The Monacelli Press, Inc, New York.

M. Christine Boyer, "CyberCities" was first published under the title 'The Imaginary Real World of "CyberCities," © 1996, M. Christine Boyer, in CyberCities: Visual Perception in the Age of Electronic Communication by M. Christine Boyer, Princeton Architectural Press, New York.

Special thanks also to Caroline Mallinder and Michelle Green for shepherding the book through its many stages and Sarah Wray for her patience and diligence in dealing with editors who were not always as patient and diligent.

Chapter 1

Introduction

Edward Robbins and Rodolphe El-Khoury

Cities are shaped in many ways. Economics, politics, society and culture all play crucial parts in this process. Whatever the forces and practices, cities are always the result of design. The design may be conscious and formal, undertaken by architects and planners, as in the case of much of Philadelphia, Barcelona, Brasilia and the Asian Megacities discussed by Richard Sommer, Joan Busquets, Farés el-Dahdah and Richard Marshall in their essays. Alternatively, it may be the result of informal cultural, social and economic practices, as illustrated by Paulette Singley in her discussion of Los Angeles, Charles Waldheim in his essay on Detroit and Rem Koolhaas in his discussion of Atlanta. Informal practices also create a new form of urbanism in cyberspace, so well depicted here by Christine Boyer. Design may be the result of social conflict, as described by Sarah Whiting writing about Chicago, or conversely it may be embedded in the search for the security suggested by Edward Robbins in his analysis of the New Urbanist City.

Cities also are shaped by the ways of seeing and understanding we bring to them. Depending on our experiences and our viewpoint, we come to see and understand cities differently. We in effect shape and design the same city differently. Even the same site can be seen through different lenses and experienced through different mindsets. These differences and the way they play crucial roles in the physical design of cities and the mentality through which we shape those designs is at the heart of the essays in this volume.

Urban design, as the essays also reveal, is not defined simply by the acts of urban designers, and nor is it limited to (although it includes) the formal acts of urban intervention taken by governments and by private developers.

Urban design is also the result of the actions taken by individuals and communities in their attempts to create a salubrious and supportive physical and social environment.

Cities are incredibly complex and textured. Any attempt in image, plan or text to fashion an easily ordered, unified and singular whole out of what is often a disordered, spontaneous, and almost infinite variety of places, people and practices parodies the richness of urban design and urban life. Within even one city there is a multiplicity of physical forms, social practices and cultural responses. Any attempt to examine and understand urban design is therefore presented with a dilemma. Much urban design is the result of governmental and institutional practices that attempt to look at the city as a totality, and to design with that totality in mind. Yet the city is also constantly being shaped at specific moments by particular local actions and developments. The essays in this book all grapple with this contradiction in a variety of ways. They recognize the complexity of the city, yet do not relinquish a sense of the totality and the importance of grand design.

Similarly, there is the contradiction wrought by time and history. On the one hand, every day the city is made and remade through the active workings of its inhabitants, by those who write about the city, and also by professional designers. More often than not we do this blithely unaware of the historical processes through which the city has come to be shaped. Nonetheless, that history provides the stuff upon which we act, even if unawares. Thus there is a contradiction between the way we often look at and act in our cities as though they are timeless and without any history, and the important roles that time and history play in setting the stage for our actions. Aware of the weight of history and the exigencies of the moment, the essays are strategically situated between history and theory. The critical interpretations and analyses they present provide avenues through which to rethink and realize urban design.

This book is the result of a series of conversations that we, the editors (one an anthropologist and the other an architect and urban designer), have had over the years about the shaping of cities and the making of particular cities and their parts. We felt that most books about urban design dealt primarily either with urban form as a kind of autonomous phenomenon or with urban design as a technical and professional practice. There was strong agreement that there was little in the literature that addressed the contradictions and dilemmas of urban design. We were certainly aware that there could be no one book about urban design that could claim to encompass the whole and all its parts. What we hoped we could do was present a series of essays that, in different ways and by addressing different themes, would provide an introduction to the rich variety and contradictions that are a part of the shaping of the city – i.e. urban design.

We wanted to address the rich variety of critical issues and approaches within urban design, which can be exemplified by different cities. We therefore asked the contributors to present visions and ideas of urban design associated with the different cities or historical moments that they have come to exemplify. The goal was to derive from the context vivid demonstrations of theoretical constructs in their physical and/or cultural manifestation; not exhaustive historical accounts or analytical descriptions of the cities themselves. Thus what follows are not complete descriptions of the urban design of particular cities, but a series of articles that epitomize the world of urban design for student, professional and layperson. Moreover, although it is critical to emphasize the variety and complexity of urban design, we need to be constantly reminded that there are a number of core issues that have persistently reappeared in the discourse about urban design. The essays in this book engage a number of those critical themes.

Central to much urban design is the belief that an understanding of the planning process is central to any discourse about the city, as in the work of Busquets and Sommer. Others would argue that there is a danger in an uncritical adherence to planning regulations, and this is addressed by Schwarzer. A number of the essays struggle with the tension between the plan and its reality. El-Dahdah reveals that what appears as a rigid plan provides a context for its mutation. Waldheim argues that what we see as an unstructured process for shaping the city is rather a highly determined result of the laws of capital. For Singley, the lack of structure is a problem of representation. What appears as an absence of plan is the result of methods of mapping that simply do not address this new form of urban design. Others deal with the implications of scale and size and the cultural and social assumptions that underlie them. Marshall discusses intoxication with "big," while Robbins addresses the reactionary infatuation with "small." Finally, a number of essays address how new economic realities and technologies challenge the very notions of urbanity and urban design as an effective practice. Koolhaas describes the erosion of traditional urban cores by suburban typologies, while Boyer raises questions about the extent to which cyberspace will transform the traditional city.

It is equally critical for the design of this book that different themes and ideas are associated with different styles of writing and presentation. Just as different theories of urban design are associated with different contexts, different ideas about urban design are perforce related to a variety of intellectual approaches and styles of writing consistent with those approaches. For some contributors a more formal and social scientific approach was appropriate; others preferred a more journalistic, plannerly or literary style. The variety is not accidental. It seemed to us, as editors, important to present a volume that not only encompasses the variety of forms of urban design, different urban contexts and different ways of understanding the shaping of the city, but also allows the reader to engage the range of stylistic and textual approaches that attempt in various ways to make sense of urban design. All the variety, though, leads to one theme: urban design and its role in shaping the city.

The cities represented in this volume were chosen opportunistically as vehicles for important lessons about urban design and ways of thinking about urban design.

Chapter 2

Atlanta

Rem Koolhaas

Sometimes it is important to find what the city *is* – instead of what it was, or what it should be. That is what drove me to Atlanta – an intuition that the real city at the end of the 20th century could be found there . . .

- Atlanta has CNN and Coca-Cola.
- Atlanta has a black mayor, and it will have the Olympics.
- Atlanta has culture, or at least it has a Richard Meier museum (like Ulm, Barcelona, Frankfurt, The Hague, etc.).
- Atlanta has an airport; actually it has 40 airports. One of them is the biggest airport in the world. Not that everybody wants to be *there*; it's a hub, a spoke, an airport for connections. It could be anywhere.
- Atlanta has history, or rather it had history; now it has history machines that replay the battles of the Civil War every hour on the hour. Its real history has been erased, removed, or artificially resuscitated.
- Atlanta has other elements that provide intensity without physical density: one building looks innocent from the outside – like a regular supermarket – but is actually the largest, most sophisticated food hall in the world. Each day it receives three cargo planes of fresh products from Holland, four from Paris, two from Southeast Asia. It proves that there are hundreds of thousands, maybe millions, of gourmets in Atlanta.
- Atlanta does not have the classical symptoms of city; it is not dense; it is a sparse, thin carpet of habitation, a kind of suprematist composition of little fields. Its strongest contextual givens are

vegetal and infrastructural: forest and roads. Atlanta is not a city; it is a *landscape*.

- Atlanta's basic form – but it is not a form – its basic *formlessness* is generated by the highway system, a stretched X surrounded by an O: branches running across the city connecting to a single perimeter highway. The X brings people in and out; the O – like a turntable – takes them anywhere. They are thinking about projecting a super-O somewhere in the beyond.
- Atlanta has nature, both original and improved – a sparkling, perfect nature where no leaf is ever out of place. Its artificiality sometimes makes it hard to tell whether you are outside or inside; somehow, you're *always* in nature.
- Atlanta does not have planning, exactly, but another process called zoning. Atlanta's zoning law is very interesting; its first line tells you what to do if you want to propose an exception to the regulations. The regulations are so weak that the exception is the norm. Elsewhere, zoning has a bad name – for putting things in their place simplistically: work, sleep, shop, play. Atlanta has a kind of reverse zoning, zoning as instrument of indetermination, making anything possible anywhere.

Atlanta has changed at an unbelievable speed, like in a nature film when a tree grows in five seconds. It reveals some of the most critical shifts in architecture/urbanism[1] of the past 15 years, the most important being the shift from center to periphery, and beyond.

No city illustrates this shift, its reasons and its potentials, better than Atlanta. In fact, Atlanta shifted so quickly and so completely that the center/edge opposition is no longer the point. There *is* no center, therefore no periphery. Atlanta is now a centerless city, or a city with a potentially infinite number of centers. In that way, Atlanta is like LA, but LA is always urban; Atlanta sometimes post-urban.

When I first went there in 1973, the notion of downtown in America was in crisis. Downtown Manhattan, downtown Boston, downtown San Francisco: the cores of most American cities were in total, demonstrative states of disrepair – crime, rotting infrastructures, eroding tax bases, etc. There was an apocalyptic atmosphere of downtown doom, doubt that they could ever be rescued.

But Atlanta was an exception. Construction was resuming in former disaster areas. Block by block, downtown was being recovered (literally, some downtowns looked like accidental checkerboards: half-full, half-empty) and actually rebuilt. Atlanta was the test case for an American renaissance, for the rebirth of the American downtown. And you can't talk about Atlanta's rebirth without talking about John Portman.

John Portman, artist-architect, is said to be a very rich billionaire, his story shrouded in rumors of bankruptcy. He works in offices crowded with his own Pollock-like paintings.

He is undoubtedly a genius in his own mind.

In a book on John Portman by John Portman, John Portman writes, "I consider architecture frozen music."

The lobby of his newest building downtown is a private museum for his own sculptures, gigantic homages to fellow artists such as Dubuffet, Brancusi, and Stella: megalomania as welcome.

John Portman is a hybrid; he is architect *and* developer, two roles in one.

That explains his tremendous power: the combination makes him a myth.

It means, theoretically, that every idea he has can be realized, that he can make money with his architecture, and that the roles of architect and developer can forever fuel each other.

In the early seventies, to a power-starved profession, this synthesis seemed revolutionary, like a self-administered Faustian bargain.

But with these two identities merged in one person, the traditional opposition between client and architect – two stones that create sparks – disappears. The vision of the architect is realized without opposition, without influence, without inhibition.

Portman started with one block, made money, and developed the next block, a cycle that then triggered Atlanta's rebirth. But the new Atlanta was a virgin rebirth: *a city of clones*. It was not enough for Portman to fill block after block with his own architecture (usually without very interesting programs), but as further consolidation, he connected each of his buildings to each of his other buildings with bridges, forming an elaborate spiderweb of skywalks with himself at the center. Once you ventured into the system, there was almost no incentive to visit the rest of downtown, no way to escape.

John Portman is also responsible for single-handedly perfecting a device that spread from Atlanta to the rest of America, and from America to the rest of the world (even Europe): he (re)invented the atrium.

Since the Romans, the atrium had been a hole in a house or a building that injects light and air – the outside – into the center; in Portman's hands it became the opposite: a container of artificiality that allows its occupants to avoid daylight forever – a hermetic interior, sealed against the real. Actually, the evacuation of the center implied by the atrium, the subsequent covering of the hole, the mostly cellular accommodation of its perimeter – hotel rooms, office cubicles –

make it a modern panopticon: the cube hollowed out to create an invasive, all-inclusive, revealing transparency in which everyone becomes everyone else's guard – architectural equivalent of Sartre's *No Exit*, "Hell is other people . . ."

Downtown becomes an accumulation of voided panopticons inviting their own voluntary prisoners: the center as a prison system.

Portman's most outrageous atrium is the Atlanta Marriott, a tour de force transformation of the slab – democratic, neutral, anonymous – which he splits in two halves, then eviscerates to bend its carcass into a sphere – as nearly as concrete permits.

This interior is not "frozen music" but "arrested maelstrom." Its accumulated architectural intensity is beyond a single perceptual grasp. Is the result of this convulsive effort beauty? Does it matter?

The new atrium became a replica as inclusive as downtown itself, an *ersatz* downtown. Downtown's buildings are no longer complementary; they don't need each other; they become hostile; they compete. Downtown disintegrates into multiple downtowns, a cluster of autonomies. The more ambitious these autonomies, the more they undermine the real downtown – its messy conditions, its complexities, its irregularities, its densities, its ethnicities.

With atriums as their private mini-centers, buildings no longer depend on specific locations. They can be anywhere.

And if they can be anywhere, why should they be downtown?

At first the atrium seemed to help rehabilitate and stabilize Atlanta's downtown, but it actually accelerated its demise.

That was Portman's Paradox.

The rediscovery of downtown quickly degenerated into a proliferation of quasi-downtowns that together destroyed the essence of center.

By the eighties, building activity had moved away from Portman's part of the city, north toward the perimeter highway, then beyond . . .

Atlanta was the launching pad of the distributed downtown; downtown had exploded. Once atomized, its autonomous particles could go anywhere; they gravitated opportunistically toward points of freedom, cheapness, easy access, diminished contextual nuisance. Millions of fragments landed in primeval forests sometimes connected to highways, sometimes to nothing at all. Infrastructure seemed almost irrelevant – some splinters flourished in complete isolation – or even counter-productive: in the middle-class imagination, *not* being connected to MARTA, the subway system, meant protection from downtown's unspeakable "problems."

The new program was usually abstract – offices for companies that were no longer tied to geography, fueled by an unlimited demand for insurance (cruel equation: hell for the insured – Elsewhere; paradise for the insurers – Atlanta).

Sometimes an area becomes suddenly popular. Attractors appear: it might be the proximity of a new, or even a rumored highway, beautiful nature, or comfortable neighborhoods. Attraction is translated in building. Sometimes the nature of the attractor remains a mystery; seemingly *nothing* is there (that may be the attraction!) – it might be the building itself. Suddenly clumps of office and residential towers spring up, then a church, a mall, a Hyatt, a cineplex. Another "center" is born, stretching the city to apparent infinity.

North of downtown there is a place where a highway starts to fork, leaving downtown behind. There is an area of nothingness, and beyond the nothingness you see outposts of a new architecture that has the intensity of downtown, but it's not downtown. It's something totally different.

In 1987, somewhere near here, two skyscrapers were built facing each other, one hyper-modern (i.e., clad in mirror-glass), the other almost Stalinist (covered in prefabricated concrete). They were built by the same firm for different corporate entities, each searching for its own elusive identity.

Two buildings, so close together, built by a single firm in opposite languages . . . A new esthetic operates in Atlanta: the random juxtaposition of entities that have nothing in common except their coexistence, or – favorite formulation of the surrealists – " the accidental encounter between an umbrella and a sewing machine on a dissecting table."[2]

I wanted to find out what kind of firm could design with such equanimity, what kind of firm could generate the same enthusiasm for such different architectures. So I made a tour of Atlanta's architects' offices.

They were usually located in idyllic situations – dense forests, hills, on lakes. Designed as corporate villas, they were large, sometimes very large: 250–300 people. The typical architect was a southerner, 26, laundered at an Ivy League school, who then returned to Atlanta to produce buildings like these two towers. They could generate an entire oeuvre in one afternoon – receiving instructions over the phone – then have it rejected without pain. They would plan symmetrical projects, then find them distorted overnight by economics – shrunk by failure, inflated by success – and have to perform adaptive amputations or stitch on additional limbs with the urgency of a field hospital: infantry on the frontline of an architectural panic.

The partners were very accessible and eager to talk about Atlanta, their work, the present situation, the dilemmas they faced – a cluster of issues that formed a very plausible argument for the emergence and consolidation of postmodern architecture, the only architecture, it seemed, that could be generated quickly enough to satisfy the needs of the clients.

In a situation where architecture is no longer the construction of city but, like a new branch of physics, the outcome of the dynamics of force fields in perpetual motion, that precious professional alibi of the architect – the mystical "spark" of inspiration – is obviously outdated. No one can wait for it, least of all the architect. His task is truly impossible: to express increasing turbulence in a stable medium.

Architecture has always equated greatness with the breaking of rules.

Now you can be great through their effortless application.

Only a postmodern architect can design building proposals of huge scale and complexity in a day, any day. Postmodernism is not a movement: it is a new form of professionalism, of architectural education, not one that creates knowledge or culture, but a technical training that creates a new unquestioning, a new efficacy in applying new, streamlined dogma.

Post-inspirational, past erudition, intimately connected with speed, a futurism, postmodernism is a mutation that will be from now on part of architectural practice – an architecture of the flight forward.

One of the offices I visited had a room: it was locked. Inside was a model of a large piece of Atlanta – particular features: none. Twelve people were working on four schemes, each as big as the Rockefeller Center, each composition hyper-symmetrical but placed arbitrarily on the huge map, surrounded by single-family homes; there was no sign of highways . . . At the last moment the table had been enlarged to make room for one additional Rockefeller Center.

The model was a complete inversion of metropolis as we know it – not the systematic assembly of a critical mass but its systematic dismantlement, a seemingly absurd dispersion of concentration. Alarmingly, it suggested that the elements that had once *made* the city would now cease to work if they got too close together. Spaced out, far apart, they needed the neutral medium of nature or (at the most) the single-family house to ensure further their noninterference.

The reason that the room had to be secret – the only vault in the otherwise open office landscape – was that none of the clients of these five centers knew that the other projects were being prepared. The architects believed that there were probably still other architects working on similar projects, maybe for the same neighborhood – in similar rooms in other offices – but nobody could really be sure.

This deliberate disinformation, lack of adjustment, represents a revolutionary reversal of the role architects traditionally claim. They no longer create order, resist chaos, imagine coherence, fabricate entities. From form givers they have become facilitators. In Atlanta, architects have aligned themselves with the uncontrollable, have become its official agents, instruments of the unpredictable: from imposing to yielding in one generation.

Working on the emergence of new urban configurations, they have discovered a vast new realm of potential and freedom: to go rigorously with the flow, architecture/urbanism as a form of letting go . . .

Atlanta is a creative experiment, but it is not intellectual or critical; it has taken place without argument. It represents current conditions without any imposition of program, manifesto, ideology.

As extrapolation, each site in Atlanta is exposed to a theoretical carpet bombardment of "centers," possibilities hovering somewhere, waiting to be activated by a mysterious process – only vaguely related to money – according to laws not yet identified, at least not by architects.

It is now possible, at any point in Atlanta (and Atlanta is just a metaphor for the world) to create a brutal, often ugly container that accommodates a wide variety of quasi-urban activities and to turn anywhere, with savage competence, into a point of density, a ghost of city.

In the future, a "realistic" frisson[3] about the periphery as a new playground for architects, a field of one-liners, will not be enough. If *the* center no longer exists, it follows that there is no longer a periphery either. The death of the first implies the evaporation of the second. Now *all* is city, a new pervasiveness that includes landscape, park, industry, rust belt, parking lot, housing tract, single-family house, desert, airport, beach, river, ski slope, even downtown.

Atlanta's is a conclusive architecture that will eventually acquire beauty. Sometimes there are prefigurations, occasional schemes that seem to intellectualize the new freedoms: a project by I. M. Pei for a chain of skyscrapers very close to the highway, causing short, stroboscopic sensations for passing cars, even at 55 mph.

Paradoxically, a more convincing premonition of this potential architecture is the prefabricated landscape that is being prepared to receive it. Atlanta has an ideal climate. Because it approximates jungle conditions it was used as training ground for the war in Vietnam. Everything grows there immediately and energetically. Landscaping carries authority, the vegetal sometimes more robust than the built. A thick tapestry of idyll accommodates each architectural appearance and forms its only context; the vegetal is replacing the urban: a panorama of seamless artificiality, so organized, lush, welcoming, that it sometimes seems like another interior, a fluid collective domain, glimpsed through tinted glass, venetian blinds, and the other distancing devices of the alienated architecture – *almost* accessible, like a seductive fairy tale.

Imagine Atlanta as a new imperial Rome – large urban figures no longer held together by small-scale urban cement but by forest, fragments floating in trees.[4]

After John Portman rescued the center, he could only react to its explosion as a developer must – by following the "demand." To outbid its centrifugality he proposed an entirely new city way up north, beyond the periphery even, and named it Northpark.

It is presented in an impressionistic brochure with a conscious fuzziness (derived from recent breakthrough in science?).

"The first of the series symbolizes the gaseous state," says the caption, "beginnings of an idea with only a hint of structure. The second expresses the solidification of ideas into emerging forms. And the last adds shading, form, and structure, bringing Northpark closer to reality."

Looking at the Northpark renderings, you may laugh, but you may also think, "Where have we seen these forms before?" Are they ugly or accidentally, unbelievably beautiful? Is this the reappearance of the sublime? Is it finally possible to identify them as the same shapes that Malevich launched at the beginning of the century – Architectons – abstract pre-architectures, the vacant but *available* volumes that could contain whatever program the century would generate in its ruthless unfolding?

If the forms of Northpark can be traced back to Malevich's Architectons, the most extreme streak of modernism, Atlanta itself can be described as a mixture of the imaginations of Malevich and Frank Lloyd Wright, whose Broadacre City described the American continent as a continuous urban – that is to say, artificial – condition: homogeneous, low intensity, with an occasional high point of visible concentration. In other words: there was advance warning. It did not come as a surprise. Atlanta is a realized prophesy.

Are these inhabited envelopes in their thick forests the final manifestation of modernization? Is this modernity?

Modernity is a radical principle. It is destructive. It has destroyed the city as we know it. We now inhabit "what used to be the city." In a bizarre way, Portman's Northpark – in fact, Atlanta as a whole – comes close to fulfilling that kind of modernity, a post-cataclysmic new beginning that celebrates revolutionary forms in liberated relationships, justified, finally, by no other reason than their appeal to our senses.

Portman lost his nerve with Northpark.

Maybe it was the economy, or maybe he never believed in it. He returned to the center, this time applying the esthetics of the periphery: a singular tower no longer interested in belonging, in being part of his web, but a needle, standing simply on its own.

It is *in* downtown, but not *of* downtown.

Downtown has become anywhere.

Hiding behind it, a private dream: his very last, most secret project is a touching relic – it shows the depth of his own misreading.

Now, maybe as a personal testament, he wants to bring the European city to the heart of Atlanta: arrogance or sentimentality? A rip-off of Leon

Krier's "community" emblem: glass pyramid over pedestrian plaza supported on four pylonlike buildings. When I asked in Portman's office whether he was inspired by Krier, I was officially told, "Mr Portman doesn't need inspiration."

Portman has three identities according to Portman: artist, architect, developer. He has yet to discover a fourth: that of the thinker or theoretician. He could assert that *each city is now an Atlanta* – Singapore, Paris – what is the Louvre now if not the ultimate atrium?

He could have been – or maybe is – disurbanist to the world. **1987/1994**

Notes

1 Of course, the word *urbanism* – which somehow suggests a minimum of steering – does not apply. For now, we could adopt the term *disurbanism* which, in the twenties, described a branch of constructivist urban theory aimed at dissolving the city.

2 Comte du Lautréamont, *Les Chants de Maldoror*, 1868–70.

3 During the eighties, critics like Alexander Tzonis and Liane Lefaivre began to suggest that the periphery might be the appropriate territory for a disabused architecture of Dirty Realism, so named after its eponymous literary equivalent.

4 The purity of this contrast may soon be compromised by the extravagant, palatial frenzy of Atlanta's residential architecture, now generating colossal mansions in absurd proximities at the potential expense of the vegetal. But then, that may make the city ultimately even more Roman.

Chapter 3

Barcelona – Re-thinking Urbanistic Projects

Joan Busquets

In the 1980–2000 period, the city of Barcelona developed a series of urbanistic strategies which sought to reinterpret existing urban structures and to restructure primary functional systems in order to face up to the start of the new century. In a description of this process it is vital to bring a new approach to certain of the city's urban planning projects, with a view to including new urban dynamics.

Barcelona's urban planning process over the last two decades led to many reflections on the necessity of disciplinary changes. The spaces of city planning, whether in terms of urban architecture or the urban project, have undergone a highly interesting development and are potential points of reference for future evolutions.

There are a number of important approaches to the issue of city-making that are a part of the recent discussions in Barcelona, as well as Europe as a whole. These include the following.

1 The *existing city* is a point of departure for future planning rather than a passive datum in the long-term project. An understanding of its forms and its capacity for modification and transformation can provide the basis for valuable projects of intervention and urban improvement.

This approach sees the city as an entity comprising *different morphologies*. According to the intrinsic conditions of their historical

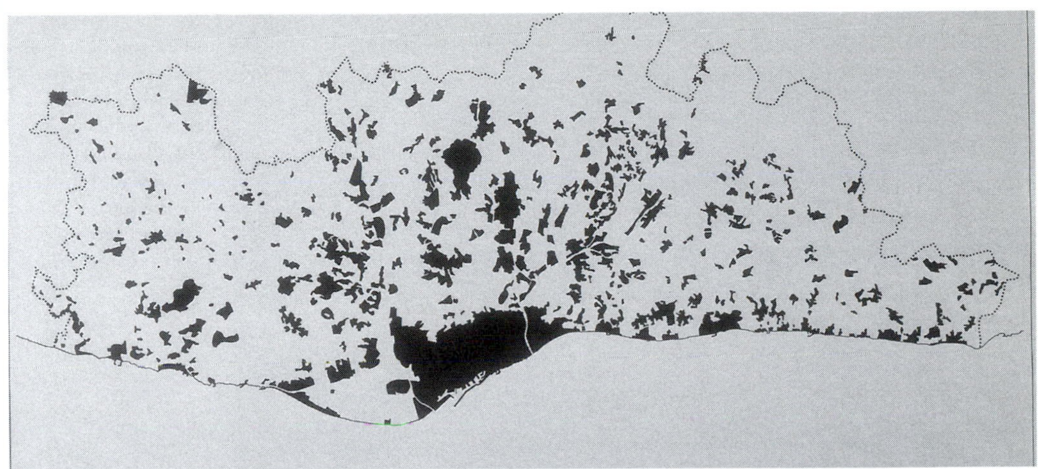

3.1
Barcelona region. Compact central town and city system around it

origins and the way in which their construction materialized, strategies of change can be introduced in the form of specific projects. So morphologies have different forms of organization and act as relatively autonomous urban units. The Italian school of the 1970s, represented by A. Rossi and C. Aymonino, blazed a trail for this kind of disciplinary development.[1]

2 *Infrastructures* are the means to ensuring the functioning of the city, and sometimes explain its origin. Their importance led the Modern Movement to use them as the basis for their propositional structure: Le Corbusier described infrastructures as communicating with seven levels or "ways," corresponding to different levels in their organizational hierarchy. Conventional planning still accords infrastructures a demiurgical value in ensuring the correct functioning of the whole. It was according to these principles that networks of motorways were planned for post-war European cities, sometimes generating greater urban destruction than the war itself. Above all, they established gaps between the infrastructure – the terrain of engineers – and the spaces between the roads to be developed by architects for residence, industry, amenities, etc.

It is true that certain levels of efficiency have to be guaranteed, but we are discovering that there are different ways to ensure sufficient levels of service and a need to evaluate the material, social and cultural costs of transforming infrastructures. The city has to be efficient but also habitable, and the use of infrastructures is more adaptable than we ever imagined. By way of example, the

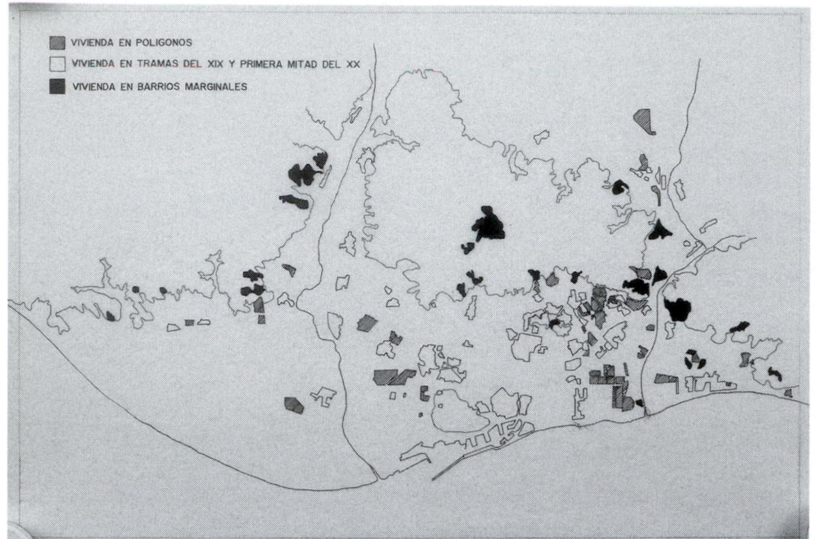

3.2
Metropolitan Barcelona and housing development in the 1960s: housing estates, row houses and informal sectors

discussion between public transport and private mobility is, in Europe, finding innovative and exemplary formulas of commitment. At the same time, the evolution of the various infrastructures – communication between parts of the territory – is changing at a dizzying rate.

It seems necessary to reinstate the role of *infrastructure as an integrated element* of the city, which is attributed the power of articulation and the weight of urban significance, rather than being an element of separation between adjacent parts. This is one of the major targets of today's urbanistic discipline, which is recovering the strategic, dynamic value of infrastructures, but also their innovative capacity within the urban and territorial landscape. This leads to the hypothesis that urban systems have to be designed in "networks" that on the one hand ensure their complementary nature, and on the other allow their definition as multipurpose units which are firmly implanted in their territory.

3 A new understanding of the *city's fit within its macrogeography* – to apply a similar interpretation to that of F. Braudel[2] – seems to be the motive behind the orientation of major urban projects in Europe. The issues of the greater landscape and the relationship with the territory are, once again, basic: this explains the force behind the recovery of the line between cities and water (the famous waterfronts), the connection of ports with historic cities, and the reservation of

3.3
Aerial view, 1998

valleys and watercourses, etc. These are themes which appear as leitmotifs in strategic operations in Barcelona, Lisbon, Lyons and many other European cities.

4 Recognition that the complexity of the project in the city calls for the intervention of *various actors*, including the public and private sectors but also associative and cultural sectors. It is only on the basis of the judicious involvement of these agents that the urban project can achieve the revitalizing effects in economic and social terms that are so often pursued. This explains its importance for the communicative action that is so relevant in the Anglo-Saxon context, as represented in the work of John Forester, Patsy Healey or Jordi Borja.[3] This capacity for dialogue of the projects does not

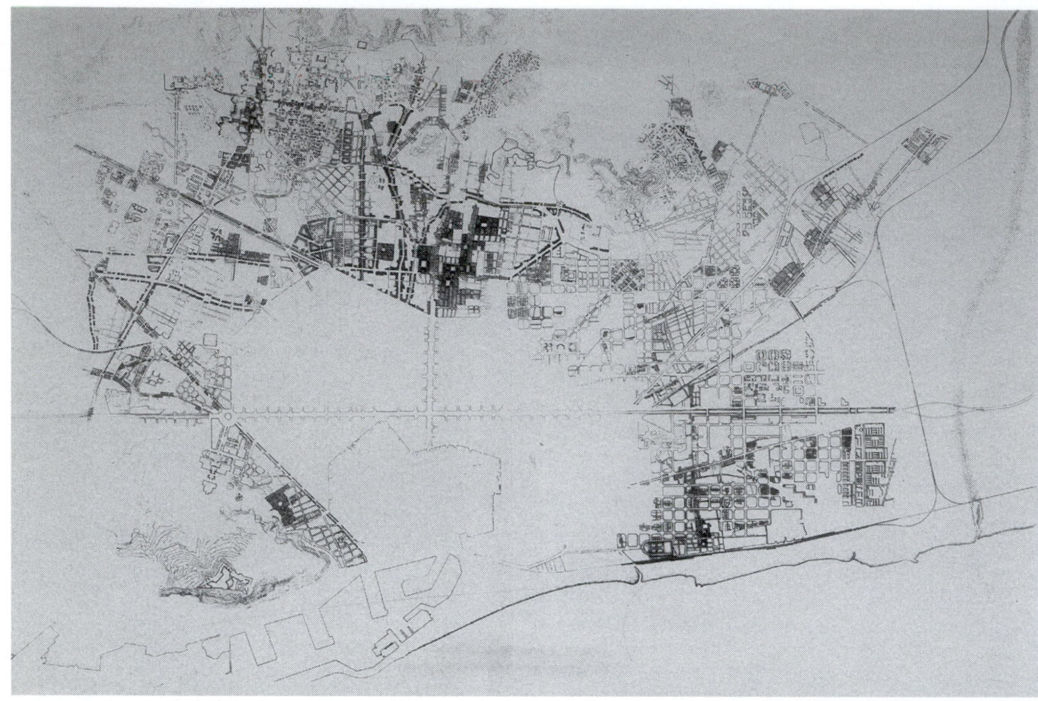

3.4
Suburban fabrics, made of different types of urban projects

signify the propositional negation that occasionally confounded advocacy planning in the 1970s, as "consensus" is only effective if there is a prior proposal which can be submitted for critical discussion. This is also the root of the force of image to which urban projects are subjected, on occasion succumbing to the temptations of the media and overlooking the rigor that is vital to their disciplinary argumentation.

5 The evolution of projects in the city is subject to an ever-increasing *multicultural tension*. The "ideas of force" in each context vary very quickly. The discussion between global innovation conveyed by the international media, sometimes acting as leader culture, and the intrinsic value of that which is local, contextual and unique is a central issue. Writers such as François Ascher[4] seek to distinguish the consequences for the urban planning model, while others such as Joel Garreau advocate the innovative strength of this tension, which, in keeping with its argument, takes place outside the city in the form of "edge cities" where "the new" seeks the best space.

Yet it is true that the city today is more than ever a "multicultural" place, due both to the composition and origin of its residents,

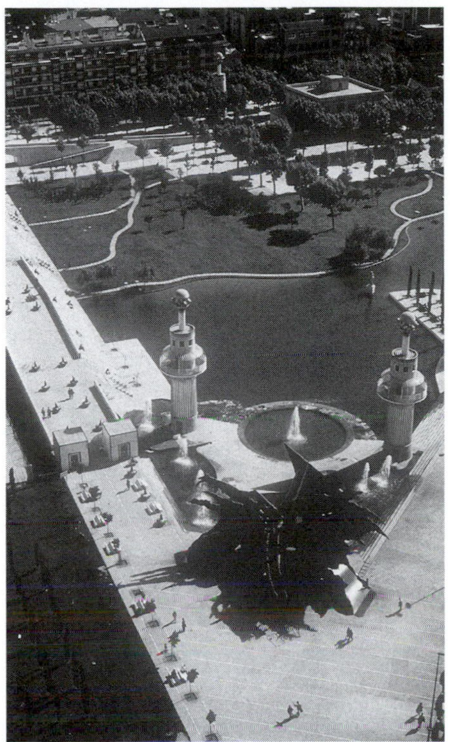

3.5
Urban park, placed within the suburban fabric

and to the variety of people who visit and use it in very different ways. This leads to the need to recover in projects a capacity for symbiosis – in other words, an active state of these situations seeking recognition of their values in their differences.

6 The general objective of projects with the most progressive ambitions is to seek a *rebalance* between the various parts of the city, according to which a fair city is not one that is equal in form but one that offers a fairly homogeneous level of service and use. These principles of "social justice" advocated among others by David Harvey[5] on the basis of a Marxist interpretation of urban evolution are based on more general strategies as to the indexes of land or the rates of urban development and socialization of the surplus value, etc. This is where the legal framework has to back the plan and the urban project in order for these aims to be achieved.

It might be said that, in our context, the legal framework is defined by laws which happen to take their name from "land," giving us an idea of how important this factor is in urban development. It has on occasion been these laws which have dictated the formal structure of plans and projects for the city, but we need to reinterpret them as the framework according to which more rational and balanced development can come about without overlooking other variables.

7 Recognition of the seminal value of cities' "historic" planning projects, which act as distinguishing references but also as models for their modern-day development. This is the case of the influence of Cerdà's project on the Barcelona of 1855, or Wagner's for Vienna at the turn of the century.[6]

The interpretation of some of these projects will be key to the interventions described below.

Recovering the city

These salient factors or dimensions go to explain the theoretical "framework" in which urbanistic projects are taking place. We are, then, a long way from having a single, precise, well-defined "theory," and are working in a context which is multidimensional and above all "non-linear," as it was thought after the war, to produce proposals for urban transformation and rehabilitation.

3.6
Plaza intervention to recover left over spaces

It is important to realize that among these factors, the project or the plan for the city and its parts revived a concern with the physical aspect which two-dimensional "planning" had practically forgotten. Today the urban project seeks to discern, within this complexity, criteria of physical coherence, urban composition and spatial priority that suggest a rebirth of the practice of "urban urbanism"[7] and "urban architecture." This direction, not without its difficulties, centers the discussion of the project for our cities on the turn of this century. The recovery of a degree of protagonism of the physical dimension of the project or the urban strategy to a large extent involves emphasis on the development of the public space as a privileged space in the urban event, be it in the city center or on the suburban outskirts. Its recomposition answers the above-mentioned criteria of integration and symbiosis, more than the criterion of order in urban composition in the second half of the nineteenth and early twentieth centuries, Multidimensionality, a differential use of spaces and their adaptability oblige us to consider other criteria in the composition of spaces of this kind.

The different scales of the urban project

Recent urbanistic practice has been based on proposals which correspond to fields of a different scale and different levels of definition according to the needs of the brief. While we describe the factor of context, plans and projects are subject to their individual times of development. We might almost say that a city works with *"visions" of its future in the mid-term*, which are linked to fairly precise proposals for some elements – infrastructure, landscape, macrogeography, etc. – and on the basis of which a general "consensus" can be established, such as, for example, the opening up to the seafront of Barcelona, which then went on to take the form of plans and projects with more specific briefs.[8] However the city works at the same time with *strategies of improvement* and rehabilitation, which are based on *the internal logic* of the existing construction of its fabrics and neighborhoods.

An interpretation of the contemporary urban planning experience of Barcelona

This chapter now goes on to describe a series of actions on the fabrics and empty interstices of today's Barcelona in an attempt to explain how it can operate on different levels: projects to improve and renovate neighborhoods, programs to improve mobility, and areas of new centrality supported by large obsolete spaces left between districts.

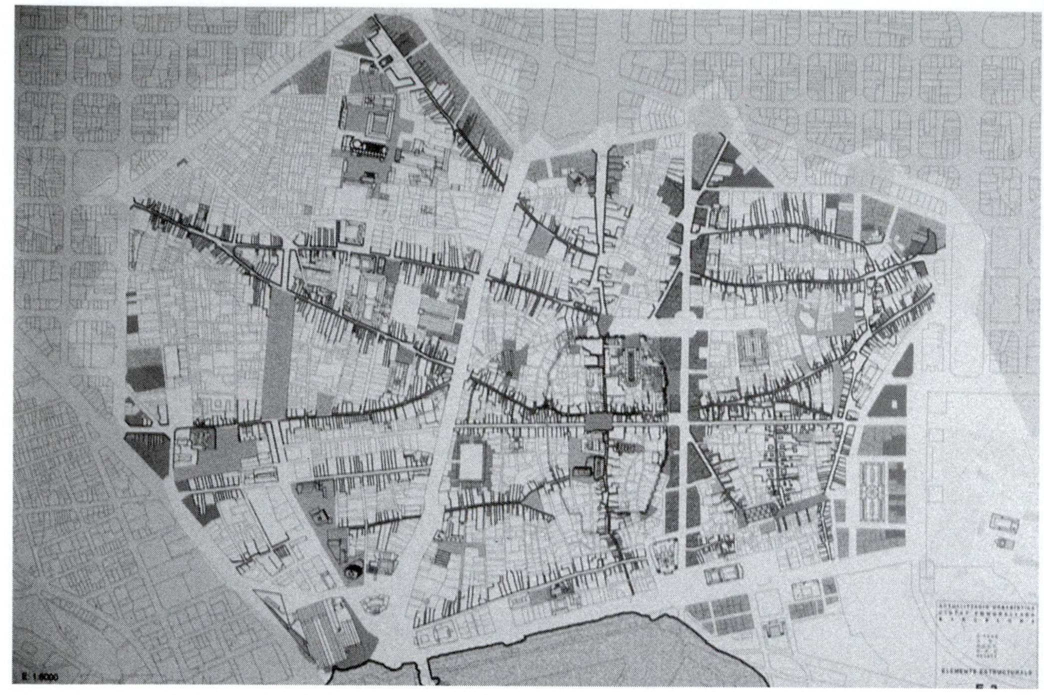

3.7
Old City reinterpretation

Suburban fabrics and the residential periphery

Barcelona, like most cities, can be considered on the basis of the construction of its various districts. In 1981, at a seminar at the School of Architecture,[9] we worked on an interpretation of Barcelona on the basis of its main morphologies: the old town, the Eixample, the suburban fabrics and the residential periphery. The "suburban Barcelona reading" stands out in particular: in the second half of the nineteenth century the old boroughs around central Barcelona (Poblenou, Sagrera, Sant Andreu, Horta, Gràcia, Sarrià, Sant Gervasi, Sants, Poble Sec, etc.) mainly developed a series of interesting urban planning parts, constituting the base which is sometimes referred to as "other Barcelonas." The work shows the many latent or explicit projects and plans on which the traditional Barcelona, comprising its present-day Districts, was built, modified and transformed,[10] with the urbanization of streets and roads, projects for squares, the creation of new streets through districts, drawn-back facades, avenues to connect the entire city, housing projects with squares, major amenities or residential complexes, etc. It explains the continual propositional capacity which is so often based on a conflicting logic but which, finally, after differing periods of time, produces and renovates the city. These projects are sometimes considered "minor" in comparison with large urban planning proposals, such as the expansion of the Eixample across the plain, but together they represent a projectual articulation of comparable entity which should perhaps not be seen as exclusive. In this way a fundamental part of Barcelona was woven from medium-density housing with shops, amenities and production and industrial centers on the same scale.

It is on the basis of this logic that we have to reinterpret the PERIs (Internal Renovation Plans) of the city districts carried out in the eighties with the idea of "adding" new elements to the existing city in order to ensure its rehabilitation and renovation.[11] The specific aims vary a great deal: from the rationalization of the existing street layout to the reuse of unoccupied land within these districts for amenities and gardens.

Interventions in squares, parks and gardens

The planning logic and legal framework for a hundred or so squares, parks and gardens throughout these districts in *the internal process* of this suburban Barcelona constitute an updating of its original structure, conforming a metropolitan whole with the central city. This process judiciously pieces together a puzzle in which we can highlight the following types.

Urban parks

These parks, set in the urban fabric, with dimensions of between six and ten hectares, correspond to the re-use of industrial and service enclosures. Obvious examples include the Escorxador (a former abattoir), España Industrial, El Clot, Pegaso and Renfe-Meridiana.

The foremost purpose of these parks was to turn a situation of "urban backs" – historically created by the walls of these enclosures – into a permeable urban element capable of offering a new service to the surrounding neighborhoods.[12]

Squares and gardens

These are small operations totally integrated into the city's various residential fabrics. The sheer quantity of works carried out – over 150 – and their quality supposes a thorough-going rehabilitation of the urban space of Barcelona.

Despite their limited size, their central positions in each district fragment has the quite remarkable effect of generating increased urbanity. The squares respond to clear functional needs to systematize traffic and overground car parking, and set out very varied spaces.

Most of the projects manifest a particular concern with restoring the symbolic values of the square, such as the incorporation of especially significant elements like sculptures, which had previously disappeared with excess functionality of design.

Gardens with amenities

These include a series of old private properties which are now re-used as public spaces in the city. The old buildings are converted for use as communal amenities. The specific theme of the project is the adaptation of a garden that was designed for exclusive use to new functional and urban requirements.

Urban axes

These interventions systematize the intermediate street layout in order to increase the protagonism of pedestrian space in some principal elements of the urban form. They are predominantly linear projects whose most significant decisions involve the design of the cross section. In turn, the project always tables a new discussion with the general street layout and public transport; and with parking opportunities and the tangential uses of the commercial ground floors. It is, then, easy to see how this introduces a degree of complexity into the management process.

Particular mention should also be made of Via Julia and Carrer de Prim, two newly designed urban axes on Barcelona's periphery. Their construction has turned abandoned spaces between building into civic axes, which give a new lease of life to the areas of Nou Barris and El Besòs, respectively.

Large-scale parks

These larger interventions change Barcelona's overall proportion of green. They include: the seafront, with its conversion into a great linear park and public access to the new beaches; the western side of Montjuïc overlooking the Llobregat delta, where the Olympic sports amenities were installed; the Vall d'Hebron in the northern part of the city, where residential land has been used to build a great park with amenities in one of the most built-up sectors; and the Diagonal park in the western extreme, which completes one of the city's large sports areas.

The restructuring of Ciutat Vella

The strategy of recovering the suburban districts and peripheral areas was to find a special complement in Ciutat Vella and the Eixample.

Urban areas such as the district of Ciutat Vella (the old town) called for more resolute action, in view of the fact that they were in a very advanced state of decline. Here the "projects" sought "internal reform," which consisted of evacuating strategic blocks to improve living conditions (the sunlighting and ventilation of houses that J. L. Sert and the GATCPAC had called for in the 1930s for these very same sectors), based on the theory that this was the only way to bring about a change in the process. In the face of the disinterest of proprietors, who considered these districts to have no future and to be des-

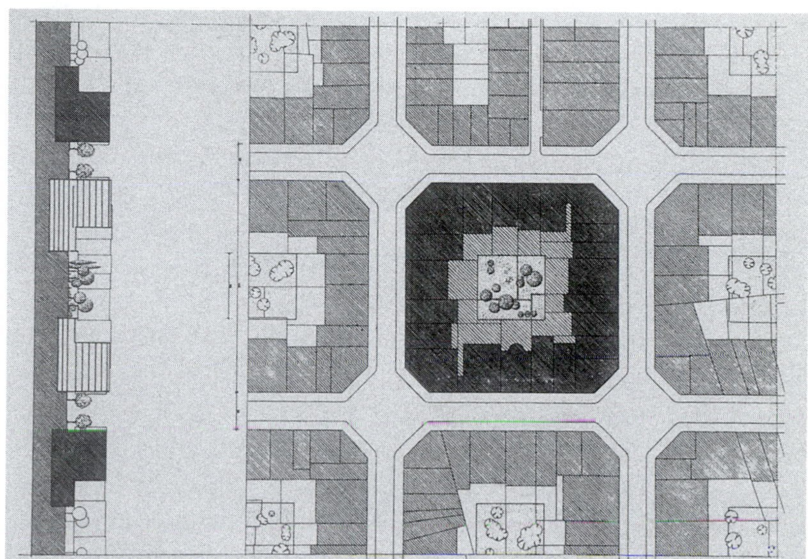

3.8
Building code to green internal courtyards for Barcelona's Eixample

tined to become ghettos, reorganization meant major public investment. These interventions led to others which reinforced the historically central functions based there. To this end, new cultural functions were developed, like the Centre de Cultura Contemporània and the Museu d'Art Contemporani in the old Casa de Caritat hospice buildings, and agreements were promoted to encourage the universities to relocate faculties there to attract students and lecturers to these spaces. Reconversion has reached an advanced stage, yet it is a project which still needs time to become irreversible.[13]

"Rehabilitation strategies" were also undertaken in the famous Eixample, the city extension designed by Cerdà in the mid-nineteenth century, which was the point of reference of a seminal "urban plan" for Barcelona. The Eixample had its own economic dynamic in which, like so many modern downtowns, residents were tending to get pushed out by the pressures of more powerful tertiary activities. Intervention in interior spaces, turning inner courtyards into mainly private gardens with a dozen or so for public use, gave a new incentive to residence, the strategy being accompanied by other means of support for housing and detaining the tertiary sector – which was later to find more convenient premises in the new downtowns.

From the Cerdà Plan to Barcelona's Eixample

The value of the area of the Eixample in the formation of contemporary Barcelona requires attention to both the dimensions of the project and the present-day urbanistic result. Let's compare the plan to the built city.

Ildefons Cerdà devoted over twenty years to generating the ideas in his project and making its implementation viable. It is beyond doubt a fundamental project in the formalization of contemporary Barcelona, but it is also a pioneering work in modern urban planning theory.

Cerdà planned a thorough reworking of Barcelona, on the scale and dimension expressed in his powerful concept of city. At the same time he was introducing the first set of modern urban planning instruments, where the project for the new city involved an analytical approach to reality and cities which was neither deterministic nor univocal.

The advances made by Cerdà have recently been discussed in the light of documents discovered in various archives.[14] These prove that he was a singular figure in European urban planning, and one who has been underestimated to date – due perhaps to the difficult gestation of his project.

We have to bear in mind the fact that the "founders" of modern urban planning generally mentioned in the history books – R. Baumeister (1874), J. Stübben (1890), R. Unwin (1909) etc. – carried out their work after Cerdà and probably did not have information about Barcelona's urbanistic process.

The theory of urban development on which Cerdà was working regarded prior conceptual formulation as being vital to the drafting of a city project.[15] His theory included the 1859 *Teoría para la Construcción de la Ciudad* (Theory for the Construction of the City) and the 1879 *Teoría General de la Urbanización* (General Theory of Urbanization).

For Cerdà, each work of "theory on" required its "application to" a specific case, and his theoretical approaches in turn had to be proved to be viable; in his own words, "the best idea is useless unless the means to carry it out are presented at the same time."

He developed his theory according to three principles:

1 Hygiene, based on the critique of the existing urban situation, with sound precedents. Cerdà wrote the *Monografía estadística de la clase obrera* (Statistical report on the working class) which accompanies the description of the preliminary project in which he minutely studies living conditions in the walled city. In addition, the description of the preliminary project presupposes an in-depth geographical analysis of the position and siting of the city, as well as its climatology and sunlighting. His ultimate purpose was to produce a thorough-going urban analysis to help him make propositional decisions. This concern with information based on disciplinary research led him to a further study of other cities such as Paris, and to interpreting maps of such far-flung cities as Boston, Turin, Stockholm, Buenos Aires and Saint Petersburg, among others.

2 The second component of Cerdà's theory was traffic flow. The profound impression of the steam train, with which he became acquainted on its introduction in Barcelona, led him to think about how to prepare the city for this great instrument of mechanical mobility.

3 Finally, Cerdà introduced a new idea of city which saw it spread right across the Barcelona plain: the already constructed and the yet to be built. We might say that his project involved the refounding of Barcelona.

This idea of a hygienic, functional city was, according to Cerdà, to produce conditions of equality among the residents using it; his proposal was therefore to cover the entire territory so that all the forms of settlement would fit into this homogeneous fabric.

Cerdà's proposal for the natural space consisted of organizing the city by means of street layout and regulations:

1 The basic layout comprised a system of street blocks situated between axes of 113.3 meters and streets of 20 meters. Its directrices correspond to the dominant lines of the plain, and are turned through 45° from the north, repeating the Roman orientation. The general or regional layout comprised a greater breadth of layout – 50 meters – to establish the main functional relations: Gran Via, Diagonal, Meridiana and Paral·lel. These two latter layouts correspond, as their names indicate, to their geographical position, and explicitly manifest the idea of bringing a global design to the city by integrating the different scales of interpretation.

2 When finally passed in 1860, Cerdà's proposal included a series of construction regulations that differed from those established by the urban police, which had traditionally formed part of a single juridical *habeas*. At the same time, he purported to guarantee good hygienic conditions, and proposed that only 50 per cent of the plot in the center of the block be developed. Cerdà trusted that the scope of the great Eixample would introduce large tracts of land into the market, thereby making cheap land available for affordable housing.

3 Economic thought aimed to put into practice Cerdà's constant idea that projects should be viable. The distinguished engineer's concern with this issue had been revived by his visits to Paris, where he had been a privileged observer of the fundamental changes that Baron Hausmann was carrying out in the French capital. Here, there were two interesting extremes. The first was the need for property-owners

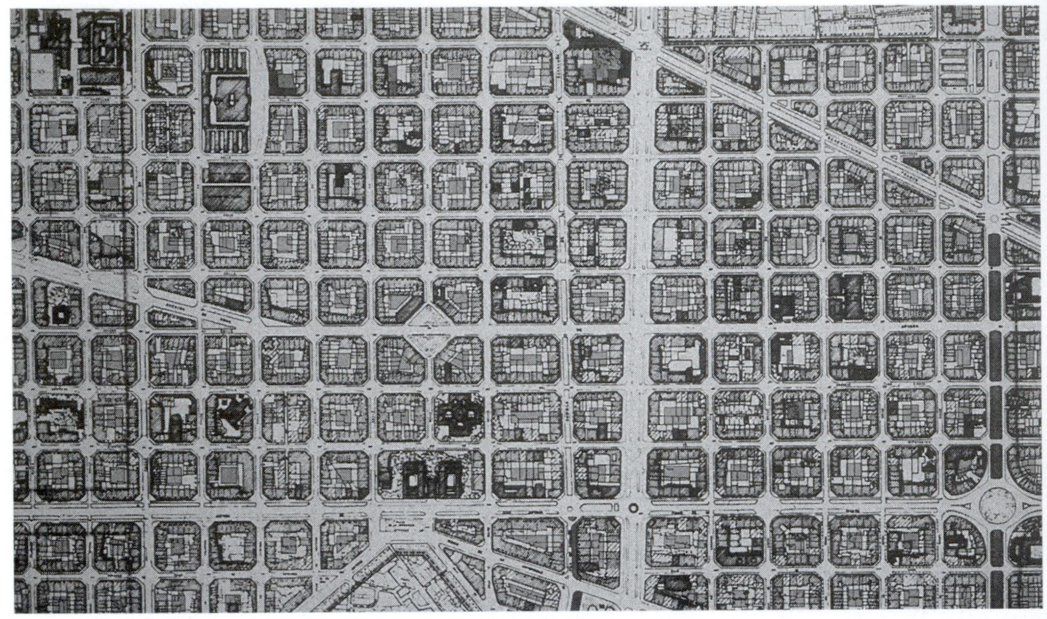

to contribute to the development scheme – a bold and highly socializing proposal for the time. The second controversial idea was his determination to make the renovation of Ciutat Vella economically viable by associating it with the dynamics and benefits of the extension of the city over the plain. The very ambitious scope of this proposal came up against an overwhelming reaction on the part of property-owners in the old town, who finally vetoed the situation, and the "Renovation" part of the Cerdà project was never passed.

3.9
Intervention on existing blocks to improve residential quality

This was one of the great urban planning projects in nineteenth-century Europe, which, having been approved in 1860, after 140 years of construction has now produced an admirable complex known as "Barcelona's Eixample." However, during the process of development, the complex became built up beyond the limits originally planned, and some of the principal ideas of the project lost definition.

As it stands today, the central Eixample covers half the area planned by Cerdà; however, in terms of building and activity it has multiplied by four. It covers 880 hectares, or 550 street blocks, and in the order of 125 kilometers of street; there is a resident population of about 350,000 inhabitants, and 300,000 people are employed there. Another indicator of use, activity and structure is traffic: some 600,000 cars pass through this area. This highlights the importance of this center, and the major presence of both residential and work functions.[16]

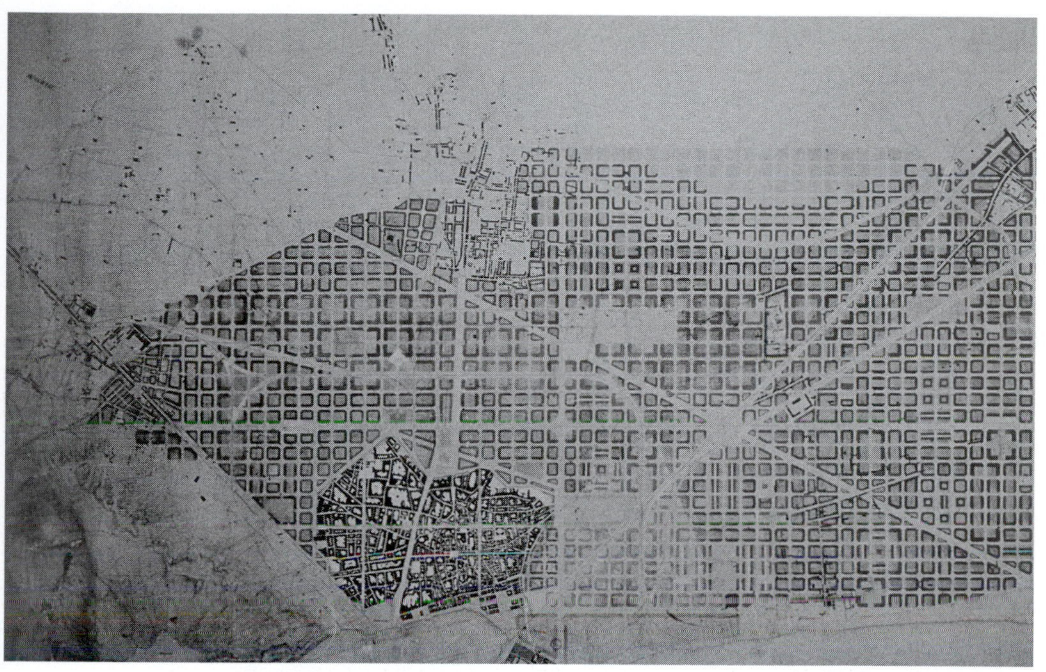

3.10
Cerdà Plan, designed in 1855

The significance of this major project and the different reality it actually produced illustrates the importance of this urbanistic episode, and also explains other elements of the rehabilitation of Barcelona. Its protagonism in the urban form and second its influence on the morphological transformation were effected by the large-scale projects described below.

Large-scale urbanistic projects

We must also look at the situation from the reverse or complementary point of view. The urban form can be understood by its empty spaces, and we must bear in mind the problems of function or brief arising in each situation. Let's take a look.

The empty spaces between "urban pieces" usually comprise vast tracts of land which are unused or have an obsolete function – industries that have fallen into disuse, dismantled railway spaces, old port land, and so on. Here we have spaces of opportunity, providing potential for endogenous development in the city. However, in Barcelona there were also problems of traffic access and a shortage of public transport between different areas of the city. Through-traffic was still using the Eixample to the extent that it attracted commerce and services, and spoiled its residential quality.

A series of large-scale projects were drawn up, endeavoring to combine increased connectivity of traffic and public transport between districts with the development of a series of new downtowns in empty or obsolete

3.11
Barcelona, plain designed by Cerdà as preparation for the Plan

central areas. A system of large connector roads (the Ronda) was also to provide a means of bypassing the city.

This program of multiple "centrality" meant that the increase in value of interstitial areas as a result of new accessibility was not totally privatized. Each new downtown would offer facilities and parks in the newly introduced areas and decentralize the overcrowded tertiary sector.

The program meant that the waterfront – previously occupied by nineteenth-century industry – was now brought into use, and development included new residential areas and the necessary infrastructures to provide access to the city's beaches.

These projects were all furthered by these: election of Barcelona as the 1992 Olympic host city, which served to concentrate a great many of the strategies of the various public and private operators.

A highlight among these schemes was the recovery of the city's port and seafront. Barcelona is proud of its role in the development of Mediterranean urban civilization, yet any possible relation with the sea was blocked by the old railway line, the port and the old warehouses, and the drainage system emptied straight out into the sea. This question had for decades been the center of ideas aspirations, but the problems of infrastructure and land ownership were difficult ones to solve.

The Barcelona of the 1980s threw itself into the task with a series of successive projects. First of all, the project for the Moll de la Fusta wharf created a new link between Ciutat Vella and the port, through-traffic was taken to a semi-underground level, and work was started on a model which was later extended to the Ronda ring roads: separating through-traffic from urban traffic heading for neighboring sectors. This urban project was the basis for the reform of the port, which was completed in 1995 by the Viaplana-Piñón team with a leisure and recreation complex called Port Vell.

Meanwhile, by 1985 work had started on designing the infrastructure ready for the construction of the Olympic Village and regeneration of the city's beaches. The project team, headed by O. Bohigas, systematized the route of the Rondas, the rail tracks were taken underground, a sewage plant beside the river Besòs freed the beaches of pollution, and its geometry was drawn out on the basis of a series of dikes which followed the rhythm of the Eixample. The construction of the Olympic Village involved the collaboration of a dozen teams of architects, and the different buildings follow Cerdà's urban scale, reducing density and producing a housing district which incorporates the services of the present-day central residential area.

At the same time, other new downtowns were developed in empty interstices such as Glòries, Carrer Tarragona and in Diagonal, with the project for L'Illa by M. Solà-Morales and R. Moneo. Each project worked with specific functional briefs in which the objective requirements of the development were common to certain urbanistic conditions of this new "urban piece" in relation to others surrounding it. This was perhaps the way to promote a public–private partnership in which the quality of spaces and buildings was not an incidental component. In the case of L'Illa, the building became a landmark in the city's most important avenue, and, as part of the development, the project includes two public schools, a new street underpass connection, and a huge public garden in a dense residential area that needed opening up.

The experience of Barcelona reveals the need to bring together the solution of major infrastructures (traffic, drainage, etc.) and services (parks, schools, etc.) with the urban space that surrounds them, not merely as a condition of context, but also, and above all, because it is these spaces that can give them their real urban meaning.

This premise leads to new relationships, such as the one between built artefacts and environment in the case of Foster's Communications Tower set in the midst of the Parc de Collserola, justifying the effort of creating a 268-meter high element at the top of the hill with a minimum shaft of 4.5 meters in diameter to reduce its environmental impact.

Barcelona's experience in the framework of Europe

In Barcelona, as in other major European urban development projects, we would seem to be looking at operations with one singular characteristic. One of them is infill of the existing city to increase its value by placing particular emphasis on improving the urban space. If at other times the dynamics of cities found expression in what happened beyond them, such as the huge urban expansions outside the cities during the 1960s and 1970s, the central theme now is reorganization of the city in itself. This does not mean that there are no processes of suburbanization on the edges of the metropolis, though they are, for the moment, complementary.

As a working hypothesis, we might suggest that these "urbanistic projects" concentrate their efforts on providing a strong projectual content, with attention to at least four components:

1 Public space is becoming the *leitmotif* of urban composition, be it in the city center or on the outskirts. It is acknowledged as the element which can voice the city's cultural capacities and respond to its functional and esthetic requirements. Here, the use of other urban spaces or the city's own historical projects serves as a point of reference for planners who have to propose layouts in their designs which may require time to take shape. Think of green and environmental systems in the city.

2 Urbanistic projects have to move around the most complex network of public and private agents ever. The present-day situation, with the superposition of various levels of government (state, regional,

3.12
Boston, mid-nineteenth century, as incorporated on Cerdà research for Barcelona's expansion

provincial, municipal, district, etc.), makes unitary administration of the urban project very complicated, but only by launching the project into this arena can possible efforts be catalyzed. The case is similar for private investors at various levels, who, with forms of partnership, have to try and go beyond the programmatic requirements of each developer.

3 Time also becomes an important factor. Urbanistic projects need time, as we all know, but if they are to last, the project has to

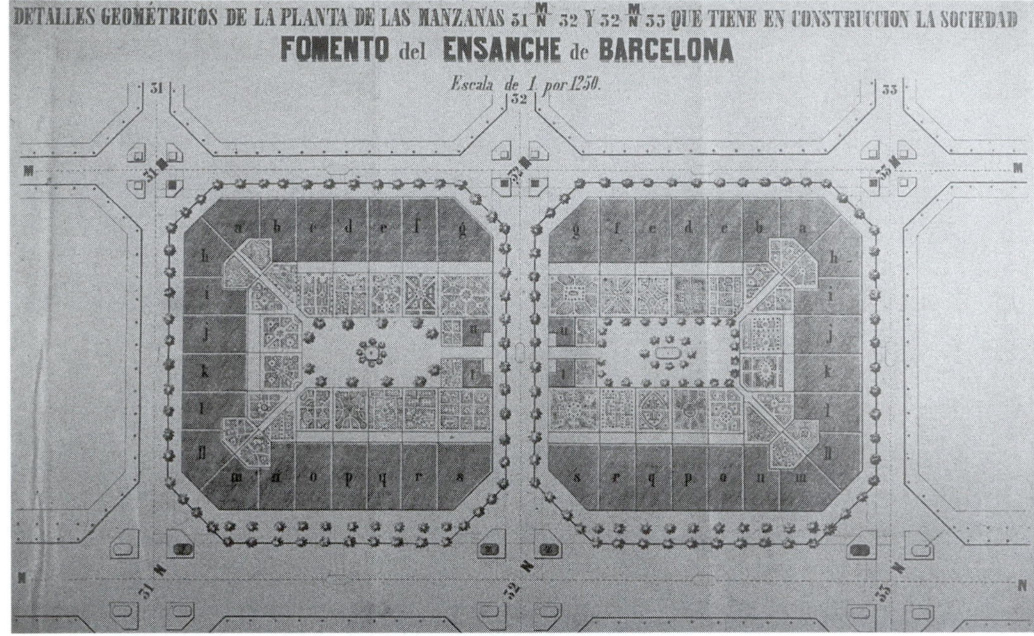

3.13
Block development, as proposed by Cerdà

channel its efforts towards "strong" elements of the urban form. We know that our thoughts and forms of action on the city often change; for "long-term" projects we have to go back to basics in the terms J. D. Burnham referred to at the beginning of the twentieth century, while our projects for intervention have to be well delimited and contextualized. This dimension has to be taken into account in urban projects, not so much to "think small" as to be aware of their capacities for implementation.

4 On the other hand, the "urban form" is once again the central element in the urbanistic project. We are coming to recognize its power of synthesis to express the urban process and make for a field of negotiation between technical, social and development agencies. But the urban form is now benefiting from the wide repertory of methodological disciplinary instruments developed in recent decades, which help to combine the discourse of the project with relevant analyses, describe morphological realities, and gauge the impact of the proposals – in short, to understand the form not so much as a final result but as a guide in an urban transformation process which is full of uncertainties that sometimes serve to cover up mediocre projects.

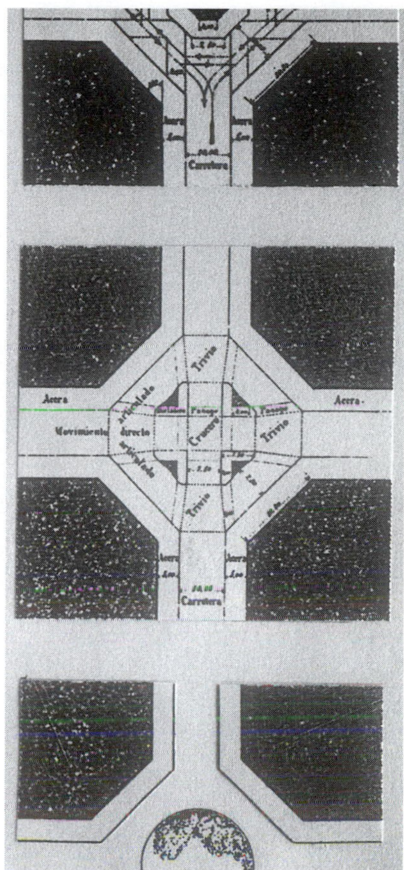

3.14
Crossing, as proposed on Cerdà (Plan)

This is where work on the "intermediate scale" comes in very useful: this means that while we establish the project on the basis of its own scale and autonomy, we force ourselves to look up to its wider context and down in a refusal to validate the project unless we are sure that it is reasonable in its viability. This exercise in planning brings us closer to the discussion concerning the traditional terms of the space of the Plan and the space of the Project.

To return to the recent Barcelona experience, there were two singular conditions: the major political capacity of the municipality, and the fact that the city's Olympic candidature for 1992 was accepted in 1986. We can see how many other cities have sought to take advantage of the spin-off of a set date: Lisbon in 1998 with its Expo, Rome in 2000 with its Jubilee, Berlin and the new capital projects, and so on. Yet we also see other major projects in Europe which have produced satisfactory results, such as K + Z in Rotterdam, or the cases of rehabilitation in Lyons, which have not had the advantage of a set date (which, on the other hand, has the disadvantage of unduly pressurizing

3.15

Barcelona's Eixample as it is now after Cerdà Plan and 140 years of development

3.16

Fragment of large-scale project on mobility

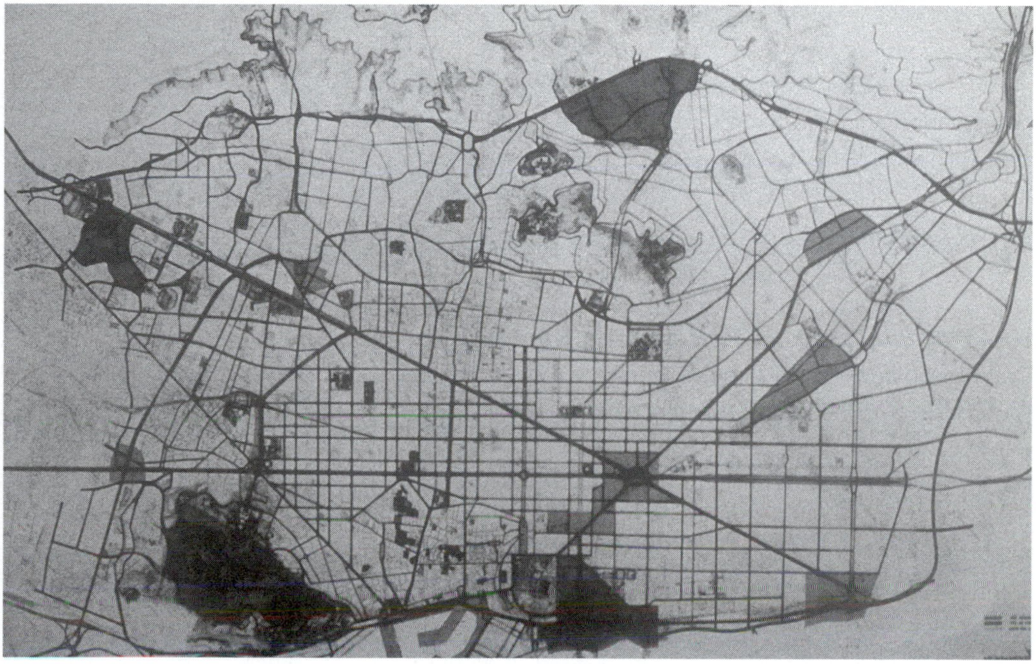

3.17
New "centrality" programe. Olympic sites were placed on four of its poles

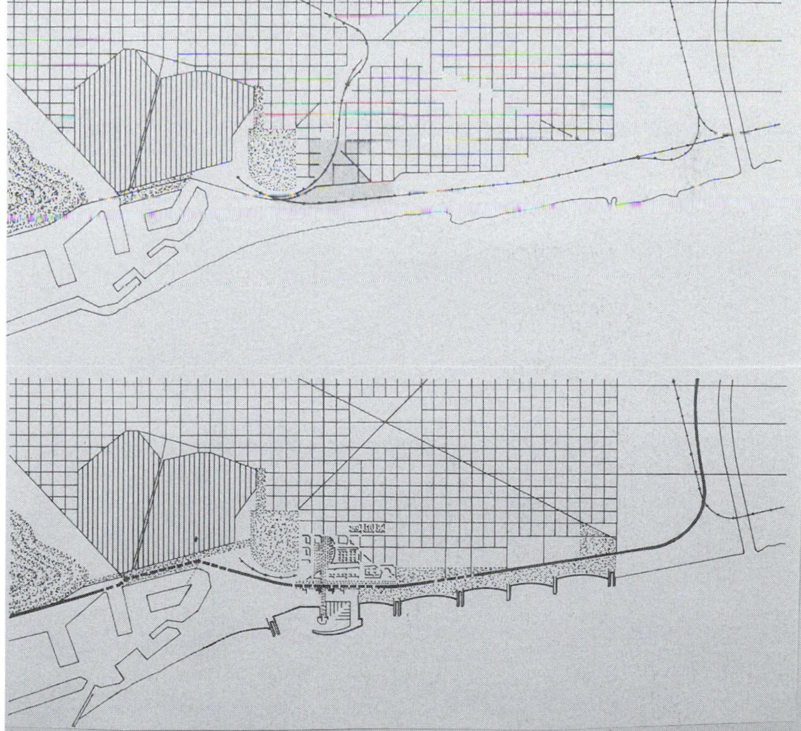

3.18
Waterfront infrastructures. Diagram representing the situation before and after the urbanistic intervention

some parts of the project and of forcing a double course of simultaneous projects, one for the event and, another for the future city).

In these projects, too, we see a search for specific objectives, attention to harmonic formulas based on well contextualized "pieces" of urban form and urban infrastructure. The logistics of these operations tend to differ from the classical bureaucratic services, and task forces are created with well-defined objectives – partly by government agencies, but also with a great many external private services.

In any case, here we have a great many of the ingredients of the discussion regarding the urban project today. These lead us to think of the vast field of work in cities, with, very different specific situations, though starting with the logic of mobilization of efforts – where existing opportunities allow us to turn some problematic points in cities into innovative, dynamic spaces.

This is a moment of far-reaching change of our urban systems in which we can appreciate the phenomena of change in their main functions and the appearance of new infrastructures almost without fixed channels which, with limited issuing centers, make for city development with unprecedented forms. Here we come up against more marked situations of discontinuity, as well as examples of heterogeneity between urban areas of different orders. We think we can understand this new territory without denying the efforts to revalue the existing city covered above, but it undoubtedly forces us to validate these new instruments of intervention in the light of new realities. This is

3.19
Waterfront view in 1985. Access to the edge blocked by old railway line and drainage emptied

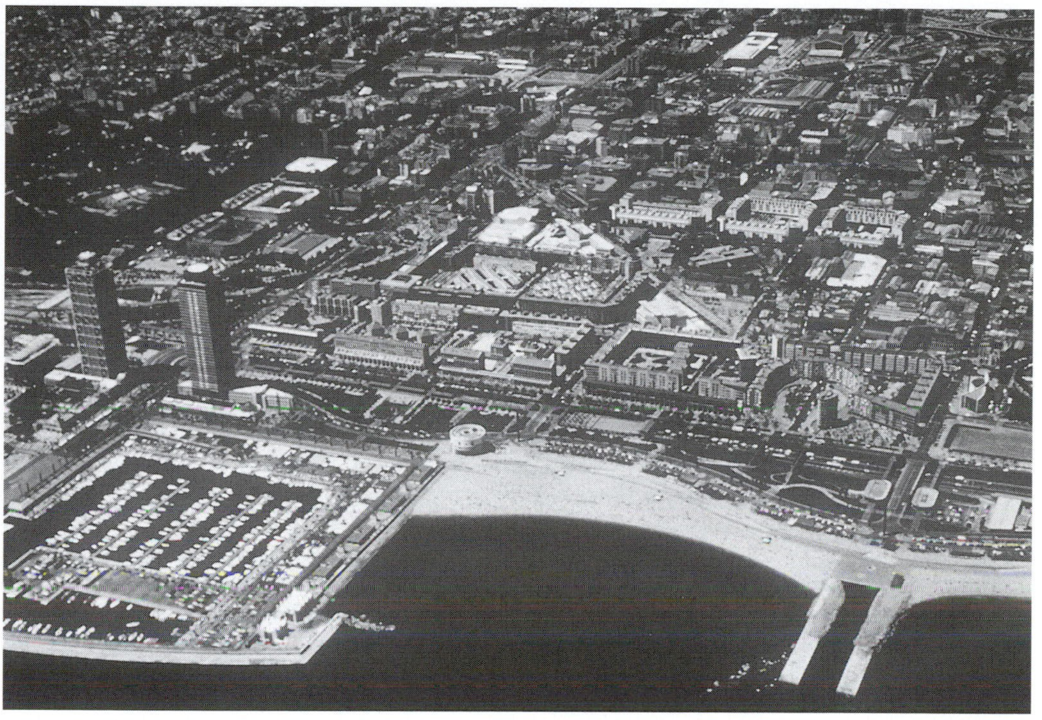

3.20
Waterfront rebuilt for 1992

where we have to be aware of the complexity of this new situation, which is so open in terms of decision-making mechanisms, and urban and market forces. Yet a major effort would seem to be in order on the part of the design disciplines to come up with rules of play that allow interesting urban results, and also the endogenous development which is characteristic of every city. This new urban culture will force us to discover the values of the city in the mutation surrounding every urban building or space, and concentrate our efforts on the "strong points" of form of these new territories – which doubtless offer other stimuli and charms. In short, each generation has to come to a new understanding of the "basic" problems of the urban territory and ambitiously articulate the proposals it can put into effect. This is the only way to see the new waterfront in Barcelona; as the carrying out of a long-range idea, with the means and skills brought to bear by the generation of the 1990s. In Barcelona and in every city, this is the starting point for new potentials and new themes for the beginning of this century.

Notes

1 See, among others, Rossi, 1982 (1st edn, 1966); Caniggia and Maffei, 1979.
2 Braudel, 1976.
3 See, for example, Borja, 2001; Healey, 1989.
4 Ascher, 1999.
5 See the recent work by Harvey, 2000.
6 Various authors; also Cerdà, 1995; Blau and Platzer, 2000.
7 Terms which are covered in detail in issues 5 and 6 of the *UR* magazine of the Laboratori d'Urbanisme, Barcelona 1988. See principally the article by M. Solà-Morales.
8 Busquets, 1992.
9 See Busquets and Parcerisa, 1983.
10 The present-day Districts were defined in 1985 within the municipality of Barcelona in order to facilitate administrative decentralization and broadly to reproduce the perimeters of the old nineteenth-century municipalities before they were annexed to Barcelona at the turn of the twentieth century.
11 A more precise description can be found in *Barcelona. Plans cap al 92* (Ajuntament de Barcelona, 1987) and, more recently, *Barcelona. La segona renovació* (Ajuntament de Barcelona, 1997).
12 Many books have been written both here and abroad about these projects. For a more complete version, see *Barcelona espais i escultures* (Ajuntament de Barcelona, 1987); *Plans i Projectes 1981–82* (Ajuntament de Barcelona, 1983).
13 Further explanation of this process can be seen in Busquets, 2002.
14 The relatively large bibliography devoted to Cerdà and his work includes: Estapé 1971, 1977; LUB, 1978; Cerdà, 1992.
15 Cerdà himself, in *Despojos* (Facsímil, Madrid, 1991) tells us at the end of his life: "I did not merely content myself with solving questions by casuistry, which is the common and most convenient procedure; instead, when I needed a theory to apply to the issue in hand, I invented it, in most cases, not to say always, with the most laborious effort."
16 Data taken from the detailed study of the evolution and present state of the Eixample, produced by a team directed by Busquets and Ordóñez, 1983.

Chapter 4

Brasilia – The Project of Brasilia

Farès el-Dahdah

Hidden beneath Brasilia's most civic of public spaces, the Praça do Três Poderes, there is an underground gallery called Espaço Lucio Costa. It was designed by Oscar Niemeyer in 1989 in order to memorialize both the winning entry of the 1957 design competition for Brazil's new capital and its author, Lucio Costa. Niemeyer suggested this space in response to the minister of culture's inquiry about eventual locations where a 50′ × 50′ model of Brasilia could be housed.[1] The model had been built as an exact replica of what the city looked like in 1987 when UNESCO declared it a World Heritage Site. The search for its permanent residency thus became the pretext for Niemeyer to find a solution that would give Costa "the tribute owed to him by the city" and be so discrete as to neither offend his modesty nor "inconveniently" compete with the Plaza's principal monuments.[1] Niemeyer's proposal consisted of a letter and a few sketches, all describing an underground space the function of which was to house the model, and the project with which the competition was won, including an illustrated text and a master plan. The subterranean room is accessed through a wide stairway, the opening of which is concealed behind by a low U-shaped bench. A marble plaque marks the entrance and dedicates the space to "Lucio Costa, Creator of Brasilia's Master Plan." One is subsequently led to a somber room almost entirely occupied by the model. What is otherwise unusual about this space is that both its interior and its dedication were respectively detailed and written by Costa and not by Niemeyer. The architects may often be mistakenly confused in terms of

Brasilia's authorship, yet their collaboration in this case is symptomatic of Costa's "modest" participation in anything related to his creation – while his words have a tendency to end up being written in stone. The text Costa submitted with his winning proposal, for example, begins with an apology to the jury, claiming that it was not his intention even to enter the competition. That same text nonetheless becomes, 40 years later, the standard upon which Brasilia can be legally protected. Costa proposed the project of Brasilia hesitantly while conceptualizing in the process the means by which his creation could survive in perpetuity. It should be noted that there were three people in charge of producing the city, an urban designer (Lucio Costa), an architect (Oscar Niemeyer), and a builder (Israel Pinheiro). All three were on government salaries and reported directly to President Juscelino Kubitschek. The architect and the builder lived on site, while the urbanist stayed behind in Rio de Janeiro.

Represented in the model is the usual image one has of Brasilia, a dragonfly-shaped plan commonly referred to as *plano piloto* (the name used in the competition's original title: *Plano Piloto de Brasília*). *Plano piloto* literally translates as "pilot plan," and simply means "master plan." It also today distinguishes the city's original form from subsequent peripheral developments, known as satellite cities. Even road signs indicate Brasilia as *plano piloto*, as if to suggest that, once in Brasilia, one theoretically lives in a "project" rather than in a city. Such semantic slippage between the name of a city and the title of its master

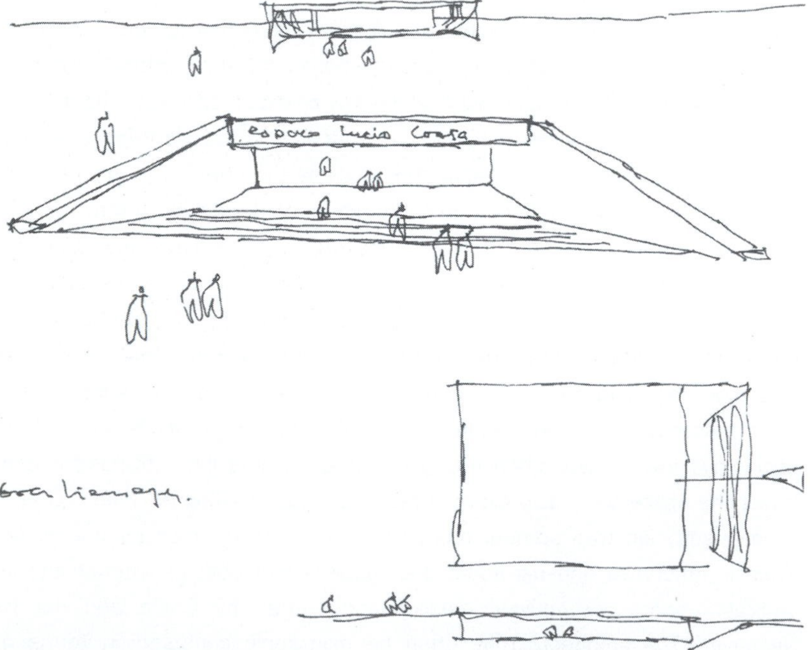

4.1
Sketch by Oscar Niemeyer, Espaço Lucio Costa

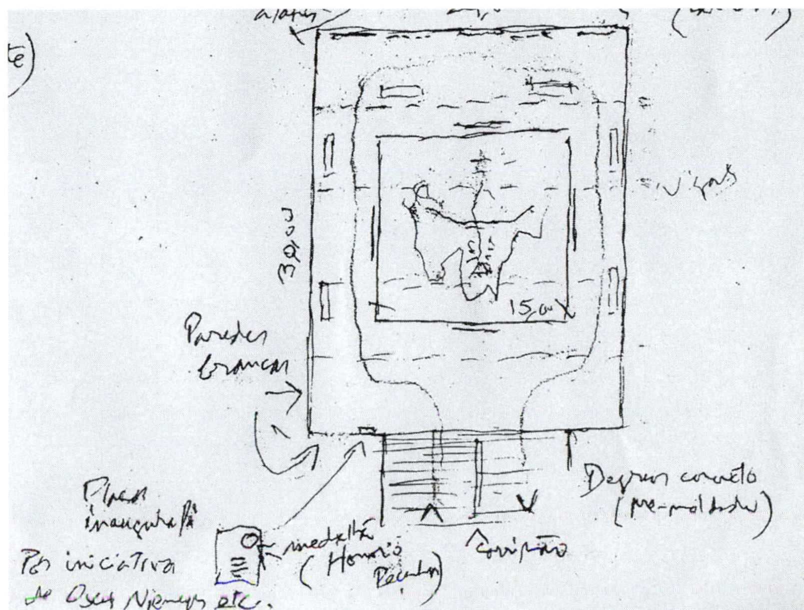

4.2
Sketch by Lucio Costa, Espaço Lucio Costa

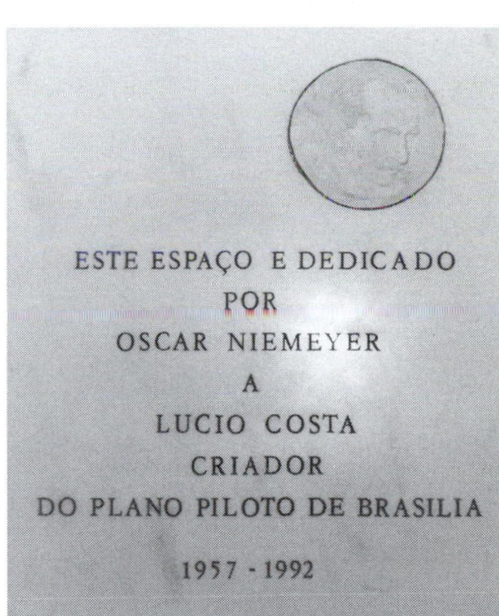

4.3
Dedication stone, Espaço Lucio Costa

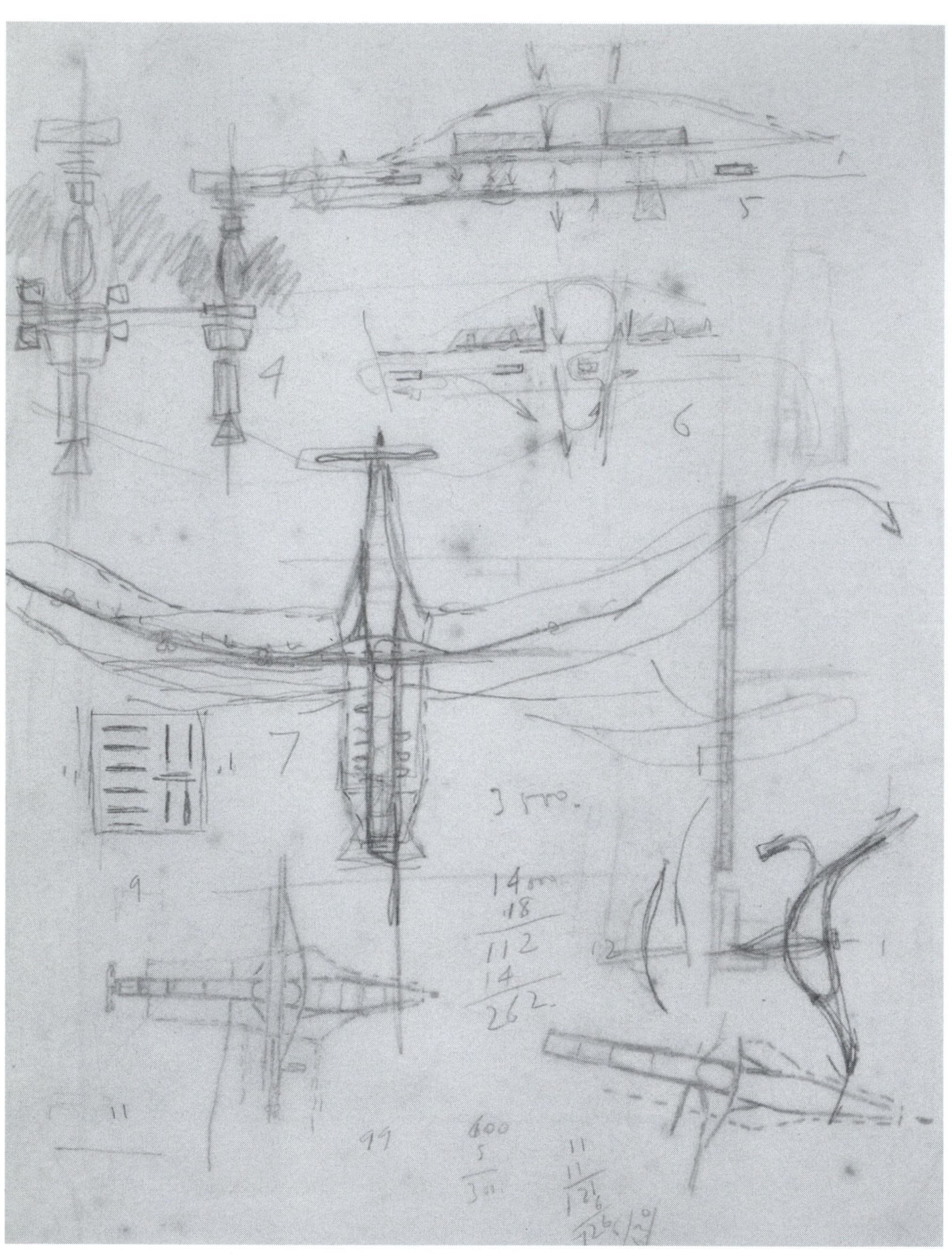

4.4
Sketch by Lucio Costa, Brasilia

4.5
Photo of Oscar Niemeyer, Israel Pinheiro, Lucio Costa, and Juscelino Kubitschek

plan is akin to saying in English "I live in the projects," however different the cultural connotation may be.[2] What is nonetheless telling about the recurrent labeling of Brasilia as *plano piloto* is that ever since its inauguration, the new Brazilian capital has always been identified with the project that Lucio Costa drew in 1957. The notion of master plan as city is not only expressed in the signs of daily life, it is also that which Brazilian preservation laws sought to protect in 1986. It is the master plan (i.e. the project) and not the city that can today be protected on the basis of cultural and historical significance. The laws that govern the protection of the *plano piloto*'s urban fabric are quite unprecedented, and may prove to be just as modern, if not more modern, than the city itself.

While Brasilia and its urbanistic conception are icons of the twentieth century, the transference of the Brazilian capital to the country's interior is a long-standing project in Brazil's history – Brasilia simply being its most material manifestation. The text Costa submitted for his competition entry, for instance, is prefaced with an exergue that situates his project as the fulfillment of an early nineteenth-century desire to found a city that as early as 1822 had already been called "Brasilia, or by some other name."[3] Throughout the nineteenth and first half of the twentieth centuries, the idea of transferring the capital was motivated by such reasons as security, integration or progress, all having as a precedent the very transfer of the royal court from Lisbon to Rio de Janeiro back in 1808. Having fled Portugal, the Prince Regent, Dom João VI, was advised by his British protectors that a capital city away from the coastline would not be as vulnerable to French invasion.[4] The project of building a New Lisbon, "in the middle of the country whence royal roads would radiate like waters that flow down from the highlands," lasted throughout the Prince

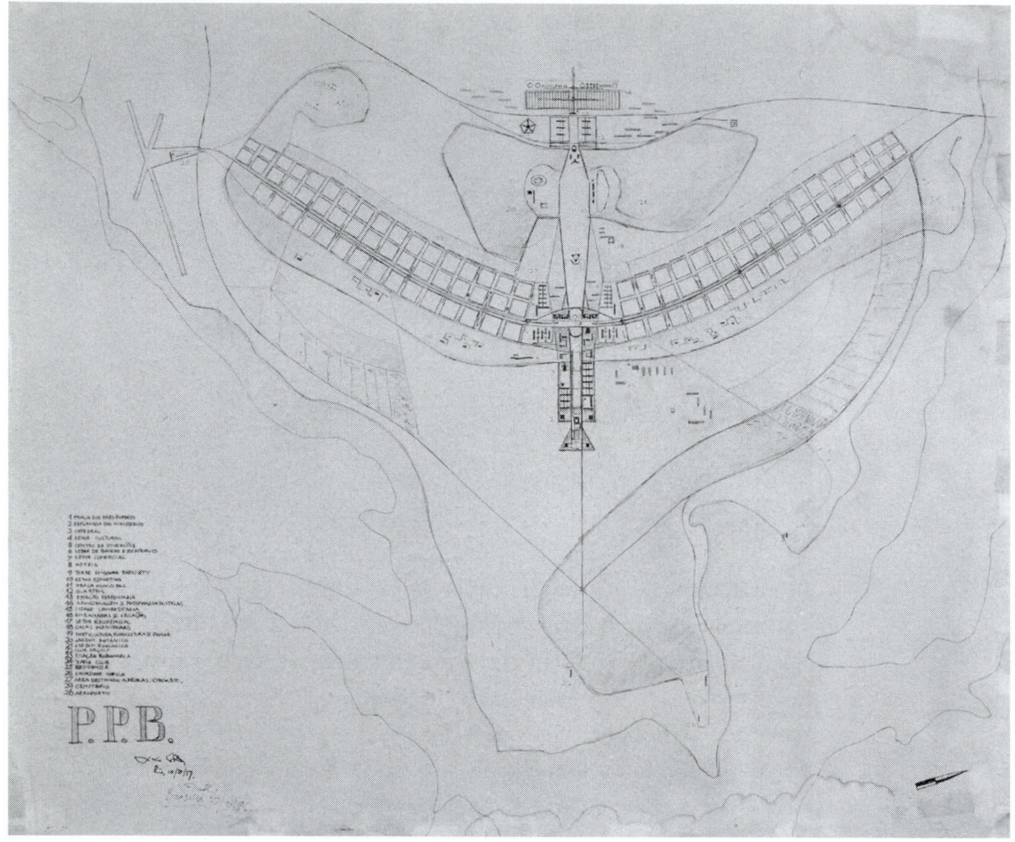

4.6
Pilot Plan of Brasilia, 1957

Regent's reign in Brazil.[4] The Portuguese Court's arrival also triggered a process of metropolitanization, whereby Rio de Janeiro itself had to transform into a "New City" in order to acquire a royal and enlightened scale.[5] An image of progress likewise, a century and a half later, motivated President Juscelino Kubitschek finally to undertake the project of a new capital for Brazil. The project remained alive throughout the nineteenth century and was even added as article to the constitutions of 1891, or, as Costa himself would say: "it was a century-old purpose, always postponed."[6] The motivation had always been a matter of progress, science, and even hygiene, that were all to provide an antidote to the turbulent and morally suspect image Rio de Janeiro had acquired over time. A site in Brazil's central plateau was subsequently demarcated by the Belgian astronomer, Louis Cruls, who published his report in 1894 and defined an area of 14,400 square kilometers known from then on as the *quadrilatero Cruls*, and later as the Future Federal District. The project was reintroduced in the constitution after the *coup d'état* of 1930. A couple of demarcation expeditions followed, yet it was not until Kubitschek's election to the presidency in 1955 that the project finally began to materialize.

4.7
View of Ministries Esplanade during construction

In his election campaign, Kubitschek promised 50 years of progress in the span of his five-year term. This was to be achieved on the basis of what was then called a *Programa de Metas* (Target Plan) that focused on expanding the country's infrastructure and intensifying the rate of industrialization: "he wanted to develop the country – fifty years in five. He had main objectives – steel, dams, ship building, highways, all sorts of activities he proposed to simulate, and the transfer of the capital was the keystone in an arch."[6] Transferring the capital to the country's interior was, in essence, the perfect pretext for building highways leading up to it, and thereby accessing vast areas of the country that had yet to be exploited. Kubitschek's road construction program ultimately tripled Brazil's transportation network. Geographic position aside, Brasilia itself reflected industrial growth. Conceived primarily in terms of uninterrupted traffic flows, Brasilia assimilated in its very form the importance of the car, whose production quadrupled during Kubitshek's mandate.[7] On 18 April 1956, soon after taking over the presidency, Kubitschek created a development company (NOVACAP, *Companhia Urbanizadora da Nova Capital*) that was given the charge of organizing and implementing the capital's construction. Oscar Niemeyer was appointed head of that agency's architecture department, and was responsible for designing the future capital's principal buildings. This choice was based on a previous collaboration with Kubitshek, who, as mayor of Belo Horizonte, had supported the project of Pampulha, which had become the benchmark of Niemeyer's notoriety. In a way, Belo Horizonte itself represented a precedent for Brasilia, since it too was the result of a capital transfer (albeit a regional one) that was accomplished in the span of four years (1893–1897).

The project of a city motivated by transport, built in the middle of nowhere, and based on automotive locomotion has coincidentally a closer precedent in Brazil – one with which Kubitshek was no doubt familiar. In 1927 Henry Ford was granted a concession of a million hectares deep in the Amazon, where a small city was eventually built from scratch and in record time. Fordlandia, as it came to be called, had "superb infrastructure, unmatchable for thousands of miles in any direction." It was complete with hospital, schools, cinema, power plants, docks, machine shops, warehouses, neatly aligned bungalows, bunkhouses, general stores, and mess halls.[8] Fordlandia was also laid out over 70 kilometers of roads, had radio and telephone communications, and even featured a "kind of modern asepsis with vast cleared spaces ... constantly sprayed by workers against all sorts of insects and pests."[9]

Kubitshek had originally asked Niemeyer to draft a master plan for the future capital, but the offer was declined. Niemeyer preferred to separate urban design from architecture, thereby assuming the responsibility of designing the city's most representative buildings while leaving the city's urbanism open to a national competition.[10] Rules for the competition were at best vague, and simply required a capital for 500,000 inhabitants, without any planning studies (which would have favored certain firms over others). Competitors were merely asked to hand in "1) a basic layout of the city, showing the location of the main elements of the urban structure, the various sectors, centers, installations and services as well as their interconnections, the distributions of open spaces and lines of communication; 2) a supporting report."[11] Voting members of the jury consisted of a representative from the Brazilian Institute of Architects, Paulo Antunes Ribeiro; a representative from the Brazilian Engineers Association, Luiz Hildebrando Horta Barbosa; two representatives from NOVACAP, Oscar Niemeyer and Israel Pinheiro; three foreign guests – William Holford (Professor of Urbanism at London University), André Sive (Professor of Urbanism in Paris), and Stamo Papadaki (American architect). The jury first met on 12 March 1957, and kept on deliberating until March 16, when it pronounced Costa's entry as the winner.[12]

The jury took its decision on the premise that Costa's entry projected an idea of a capital rather than being merely a good urban plan for a medium-sized city – or, as one of the jury members put it, "It is the only plan for the administrative capital of Brazil."[13] Among the other 25 entries far more complex and detailed projects were proposed, but none was able to encapsulate a variety of cultural tendencies as well as Costa's project. In pragmatic terms it was the only entry that took into consideration the plan of building the city in only three years, by making clear the position, size, and outline of buildings, which could plausibly be built in the middle of nowhere. Having been given the footprint of all buildings, their size, and their relationships, NOVACAP i.e., Oscar Niemeyer could subsequently take over with ease and without altering the given image of the city. Costa's entry also catered for the taste of the dominant bourgeoisie by insisting on such values as unity, proportion, harmony, and even figurativeness, despite its otherwise declared dependency on the Charter of Athens. Costa's entry, for instance, was the only one in which the North arrow on the master plan pointed unconventionally sideways, for if it hadn't Brasilia would not so readily look like the mythical figure of a plane or a bird. By his own admission, the ingredients for Brasilia's urbanistic conception were as follows:

1 However original, native, and Brazilian, Brasilia – with its axes, its perspectives, its *ordonnance* – is intellectually French in its filiation. Unconsciously perhaps, the loving memory of Paris was always present.
2 The vast English lawns of my childhood . . .
3 The purity of distant Diamantina . . .
4 The fact of having gotten to know the fabulous photographs of China at the beginning of the century (1904 +/–) – terrepleins, retaining walls, pavilions with the drawings of their distribution . . .
5 The circumstance of having been invited to participate, along with my daughters, in the commemorative festivities of the Parsons School of Design in New York and having then been able to take the "Greyhound" bus and travel the highways and interchanges around the city.
6 Being free of urbanistic taboos and biases and being imbued with the program's implicit dignity: to *invent* the definitive capital of the country.[14]

Brasilia is otherwise the undeniable product of a shift from a nineteenth-century interest in economic and social orders to an early twentieth-century obsession with technique and esthetics. In it one finds characteristics that range from Fourier's *Phalanstère to* Garnier's *Cité Industrielle*. Urban morphology is predictably exploded in order to expose buildings to sun and trees.

Streets are consequently abolished. Open spaces become background. Functions are separated in order for the city to yield better production. Circulation, itself conceived as a separate function, is designed as a network that holds the built domain together. Aside from being a technical instrument of production, it also becomes a spectacle for production, having been "composed" on a drawing board. Much like the Garden cities of Unwin or Howard, Brasilia too is circumscribed by a green belt, the purpose of which is supposedly to impede any possible coalescence with other urban agglomerations. In short, "Brasília, capital of the highways and skyways, a park and a city. Century-old dream of the Patriarch [José Bonifácio]."[15]

While it may be true that Costa's proposal won because it somehow lent itself to becoming a much-needed ideological tool for negotiating a national consensus (i.e. those who would commit to it would inevitably commit to Kubitschek's economic Target Plan), it did so by projecting an image of monumentality fit for the nation's capital. Costa, for instance, wrote in his supporting report that Brasilia "should not be conceived as a simple organism able to satisfactorily and effortlessly fill the vital functions proper to any modern city, not as an *URB*, therefore, but as a *CIVITAS* having the inherent attributes of a capital." The monumental is thereby identified as a value: "To achieve this, the urbanist must be imbued with a certain dignity and nobility of purpose which will confer real monumentality on his urban scheme."[16] The possibility of translating such nebulous things as dignity and nobility into urbanism is what ultimately seduced both jury and nation. For those who lost the competition, the notion of monumentality was enough of a key issue to be virulently criticized: "I do not believe that a capital should be a pantheon . . . I can not accept the 19th century concept of 'monumentality'."[17] Costa, for whom ideological biases were to be avoided at all cost, replied a few days later that "in reference to the concept of monumentality, I do not see why in a democracy a city must necessarily be devoid of grandeur."[18] In order to make monumentality recognizable and intrinsic to the urban fabric, Costa introduced a grammar of different scales which were to give Brasilia its distinct characters. Monumentality is recognized therefore in the monumental axis in contradistinction to the quotidian scale of the residential one – both scales having the endless horizon of Brazil's central plateau as their picturesque background. This notion of a city made up of various urban scales is implicit in the competition entry report, and is only made explicit in an interview given four years later:

> "it is the play of three scales that will characterize and give meaning to Brasilia . . . the quotidian or residential scale . . . the so-called monumental scale in which man acquires a collective dimension; the urbanistic expression of this new concept of nobility . . . Finally

the aggregate scale, where dimensions and space are deliberately reduced and concentrated in order to create a climate fit for congestion . . . We could even add a fourth scale, the bucolic scale of green spaces."[19]

However abstract, these four scales eventually turned into legal concepts for urban preservation when Costa was invited to revise the city he had designed 37 years previously. Up to that time, Brasilia had been legally protected with a simple sentence: "any alteration made to the Pilot Plan in terms of Brasilia's urbanization must be authorized by Federal Law."[20] Considering how a juridical apparatus actually works, a sentence so brief was hardly enough to control the pressures of real-estate development. In 1985 the newly elected Governor, José Aparecido de Oliveira, invited Costa, Niemeyer, and Roberto Burle Marx to complete and rectify the project as it had been intended. His strategy also included the pursuit of international recognition so that the city could be protected in perpetuity from local real-estate development forces. The Governor went to Paris and proposed to Unesco the theory that contemporary monuments such as Brasilia as a whole ought to be considered. Unesco commissioned a report in which Brasilia is described as one of the greatest events in the history of urbanism, but that it is nonetheless suffering from the absence of an urban code. The report basically dismissed the petition, arguing that Brazil could not make such a request when its own preservation laws regarding Brasilia were so abstract and ill-defined.[21]

Two sets of preservation measures were subsequently taken at State and Federal levels, and in both cases Costa's words were not far behind. At the state level, a Governor's decree essentially reiterated the recommendations that Costa himself had made earlier that year. This became the legal text that ultimately convinced Unesco to confer the title of World Heritage Site to Brasilia. At the Federal level, it was the IPHAN (that heritage bureau for which Costa once worked) that passed a law affording the city another level of national protection. The content of that law is paraphrased from a letter in which Costa suggested to the head of IPHAN what ought to be done. What is peculiar about these laws is not so much that they were in fact dictated by the urbanist whose work was being protected; it is their very content, which ends up offering a conception of the modern city, that is rather unprecedented.

The document Costa produced at the Governor's invitation begins with what it describes as the "Fundamental Characteristics of the Pilot Plan," number one among them being "the interaction between the four urban scales." It goes on to define each one of them.

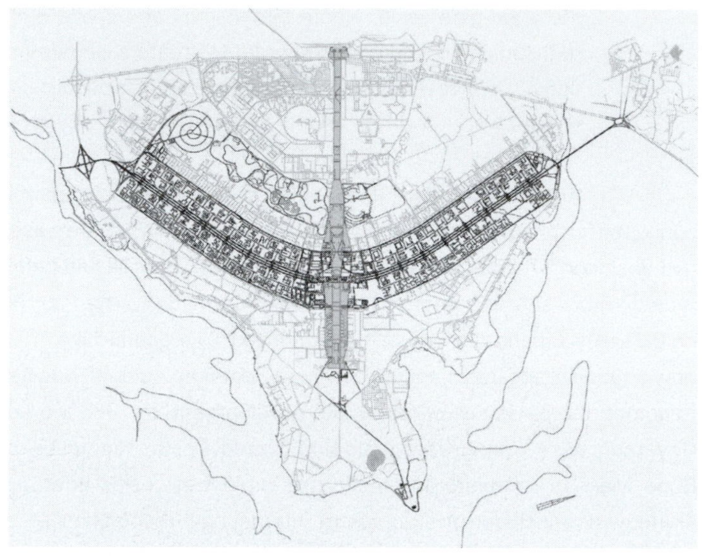

4.8
Area of monumental scale

The monumental scale, it is that which gave an emerging city the inalienable status of capital. This scale occupies the straight monumental axis and was introduced through the application of terreplein techniques, the disciplined disposition of built masses, the vertical references of the Congress and television tower, and the central green mall free of any construction as it crosses the city from dawn to dusk.

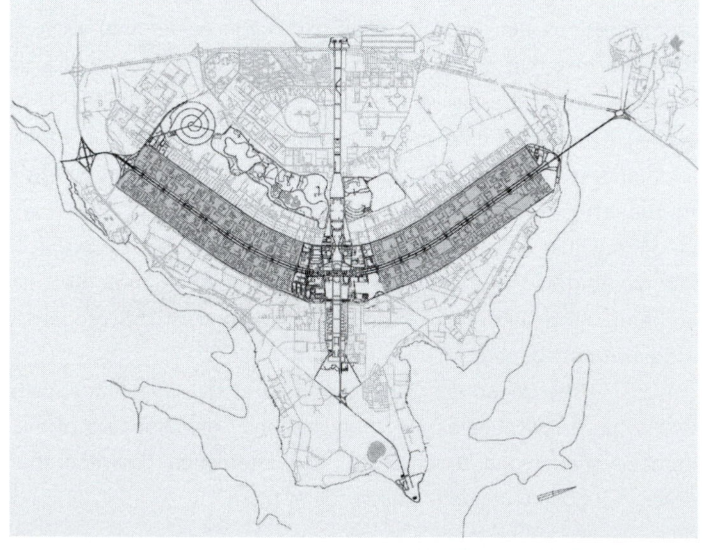

4.9
Area of residential scale

The residential scale brings about a new way of living proper to Brasilia through the innovative proposition of the Superquadra. It provides an urban serenity guaranteed by a uniformity of size and a ground made accessible to all via the generalized use of pilotis and the predominance of green areas. Its scale differs from that of the monumental, not only in terms of size but also in terms of the planimetric distribution of each quadra that is marked by a continuous green band which gives it the feel of an internal urban patio.

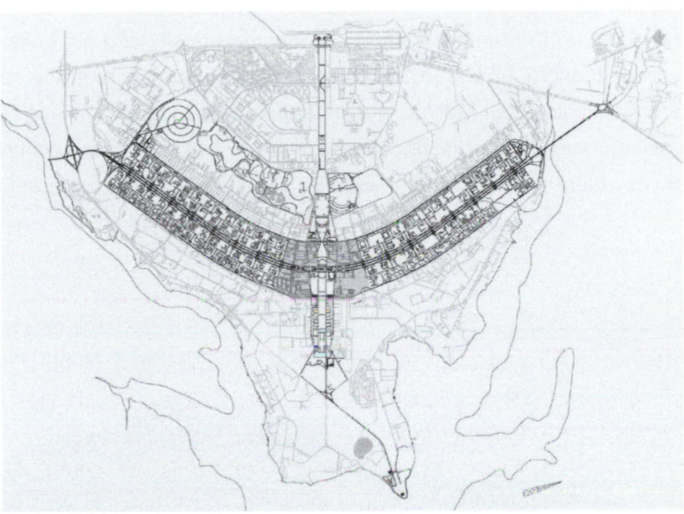

4.10
Area of concentrated scale

The concentrated scale belongs to the city center and had the intention of creating high density urban spaces that would favor encounters. It naturally occurs at the intersection of both axes.

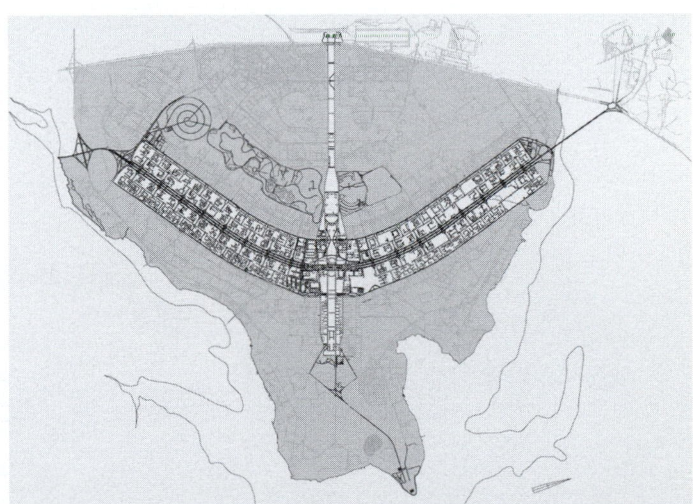

4.11
Area of bucolic scale

> The bucolic scale represents large vacant areas that are adjacent to built areas and which are to be densely planted or to have their native flora preserved. It occurs in the transition, without interruption, between the inhabited and the uninhabited.[22]

The document goes on to describe the remaining "fundamental characteristics," some of which are no less eclectic: the residential question, the lake's shore, the importance of landscape, the presence of the sky, and the rejection of suburban sprawl. The law, in the form of a Governor's decree, literally picks up the same language and identifies scale (and not buildings) as that which it ought to be protect.[23] It begins by stating that the protection of Brasilia's Pilot Plan will be guaranteed by the preservation of the essential characteristics of four distinct scales through which an urban conception of the city is made explicit. The subsequent chapters of the law are entitled accord-

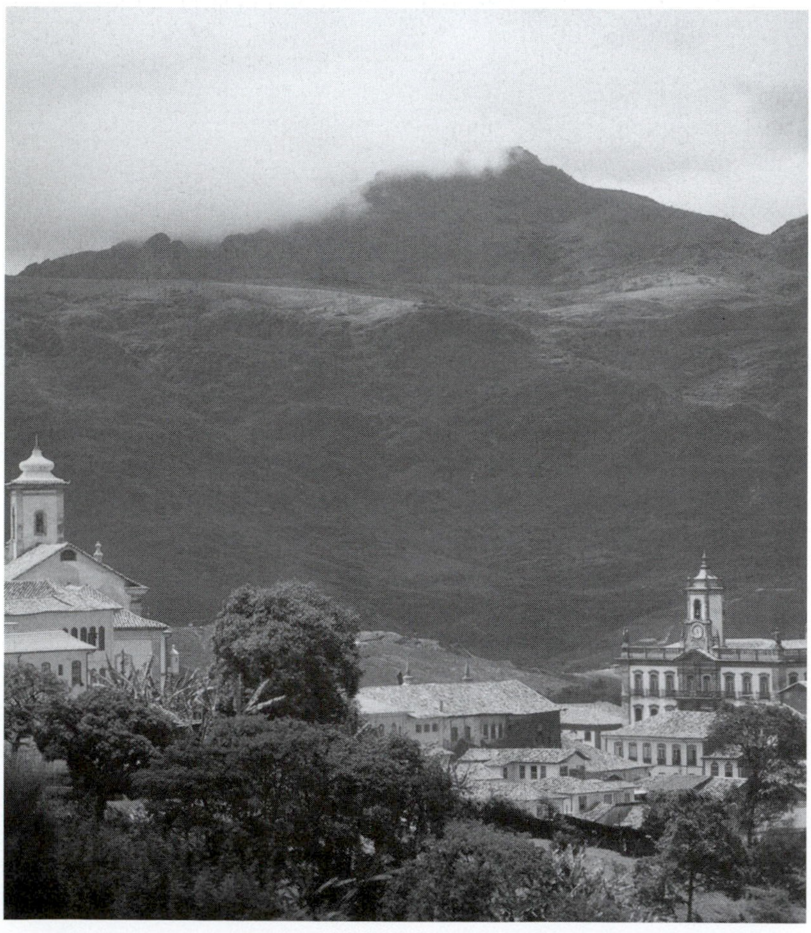

4.12
Aerial view of Ouro Preto

4.13
Aerial view of Brasilia

ingly: On the monumental scale; On the residential scale; On the concentrated scale; On the bucolic scale.

A similar operation occurred when the IPHAN decided to produce its own preservation laws. Costa and Niemeyer were again consulted. They sent their opinions and it was Costa's letter that eventually became legal text. In it, Costa made a list of what was important to him, and began by reaffirming that the four scales which governed the very conception of the city ought to be respected.[24] Federal law in turn replicated the language, and ratifies the notion that in Brasilia buildings are not protected; only their outline and the percentage rate of their land occupancy are.[25]

In terms of historic preservation, an unprecedented condition exists in Brasilia whereby any building can be destroyed as long as its scale is somehow reconstituted (except two buildings that are physically protected by law: the National Cathedral and the *Catetinho*, a wooden shack on pilotis built as a temporary residence for Kubitschek). It is the project rather than the city that ultimately survives. What the law seeks to protect is not Brasilia's urban fabric but its urban grammar, which means that in Brazil one does not protect a modern city in the same way as an eighteenth-century colonial town. The difference is that in Ouro Preto, for example (which is also on Unesco's list of World Heritage Sites), buildings are physically frozen in time, while in Brasilia they remain forever new . . . as long as the city does not transgress its project status.

Notes

1 Oscar Niemeyer, Letter to José Aparecido, 4 October 1989.
2 Critics of Brasilia often rely on a similar metonymy when arguing that living in Brasilia is like living in an architectural model.
3 Anonymous government leaflet, 1822, cited by Raul de Sá Barbosa, 1960, p. 35.
4 See Sá Barbosa, 1960, p. 33.
5 Pereira, 1946, pp. 127–129.
6 Costa, "For Brazilian Students of Architecture Residing in the United States," sound cassette recorded in 1983.
7 Alexander, 1991, pp. 189, 204.
8 Dean, 1987, p. 73.
9 Vicentini, 1996, pp. 436–437.
10 Niemeyer, 1960, p. 12.
11 "Edital do concurso do plano piloto da nova capital do Brasil," *Brasília* 3 (1957): 20.
12 Silva, 1978, p. 116.
13 Holford, 1957, p. 13.
14 Costa, 1995, p. 282.
15 Costa, 1995, p. 295.
16 Costa, 1995, p. 283.
17 Marcelo Roberto, interview by Jayme Maurício, *Correio da Manhã*, 24 March 1957.
18 Costa, "Letter to Jayme Maurício," *Correio da Manhã*, 27 March 1957.
19 Costa, Interview by Cláudio Ceccon, *Jornal do Brasil*, 8 November 1961.
20 Brazilian Law # 3.751, Article 38, 13 April 1960.
21 Peralva, 1988, pp. 105–110.
22 Costa, *Brasilia Revisitada, 1985/1987*, photocopy.
23 Federal District Decree # 10.829, 14 October 1987.
24 Lucio Costa, Letter to Ítalo Campofiorito, 1 January 1990.
25 Portaria do Instituto Brasileiro do Patrimônio Cultural #314, 8 October 1992.

Image credits

4.1, 4.2, 4.3, 4.5: Fundação Oscar Niemeyer
4.4, 4.6: Casa de Lucio Costa
4.7: Instituto Moreira Salles
4.8, 4.9, 4.10, 4.11: Nik Nikolov
4.12: Günter Heil
4.13: Tuca Reinés

Chapter 5

Chicago – Superblockism: Chicago's Elastic Grid

Sarah Whiting

The 11 September 2001 destruction of Minoru Yamasaki's World Trade Center rapidly rekindled the long-standing debate over the viability and desirability of the superblock as an urban type. Condemnations forcefully outnumbered endorsements: "Break up the 16-acre Trade Center superblock" was the dismissive refrain of many a newspaper editorial. "Restore the traditional street grid so as to restore neighborhoods [. . . and] espouse community"[1] and other such suggestions directly echoed the urban critiques penned by urban advocate Jane Jacobs 43 years ago when she took on Lewis Mumford, Clarence Stein, Henry Wright, and the rest of the Garden City movement in *The Death and Life of Great American Cities*: "The Garden City planners and their ever increasing following among housing reformers, students and architects," Jacobs complained, "were indefatigably popularizing the ideas of the superblock, the project neighborhood, the unchangeable plan, and grass, grass, grass; what is more they were successfully establishing such attributes as the hallmarks of humane, socially responsible, functional high-minded planning."[2]

That one can draw a ring around bucolic suburban Garden Cities – such as Stein and Wright's Radburn, New Jersey of 1929 – and the extremely metropolitan World Trade Center and then label the entire lot of it "superblocks" reveals the Houdini-esque quality of this term, which eludes hard definition despite its extensive use throughout the world during the twentieth century. As an urban strategy – more specifically, as a platting strategy – the term "superblock" is used to describe three completely different organizational paradigms: the park-like configurations belonging to the Garden City; the enormous slabs or perimeter blocks of housing and other programs that emerged in Red Vienna, the Amsterdam School and the Soviet Union in the early twentieth century; and the superscaled plats embedded within Modernism's gridded orthogonality. If the former is associated with Mumford and Stein (and eventually with the pastoral pretense of suburban subdivisions), the second invokes de Klerk, Karl Ehn, and Mosei Ginzburg, and the third is firmly wed to Le Corbusier, whose "towers in the park" sprouted in city centers around the world throughout the 1950s and 1960s.

Enter Chicago and its particular perpendicular proliferation of the superblock. How does Chicago fit into the superblock's multifarious genealogical tree? Simple: it doesn't. Offering examples of all types of superblocks *avant la lettre* and then some, it exposes the weak spots of this system of classification. This is not to suggest that Chicago offers the *origin* of the superblock or an especially atypical form (or forms) of this urban type. Instead, it is to highlight the special case of Chicago as a city where the superblock is more a norm than an anomaly, due to the city's settlement history as well as certain economic and political histories. The value of Chicago as a case study for the superblock emerges especially from the particularities of its grid – a grid that marks the coincidence of urban and agricultural logics as they intersected at what was once the gateway to the American west. The historically threaded textual blocks below offer a verbal corollary to the urban superblocks of the Chicago metropolis: different in scope, scale and import, each offers a freeze-frame image of the elastic grid that makes up this city.

Long division

> The Chicago plain, in common with most of the Western United States, was surveyed in mile-square sections, which in turn were cut into four square quarter-sections and thus sold to settlers. Subdividers found it convenient to adopt a rectangular block plan in cutting up these quarter-sections, and such a layout was virtually forced upon them when the one-hundred-and-sixty-acre tracts were divided into four square "forties," or into sixteen square ten-acre parcels.[3]

Platted in 1830, Chicago, Illinois was squarely set within the gridiron tradition systematized by Thomas Jefferson's 1785 Northwest Ordinance, which subdivided the Western Territories into townships of 36 square miles. This gridded system divided the landscape into commodifiable parcels, thereby facilitating rapid (and rampant) land speculation. The grid homogenized the landscape in such a way that the cityscape was liberated, unanchored from its ground. Whereas earlier examples of landownership turned a deed or a title into a metaphoric stake in the earth, in Chicago and other Western cities land became paper thin, as if each plot were but randomly dealt chances in an endless game of seven-card draw. James Silk Buckingham's hyperbolic description from the early 1830s provides a telling glimpse of the city's speculative whirlwind: "some lots changed hands ten times in a single day and the 'evening purchaser' paid at least 'ten times as much as the price paid by the morning buyer for the same spot!' "[4] Land division multiplies economies. This redundant, repetitive exchange of plots depended upon the assumption that the city's platted rectangles were both easily identifiable and interchangeable. Accordingly, the plots were numbered and, throughout the city's first real estate boom of 1836, were sold sight-unseen in auction houses in New York, oftentimes offering surprises to the owners when they eventually made their way to the city named by the Indians for its unpleasant smells.[5]

Usually . . .

> The blocks may be made 300 feet square, and *usually* not over 320 feet by 400 feet, with a 20-foot alley running the long dimension of the block. The principal streets are *usually* made 80 feet in width, though frequently as much as 100 feet where the greater width appears to be needed or desirable, and the less important intersecting streets are seldom given a width of less than 60 feet. An alley is *usually* placed in each block, 20 feet in width and paralleling the principal street system. . . .Unless planned differently, the whole system is laid out on cardinal directions . . .[6]

Despite the implied rigor of the Ordinance grid's mathematical definition, Chicago's blocks are not entirely homogeneous. The phrase "usually," oft repeated within the pages of *The Manual of Surveying Instructions* of 1947, props up the image of a uniform grid like a broomstick holding a scarecrow against the wind: the term suggests regularity but admits aberration. If New York's unyielding grid "forces Manhattan's builders to develop a new system of formal values, to invent strategies for the distinction of one block from another,"[7] Chicago's is essentially the opposite: the grid itself is manipulated in order to distinguish one project from another. Because Chicago emerged from a territorial organization (unlike Manhattan, whose organization is limited by its island configuration), the city's logic lies at a scale much greater than its urbanism. Jefferson's original Ordinance divided the Northwest Territories into a grid of squares of 100 miles; subsequent amendments reduced the township scale to grids of 36 miles, 6 miles square on each side. Townships that were sold whole alternated in a checkerboard pattern with townships that were divided into 640 acre lots (1 square mile) or "sections."[8] Only when divided do these sizes become viable for agriculture or urbanism. Forty acres, one-sixteenth of a section, became the standard module size for farms, which would thereafter appear as 40 acres or multiples thereof (hence the saying, "forty acres and a mule"). Even if cities were divided into smaller parcels, urban subdivisions to this day continue to reveal the importance of the 40-acre module. Homer Hoyt's *One Hundred Years of Land Values* of 1933 illustrates the various ways in which a 40-acre tract can be divided into urban lots (Figure 5.1). It was this practice of subdivision that led to Chicago's "usually" blocks: some areas of the city were developed and therefore subdivided at the same time, leading to homogenous block sizes for entire zones. While it was only speculation that determined such continuity, lengths of streets such as Western Avenue reveal the scale of Chicago's real estate ventures: at 24.5 miles, Western remains the

5.1
Various Methods of Subdividing a 40 Acre Tract, 1320 Feet Square. In Homer Hoyt, 1933. *One Hundred Years of Land Values,* p. 431, Figure 103, University of Chicago Press

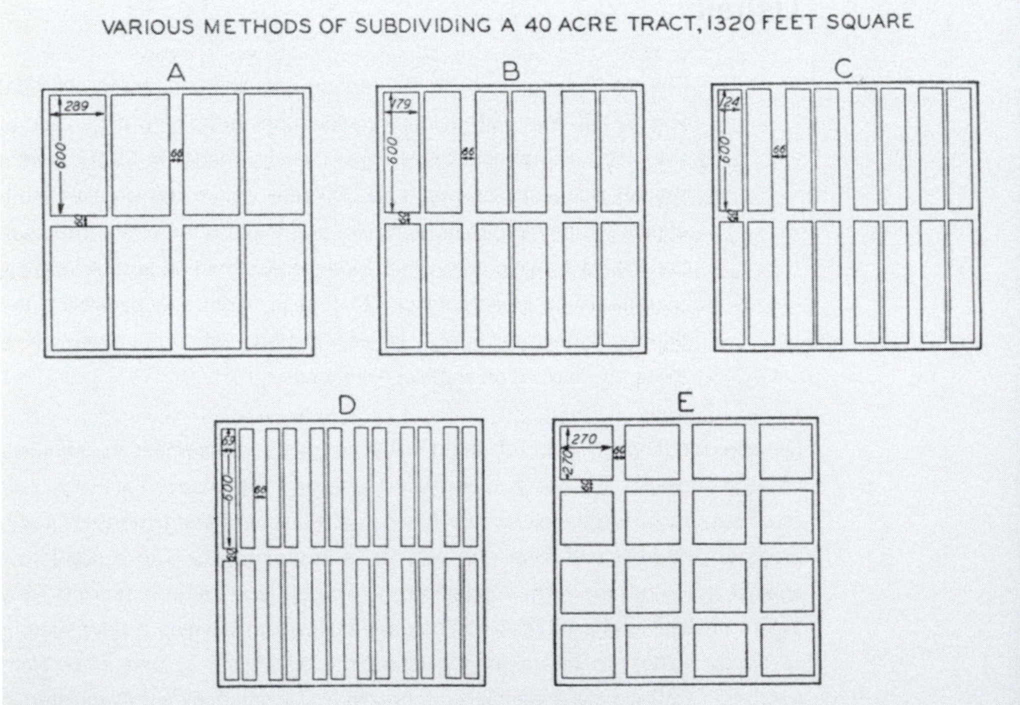

longest continuous street within city limits in the world.[9] Chicago block sizes range from 218 by 341 feet to 320 by 360 feet to what became, during the real estate boom from 1866 to 1873, the standard (or *usual*) Chicago block of 266 by 600 feet.[3]

Quarter-sections

> The site comprises a quarter-section of land assumed to be located on the level prairie about 8 miles distant from the business district of the City of Chicago. The tract is without trees or buildings and is not subdivided. The surrounding property is subdivided in the prevailing gridiron fashion . . .[10]

It was only in 1832 that Congress permitted the sale of the quarter-quarter-section, or the "forty." Until then, the primary module of land sale had been the quarter-section, or 160 acres.[11] Although the forty quickly became the favored unit for individual sales, the quarter-section remained firmly established as the module for subdivisions, as demonstrated by the City Club of Chicago's competition of 1913 for subdividing a typical quarter-section of land in the outskirts of Chicago.[10] While many of the 39 submitted entries can be considered "superblocks" in that they offer grids greater than the surrounding contextual grid of 272.5 by 610.5 blocks, one entry in particular constitutes an innovative superblock: Frank Lloyd Wright's non-competitive quarter-section plan[12] (Figures 5.2, 5.3). Wright's design maintained the overriding orthogonality of the Chicago grid system, but eschewed monotony by introducing what Wright called "picturesque variety." Wright's innovation for developing the residential section was the "quadruple block plan," which he had developed for an article that appeared in the *Ladies' Home Journal* in 1901.[13] The Quadruple Block Plan adopts not a rectangular but a square block subdivision (equivalent to Option E in Hoyt's diagram, Figure 5.1). By placing only four houses on a single small block, Wright was able to offer each house its own orientation. He pinwheeled the four around an inner core of shared utilities, thereby guaranteeing a degree of privacy while also ensuring visual variety: "[Each] building," Wright argued, "is in unconscious but necessary grouping with three of his neighbors', looking out upon harmonious groups of other neighbors, no two of which would present to him the same elevation even were they all cast in one mould. A succession of buildings of any given length by this arrangement presents the aspect of well-grouped buildings in a park, *of greater picturesque variety than is possible where façade follows façade.*"[14]

Indeed Wright created a picturesque relationship between buildings

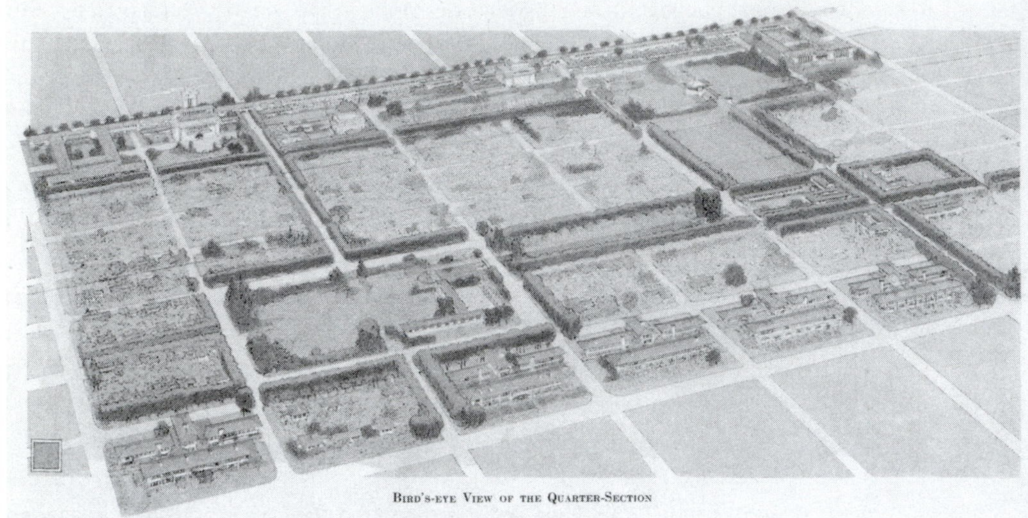

and park, but without either sacrificing the orthogonality of the grid or reducing the park to the role of mere spatial buffer. Financed by the sale of the residential property, the internalized park system weaves through the subdivision, ordering recreation features such as playgrounds, athletic fields, and a music pavilion. Balanced, although not entirely symmetrically, around a diagonal axis across the site, the park subtly segregates the residential from the civic and commercial sections of the subdivision in addition to differentiating residential zones of seven- or eight-room houses, two-flat buildings, workmen's houses, and women's and men's apartment buildings. It is this park that makes Wright's proposal a superblock prototype: the project foreshadows the two superblock types of the tower in the park and the garden city. The park reaches to the edges of the superblock but unlike the green carpets that Le Corbusier would design a decade later, this one is strategically programed: it combines low-rise and medium-rise densities with non-residential programming to animate the entire subdivision perpetually. While the park system blocks some through streets, it never creates cul de sacs like garden city superblocks would do, and thereby does not turn its back on Chicago by asphyxiating the larger urban grid.[15] While architect Albert Pope's book *Ladders* offers a provocative tableau of how the superblock can be read as a closed system, inverting the grid's centrifugal spatial field by introducing centripetal points of gravity within it, I would argue that certain developments in Chicago stem from the original platting patterns of this region and that, rather than shutting down the grid, these developments reveal this particular grid's ability to absorb and promote different scales and uses. While Wright's Quarter-Section Plan for the 1916 Competition was never executed, it illustrates the relationship between the

5.2
Bird's-Eye View of the Quarter-Section," Frank Lloyd Wright, in Alfred B. Yeomans, 1916, *City Residential Land Development: Studies in Planning*, p. 97. University of Chicago Press

5.3
Plan by Frank Lloyd Wright, in Alfred B. Yeomans, 1916, *City Residential Land Development: Studies in Planning*, p. 98. University of Chicago Press

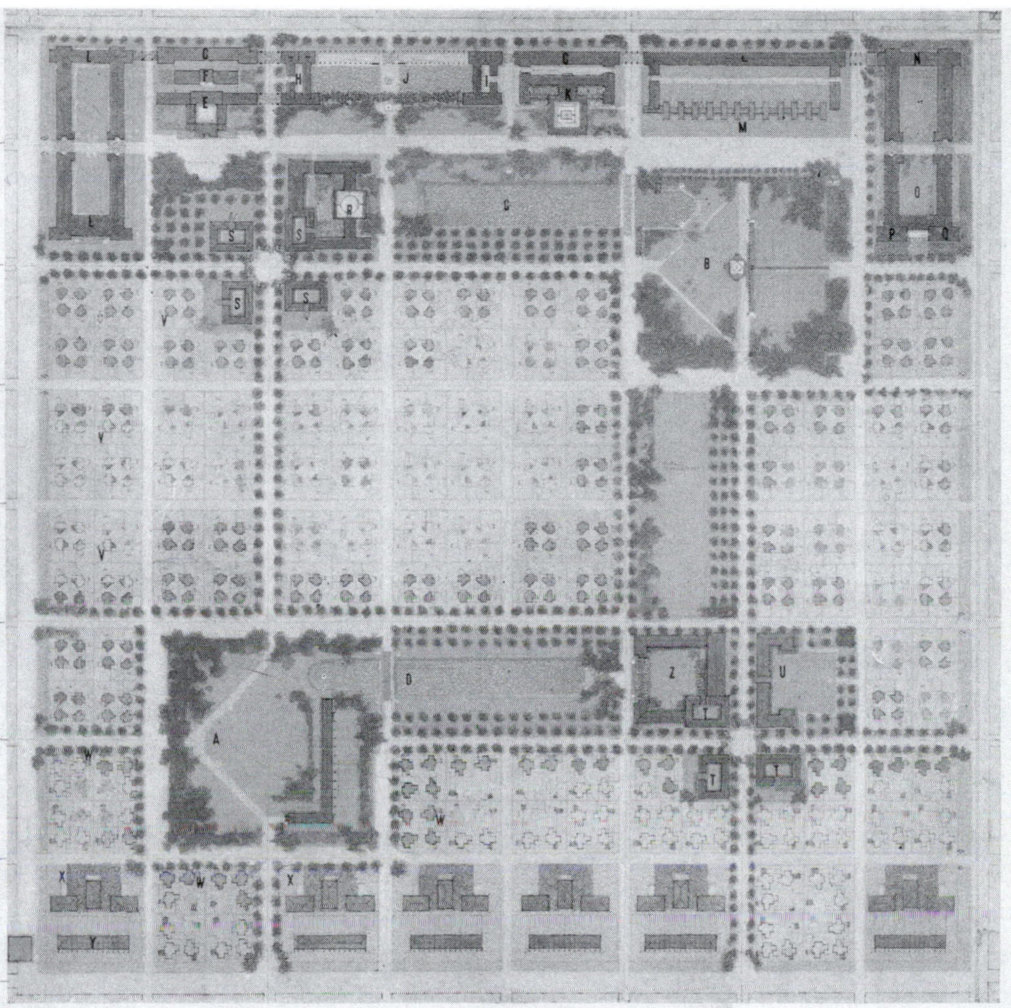

PLAN BY FRANK LLOYD WRIGHT

KEY TO PLAN

A. Park for children and adults. Zoölogical gardens.
B. Park for young people. Bandstand, refectory, etc. Athletic field.
C. Lagoon for aquatic sports.
D. Lagoon for skating and swimming.
E. Theater.
F. Heating, lighting, and garbage reduction plant. Fire department.
G. Stores, 3 and 4 room apartments over.
H. Gymnasium.
I. Natatorium.
J. Produce market.
K. Universal temple of worship, nonsectarian.
L. Apartment building.
M. Workmen's semi-detached dwellings.
N. Four and five room apartments.
O. Stores with arcade.
P. Post Office branch.
Q. Bank branch.
R. Branch library, art galleries, museum, and moving picture building.
S. Two and three room apartments for men.
T. Two and three room apartments for women.
U. Public school.
V. Seven and eight room houses, better class.
W. Two-flat buildings.
X. Two-family houses.
Y. Workmen's house groups.
Z. Domestic science group. Kindergarten.

STATISTICAL DATA

304 Seven and eight room houses.
120 Two-flat buildings, five and six rooms.
18 Four-flat buildings, four and five rooms.
6 Fourteen-family workmen's house groups.
12 Seven-room semi-detached workmen's houses.
6 Apartment buildings, accommodating 320 families in all.
4 Two and three room apartment buildings for women, accommodating 250 to 300.
Total, 1032 families and 1550 individuals (minimum).

dominant quarter-section subdivision land package and the superblock as a Chicago type. Additionally, it offers a more appropriate prototype for Chicago's boom period of superblock development during the 1940s than do the three typical models of superblock, for it demonstrates how development can work within the logic of the Chicago grid (that is, by prioritizing the most efficient sale of property) without being entirely subsumed by that same grid: Wright's superblock offers an urbanism of its own that emerges from the larger-gridded urbanism of its surroundings.

Centering the civic

> A civic center to serve Chicago where governmental and other related functions could be grouped, would promote greater efficiency in the conduct of the public's business. Its location should be readily accessible to all Chicagoans and at the same time tend to reduce congestion within the Loop.[16]

In 1943, the mayor of Chicago, Edward Kelly, was so confident that the United States would win the war he asked the Chicago Plan Commission to coordinate the city's envisioned public works projects so as to establish a Master Plan for a long-term improvement campaign. Like Daniel Burnham's famous Chicago Plan of 1909, the 1943 preliminary study included a proposal for a civic center. However, where Burnham's Civic Center interrupted the city grid – providing a Haussmannian focal point for his Plan's diagonal axes – the 1943 schematic proposal made a superblock (Figure 5.4). The whole Center occupied approximately eleven city blocks, straddling the Chicago River and Wacker Drive, both which were bridged by the project's gardens.

Six years later the Chicago Plan Commission submitted to the city a more complete proposal for the Civic Center. Covering the same eleven blocks and still a superblock, the project reveals modernism's impact on America at the war's end (Figure 5.5). The classical axes of the previous scheme were abandoned in favor of modernist slabs in a park, with each building corresponding to one part of government: Federal, State, County, and City. Additionally, there was one building for the Board of Education and another for all levels of judicial courts. The project was characterized by open siting, accessibility, efficiency, spaciousness, and diverse, flexible programming, including private as well as government offices. Sited along the river, the Civic Center foretells a new beginning, a renewal of Chicago's downtown in light of burgeoning suburban flight. The green carpet of the project deliberately offers a striking contrast to the Loop's three-dimensional density, and the Center's similar but not

5.4
Civic Center. In Chicago Plan Commission, 1943, *Chicago Looks Ahead: Design for Public Improvements*, p. 30

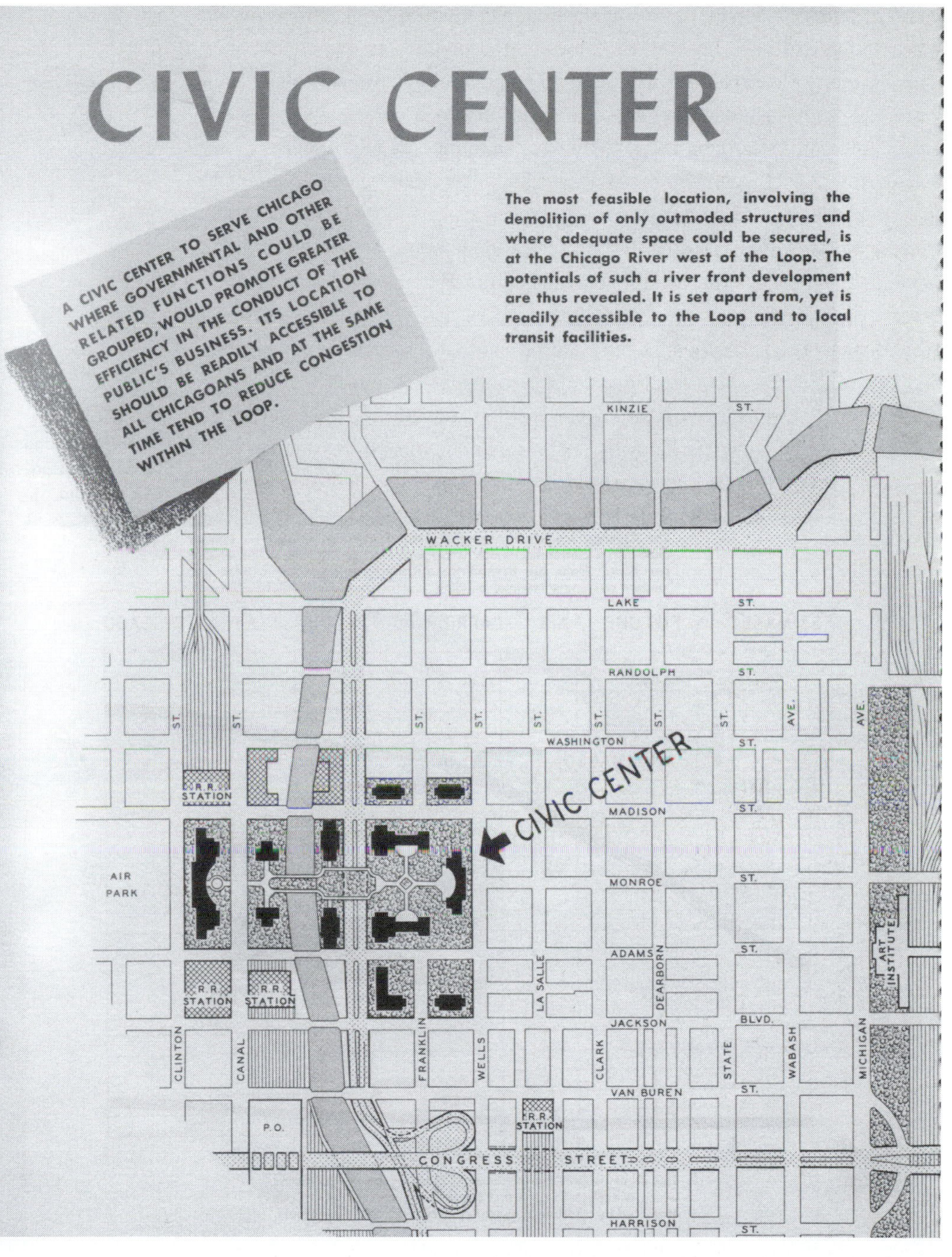
CIVIC CENTER
A CIVIC CENTER TO SERVE CHICAGO WHERE GOVERNMENTAL AND OTHER RELATED FUNCTIONS COULD BE GROUPED, WOULD PROMOTE GREATER EFFICIENCY IN THE CONDUCT OF THE PUBLIC'S BUSINESS. ITS LOCATION SHOULD BE READILY ACCESSIBLE TO ALL CHICAGOANS AND AT THE SAME TIME TEND TO REDUCE CONGESTION WITHIN THE LOOP.
The most feasible location, involving the demolition of only outmoded structures and where adequate space could be secured, is at the Chicago River west of the Loop. The potentials of such a river front development are thus revealed. It is set apart from, yet is readily accessible to the Loop and to local transit facilities.
KINZIE ST.
WACKER DRIVE
LAKE ST.
RANDOLPH ST.
WASHINGTON ST.
MADISON ST.
MONROE ST.
ADAMS ST.
JACKSON BLVD.
VAN BUREN ST.
CONGRESS STREET
HARRISON ST.
CLINTON
CANAL
FRANKLIN
WELLS
LA SALLE
CLARK
DEARBORN
STATE
WABASH
MICHIGAN
AVE.
R.R. STATION
AIR PARK
P.O.
ART INSTITUTE
CIVIC CENTER

identical buildings suggest a continuity of government without compromising the autonomy of each branch – a "proper atmosphere," as the presentation booklet notes. Modernist forms – maximal in size and minimal in articulation – were asymmetrically arranged like objects placed on a coffee table, and the space between and around these forms was as formed as the buildings themselves. The project's presentation emphasized these public spaces, suggesting that spectacles could take place in the expansive plaza and that more personal exchanges would result within the project's various social arenas, such as its restaurant and shops. The twelfth floor was a public concourse, like a street in the sky that joined all the slabs where its social and commercial amenities were concentrated. The openness of the planning, the reliance on spectacles and leisure, and the absence of traditional ornamental references were part of an effort to foster and symbolize what Sigfried Giedion had referred to as "communities of experience" in his 1944 argument for a redefined modern monumentality.[17] Indeed, underlying the project's openness and emphasis on public space was a desire to concretize post-war democracy.

5.5
Chicago Civic Center. In Chicago Plan Commission, 1949, *Chicago Civic Center*, p. 17

Looking at the scheme, it would be easy to claim that its superblock configuration was as influenced by European modernism as its building forms were; however, the classical Civic Center proposal from 1943 reveals that the superblock urbanism preceded the architecture. And it was the urbanism that remained constant even as the project underwent several more incarnations before Chicago was to get a Civic Center in the 1960s. It is not insignificant that when the Chicago Civic Center project went dormant after failing to secure the land east of the river, it was revived five years later for a site north of the river under the auspices of a privately funded business venture led by developer Arthur Rubiloff. Business was in a stronger position to design post-war democracy than government. "The Fort Dearborn Project" (even its name shed the legislative emphasis implied by "civic center") formally resembled the 1949 project (Figure 5.6). Programmatically, this version maintained the Civic Center's municipal and juridical functions, but also included significant additional programs, such as a Chicago campus for the University of Illinois. (As an aside, that campus was eventually realized west of the river in the 1960s. Remarkably, the University of Illinois Chicago campus site is exactly that of Burnham's 1909 Civic Center.) Like the 1949 project, Fort Dearborn was also never built because Rubiloff could not acquire the necessary land. Ultimately,

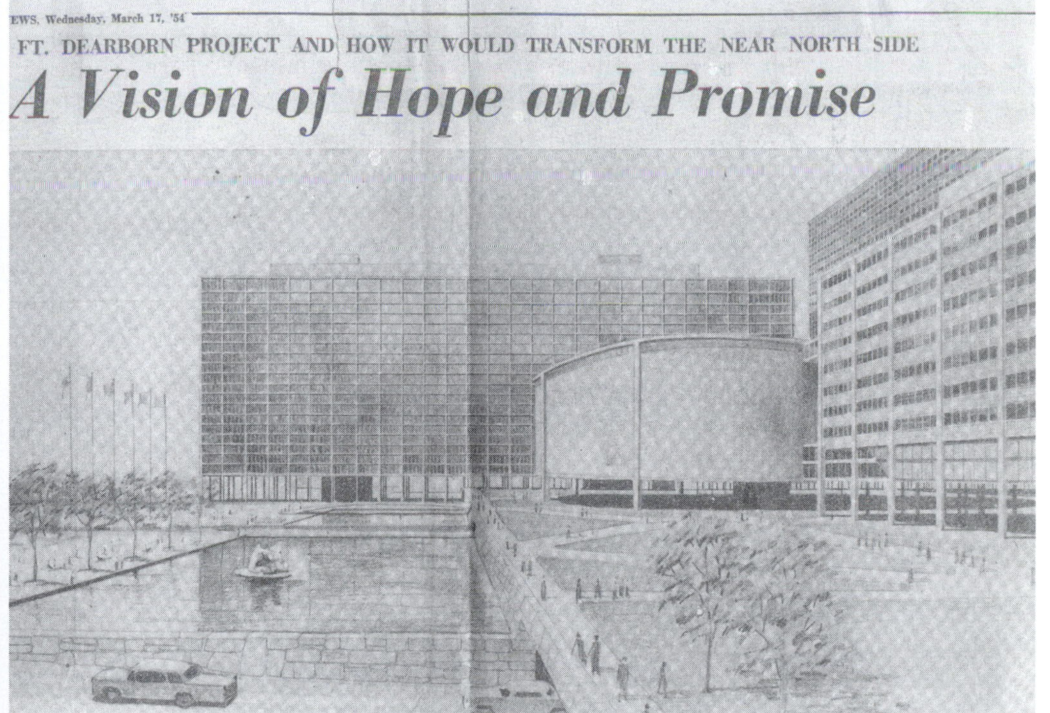

EWS, Wednesday, March 17, '54

FT. DEARBORN PROJECT AND HOW IT WOULD TRANSFORM THE NEAR NORTH SIDE

A Vision of Hope and Promise

5.6
A vision of Hope and Promise: How the Ft. Dearborn Project would appear in a view looking west from Dearborn St. Building in rear would be Federal building. Round building would be Hall of Justice. Building at right would be State building. Reflecting pool would be ice rink in winter. From The *Chicago Daily News*, Wednesday March 17, 1954, p. 60

the realized Federal Center and Civic Center, designed by Mies van der Rohe and C.F. Murphy respectively, which were built in the 1960s, dropped much of the programmatic complexity and "event-potential" of these previous schemes, but maintained the superblock configuration, albeit at a much smaller scale. Mies's Federal Center, for example, combines three buildings – an office building, courtroom building and post office – that cover a block and a half of the city. While Dearborn Street cuts the project in two, the Federal Center nevertheless reads as a single superblock of civic programming.

The conflation of public and private in these projects – most evident in the Fort Dearborn project, but even visible in the Civic Center proposal of 1949, which included shopping and restaurant facilities – was almost obligatory in the face of the large urban scale of these schemes. Like the Rockefeller Center, they were "cities within the city." While this designation may imply a fortress-like condition, these large campus-like insertions necessarily included the larger city within their borders – or, to put it differently, the boundary between the city and the city within was rarely exclusionary, particularly in the case of these primarily public institutions.

Inner-city landfill

> So I think it was a matter of passing through a space, spaces that were varying in dimension and varying in scale of height between buildings, length . . . You have a different psychological feeling when you come into a space with a high vis-à-vis a low, and vice-versa, building. So I think [Mies] was very careful, just in studying these things abstractly in blocks, cut pieces of wood . . . I was aware, yes, of what kind of space he was creating and what the effect was going to be by being in it.[18]

In 1937, after four years of trying to purchase property somewhere other than the Near South Side, the Armour Institute of Technology (later renamed the Illinois Institute of Technology or IIT) Board of Trustees concluded that the school could not afford to leave the area. With resigned optimism (tinged with a stiff shot of Manifest Destiny), President Willard Hotchkiss proclaimed that "now is the time to move forward and possess the land."[19] The 100-acre campus designed by Mies van der Rohe between 1939 and 1958 that ultimately emerged from this fortuitous decision has been recognized for its structural integrity and elegance, as well as for its innovative approach to American campus design, but it has yet to be read as a productive urban model (Figure 5.7). When studied in the context of Chicago's Near South Side of the 1940s,

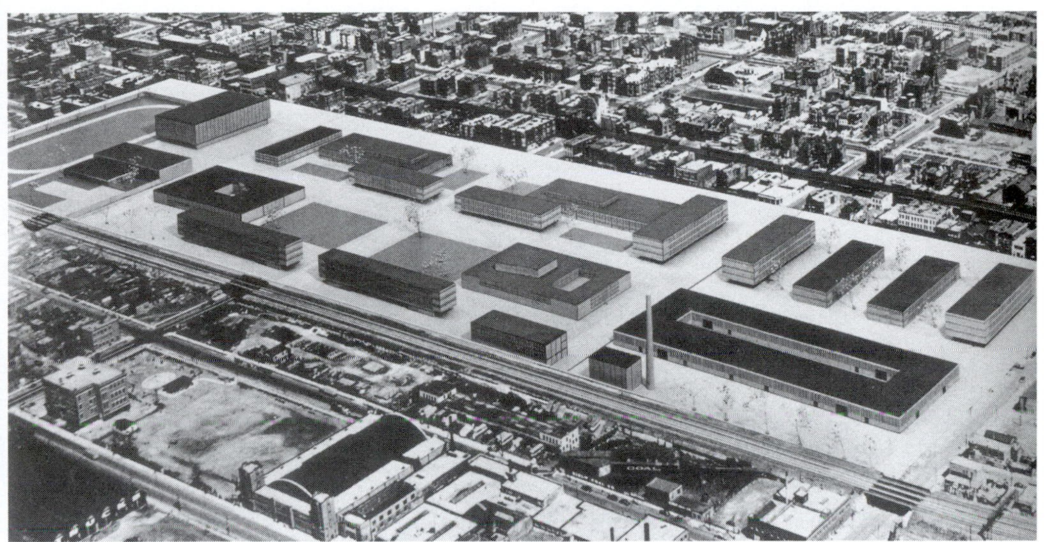

5.7
Mies van der Rohe, "IIT campus, photomontage aerial view showing model within Near South Side" (detail), 1947. Hedrich-Blessing, photographer. Chicago Historical Society HB 26823B

however, another, more effective reading of IIT emerges: rather than forming just a set of innovative buildings, the campus forms an integral component of a larger, more complex and multifarious field. Mies's plan for IIT initiated a new form of modern urbanism that represents an epitome of the Chicago superblock that is at once figural and abstract, figure *and* ground. An inner-city landfill of green carpet, the campus offers an example of how the superblock reconfigures the urban grid in order to *figure space*.[20]

Even fans of the campus describe it as an autonomous island that disregards its physical and social context. Such an interpretation is only reinforced by Mies's presentation collages, which ruthlessly eliminated 100 acres of the city's dense urban fabric in order to make way for the expansive, low-density campus. But both the size of the campus and the strategy of dispersing buildings on the site were decisions that predated Mies's arrival on the scene. IIT was one of a network of superblocks that emerged in unison on the Chicago South Side during this period (Figure 5.8). Beginning with IIT, and later including Michael Reese Hospital, the Chicago Housing Authority, Mercy Hospital, and several private-housing developments, a group of institutions collaborated to plan and execute one of the first large-scale modern urban plans in the United States. This seven-mile-square plan paved the way for federal slum clearance, redevelopment, and urban renewal legislation, including the Housing Acts of 1949 and 1954. In addition to Mies and Ludwig Hilberseimer from IIT, key figures involved in the promotion of the Near South Side Plan included Walter Gropius, planners Reginald Isaacs and Walter Blucher, real-estate developer Ferd Kramer, IIT President Henry Heald, and University of Chicago sociologist Louis Wirth, among others.

5.8
South Side Planning Board Redevelopment Plan for the Near South Side. In John McKinlay, 1950, *Redevelopment Project No. 1: A Second Report,* The New York Life Insurance Company Redevelopment Plan, p. 8

Contrary to what one might assume, once Mies was officially asked to design the campus, he did not start by designing the plan. Instead he began by studying the program, which was just being developed (and which would continue to be developed over the twenty years that Mies directed the project). After considering and testing various alternatives, he determined that a 24-foot-square module could be used to accommodate the programs of classroom buildings, lab buildings, and office spaces. Rough volumes were established and wooden blocks were cut, with gridded elevations pasted on, and then Mies and his associates played with the blocks on the "site": a large piece of paper, gridded with the same 24-foot module.[21] Although Mies once claimed that he did not think that site was "that important,"[22] the combination of the gridded background and the gridded blocks gives the impression that the blocks protrude from the paper – that the figures of the buildings emerge from the field of the Chicago grid, flipping it up 90 degrees from a horizontal to a vertical surface. Although the decision to divide the school's program into several individual buildings predated Mies's arrival at IIT, and although this choice was probably driven largely by economic concerns (it was easier to raise money for individual departments and to proceed slowly if the process was broken down into pieces), this decision was also the mechanism that allowed the design of IIT to be as much the design of a campus (or quasi-urban) space as it was a design of buildings. Mies's method of moving blocks about rather than working only in plan demonstrates to what extent he recognized the problem of the campus design to be a three-dimensional spatial issue.

At the scale of the campus, the "ceremonial" or communal programs (the library and the student union) are given significant sites, but do not serve to centralize or focus the campus as they would had they been conceived along the lines of a traditional city plan. Rather than occupying the center of the central courtyard space these programs define its edge, as well as the edge of what is referred to as Mies Alley. Presentation drawings also reveal the campus's accessible institutional identity, or new monumentality. Rather than converging onto one significant point or feature, Mies's perspectival views tend to draw the outsider into the campus; their multiple side axes promise endless possibilities lying just around the corners of the drawn buildings. When the perspectives do focus upon a building's entry, the ground plane slips through the door into the lobby, suggesting a continuum rather than a boundary. In the earliest schemes, many of the buildings were on pilotis; it was Mies's dream that the entire ground plane could be one surface, interrupted only by the glass walls of the lobby spaces and stairs, smoothly taking people up into the buildings above. Each building would then have a transitional, public/private space between the exterior public world and the interior private or academic world. Even if budget considerations eventually forced the elimination of the pilotis, the continuum was stressed: once the decision was made to put the buildings on the ground, Mies put them directly onto the ground, aligning the ground floor slab with the ground itself.[23] Even the detailing of the doors does not interrupt the flow of space between outdoors and indoors, as demonstrated by the centered, pivot-hinge doors to Lewis (now Perlstein) Hall: the door handles are kept vertical and in alignment with the doorframe, avoiding any interruption of the view. Given that the campus plan was designed as if the field and the figures were one and the same – the gridded blocks emerging from the grid of the ground plane – it was not necessary for the "ground level" of the buildings and of the landscape to remain level zero: the "ground" is sometimes at grade and sometimes raised above grade, as with Crown Hall, where the main level is half a level above street level. Even the lower levels that get used – Crown, the Commons, and Alumni Memorial Hall – are more like a ground plane that has dipped downwards rather than a basement. The use of half-levels, high clerestory windows, ramps, and shallow, wide, and unenclosed stairways turn the experience of this modulated ground plane into that of a continuous topographical surface.

In 1942, then IIT President Henry Heald wrote a letter to Mies suggesting that, for esthetic and security reasons, a wall be erected around the perimeter of the campus. In a particularly insensitive gesture toward those displaced by the demolition, Heald even suggested building the wall of recycled materials culled from former homes: "It has been suggested that a brick wall might be used, built from brick salvaged from some of our wrecking operations."[24] While no reply is documented, Mies's answer lies in the campus's permeability.[25] Just as the courtyards are not closed off with four walls, the campus as a whole is open. The field upon which IIT's buildings sit extends out from the centermost courtyards to the very edges of the campus. With such moves, Mies deliberately redirected the city grid in a positive way and at two scales: that of IIT itself, where he replaced the *tabula rasa* of the land-clearance program with a modulated abstraction, and that of the entire Near South Side, which would follow Mies's design lead.

Superscale

> Marina City was the first mixed use city center complex in the United States to include housing . . . The Marina City towers were the tallest apartment buildings in the world and the highest concrete buildings in the world at the time of construction . . . Marina City remains the densest modern residential plan in the United States, and possibly in the world, with 635 dwellings per acre.[26]

America's Midwest is the land of big vistas, Big Gulps™, and big buildings. Not surprisingly, Chicago is no stranger to superlatives. It is the home of the first mail-order company (Montgomery Ward), the largest commercial building (the Merchandize Mart), and, until recently, the world's busiest airport (O'Hare) and the world's tallest building (the Sears Tower). Bertrand Goldberg's Marina City is perhaps best known for its formal and structural innovation: the primary components of the project are two concrete residential towers shaped like corncobs (Figure 5.9). Goldberg himself underscored the project's superlative achievements: "At 588 feet, these towers were the tallest concrete buildings in the world and also the highest apartment buildings; at $10 per square foot, they were also the most economical. They were also the first American mixed-use urban complex to include housing."[27] Each tower's core carries the majority of the building's structural load: a concrete tube houses the elevators and stairs with the apartments ringing it like flower petals on a daisy. As a superblock, it maxes out a three-and-a-half acre block of the city grid. In comparison to IIT's 100 acres this size may not seem very superblock-esque, but Marina City qualifies because, like Frank Lloyd Wright's Quarter Section Competition entry, it offers a city within a city – a residential enclave with commercial, communal and recreation amenities.

As a *type*, Marina City might be compared to the Socialist superblocks of Mosei Ginzburg and others – for few people realize that the complex includes other buildings than the superscaled, iconic residential

5.9
Marina City. In Ira J. Bach, 1965, 1980, *Chicago's Famous Buildings*, p. 82. University of Chicago Press

towers and marina base. But Marina City presents the Narkomfin's resolutely capitalist cousin: its communal living occurs only at the level of recreation, rather than dining or laundry or other aspects of personal life. The apartments were envisioned for singles or childless couples, and the lifestyle of what was advertised as a "twenty-four hour city block" (to heighten the contrast with the bedroom communities surrounding Chicago) was tailored for this particular demographic. The complex includes housing, parking, an office block, commercial space, four theaters, and a restaurant, bowling alley, swimming pool, skating rink, and marina. Conceived as a city within a city, the recreation and office facilities ensured that it would *participate in* rather than *isolate itself from* the city, for the project's programs deliberately reach beyond its own constituency to draw people in from all of Chicago. As a prescient solution to both urban sprawl and urban fiscal crises, Goldberg imagined entire cities composed of such complexes. These urban complexes would increase the city's density, thereby providing the population needed to support the costs of public transportation, culture, and other urban amenities. Goldberg's initial proposal for River City in Chicago was a linear city of tower triads which, reminiscent of the Civic Center's twelfth-floor public concourse, would be connected at every eighteenth floor by bridges offering communal amenities, such as post offices, health care, and daycare facilities, in addition to having commercial and other support programs at their base. This triad scheme takes the city within a city one scale further: different identities (and amenities) are provided at the scale of the single tower, the joined triad, and the 750 residents across the three towers who define a bridge community (there are three such horizontal communities in each triad).

Superminiurbanism

> The superblock is more (and less) than a building. It has implications of size and complexity but also of the lowering of architectural voltage, because, unlike the representational buildings of the past, it is unable to acquire the status of a metaphor.[28]

Alan Colquhoun has argued that a superblock can never play a representational role within the city and that these are "rapidly destroying the traditional city." In the context of Chicago, however, the superblocks that stretch the city's original grid, causing it to absorb ever-variable, ever-evolving programs, are on the contrary constantly constructing the city, *figuring* it. The combination of grid and superblocks of all kinds works to redefine the urban understanding of background versus foreground: here the background is the grid, an ever present datum that is consistent enough to be understood, even if in reality it varies considerably. Read against this background, each superblock offers its own mini-urbanism – each constructs its own version of a different kind of Chicago grid. Colquhoun is right to say that superblocks cannot operate as metaphors, but that does not mean that they are not read or representational. Each superblock in Chicago contains an urban vision, an urban representation or snapshot of one part of Chicago. Like a tartan plaid, each one can read as a specific block unto itself, but each block also connects into the city via the grid. While the superblock has been condemned as a large-scale totalizing vision, the totalization that is Chicago is – because of the superblock's agglomeration – the most heterogeneous homogeneity of urban tableaus.

Acknowledgments

I would like to thank Albert Pope for provoking my interest in the superblock and Ron Witte, R. E. Somol and Cécile Whiting for their helpful suggestions regarding this text. Thanks also to Ed Robbins and Rodolphe el-Khoury for their generous patience and perseverance.

Notes

1 See Shiffman, 2002.
2 Jacobs, 1961, p. 22.
3 Hoyt, 1933, p. 428.
4 Buckingham, 1842 (cited in Reps, 1965, p. 302).
5 "Historians still argue over the origin of the name, some maintaining it comes from the Indian *Chicagou*, 'garlic,' while others hold that it was derived from *Shegagh*, or 'skunk.' There is general agreement, however, that the odors of the place were dreadful and that the Indians were correct in referring to it as "the place of the evil smell." Reps, 1965, p. 300.
6 Bureau of Land Management, 1947, p. 352 (emphasis added).
7 Koolhaas, 1984, pp. 20–21.
8 Johnson, 1976, pp. 42–44.
9 Condit, 1973, pp. 52–53.
10 Yeomans, 1916, p. 2.
11 Johnson, 1976, pp. 60–61. An 1804 Act of Congress established the section, half section and quarter section as units of land sale; an 1832 Amendment included the quarter-quarter section, or "forty."
12 According to Frank Lloyd Wright specialist Neil Levine, the plan is "non-competitive" (as Yeomans labels it in the competition book) because it was most likely submitted to the City Club after the competition deadline, after Wright had been solicited to offer a scheme. Wright did not participate in competitions.
13 My thanks to Neil Levine for this reference. Levine has an article forthcoming on the quadruple block plan.
14 Yeomans, 1916, p. 99 (emphasis Frank Lloyd Wright's).
15 Pope, 1996.
16 Chicago Plan Commission, 1945, p. 30.
17 Giedion, 1944, p. 568.
18 George Danforth in conversation with Kevin Harrington, Canadian Centre for Architecture Oral History Project, unpublished transcript: 96–100.
19 Willard E. Hotchkiss in *Armour Institute Board of Trustees Minutes* (1934–40), addendum 2 (17 May 1937), 11.
20 A longer version of this section appears in Lambert, 2001, pp. 642–691. This version, which concentrates less on the policies that enabled this superblock than on the figuring of space within the superblock, owes thanks to Robert McAnulty for perceptively suggesting that the thing to pay attention to in the "tower in the park" is the park, not the tower.
21 "We then also, as Mies got the program from the various departments of the school, we

made wood blocks of the volume of the building, and on a plot of the whole site I drew up, he would work those out in some arrangement within the spaces of the buildings, having had that plot from – what was it? – 31st Street down to 35th, State Street over to the tracks to the west, drawn up in a modular system that he had found workable for the contents of the program." George Danforth in conversation with Kevin Harrington, CCA Oral History Project.

22 Interview with Katherine Kuh, in Kuh, 1971, p. 35.

23 Safety considerations were an issue as well: as George Danforth notes, had the buildings been built in this manner, the stairwells would have been filled with a dangerously crushed crowd of students at the beginning and end of each class. (George Danforth in conversation with Kevin Harrington, 9 April 1996, CCA Oral History Project.

24 Letter from Henry Heald to MvdR, 30 July 1942, Heald papers, Box 17, folder 4, IIT Archives, Paul V. Galvin Library. Thank you to Phyllis Lambert for kindly pointing me to this reference.

25 It has been argued that Mies's open perimeter depended upon an urban "wall" of poché, formed by the context around the campus; see Pierce, 1998, p. 5. Given that Mies was cognizant of IIT's expansionist desires and land-purchasing efforts, I would be surprised that he would base his logic upon the campus's immediate context. Second, given that the landscape of the campus deliberately extends to the public realm, I hold to my reading that Mies envisioned it extending as far as it could.

26 Goldberg, 1985a, p. 33.

27 Goldberg, 1985b, p. 192.

28 Colquhoun, 1981, p. 98.

Chapter 6

Detroit – Motor City

Charles Waldheim

> The belief that an industrial country must concentrate its industry is, in my opinion, unfounded. That is only an intermediate phase in the development. Industry will decentralize itself. If the city were to decline, no one would rebuild it according to its present plan. That alone discloses our own judgment on our cities.[1]

In the second half of the twentieth century, the city of Detroit, once the fourth largest city in the US, lost over half its population.[2] The *motor city*, once an international model for industrialized urban development, began the process of decentralization as early as the 1920s, catalyzed by Henry Ford's decision to relocate production outside the city to reduce production costs. While similar conditions can be found in virtually every industrial city in North America, Detroit recommends itself as the clearest, most legible example of these trends evidenced in the spatial and social conditions of the post-war American city (Figure 6.1).

> Forget what you think you know about this place. Detroit is the most relevant city in the United States for the simple reason that it is the most unequivocally modern and therefore distinctive of our national culture: in other words, a total success. Nowhere else has American modernity had its way with people and place alike.[3]

In August 1990, Detroit's City Planning Commission authored a remarkable and virtually unprecedented report.[4] This immodest document proposed the decommissioning and abandonment of the most vacant areas of what

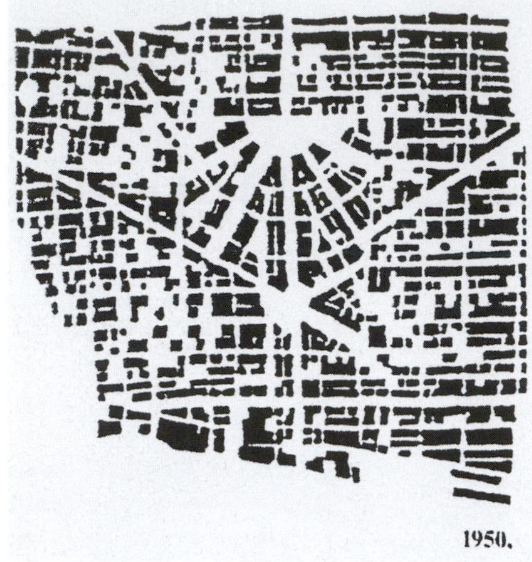

had been the fourth largest city in the US. With this publication, uninspiringly titled the *Detroit Vacant Land Survey*, the city planners documented a process of depopulation and disinvestment that had been underway in Detroit since the 1950s.[5] With an incendiary 1993 press release based on the City Planning Commission's recommendations of three years previously, the city Ombudsman, Marie Farrell-Donaldson, publicly called for the discontinuation of services to, and the relocation of vestigial populations from, the most vacant portions of the city (Figure 6.2):

6.1
Downtown Detroit figure-ground diagrams, Richard Plunz, "Detroit is Everywhere," *Architecture Magazine*, 85(4), 55–61

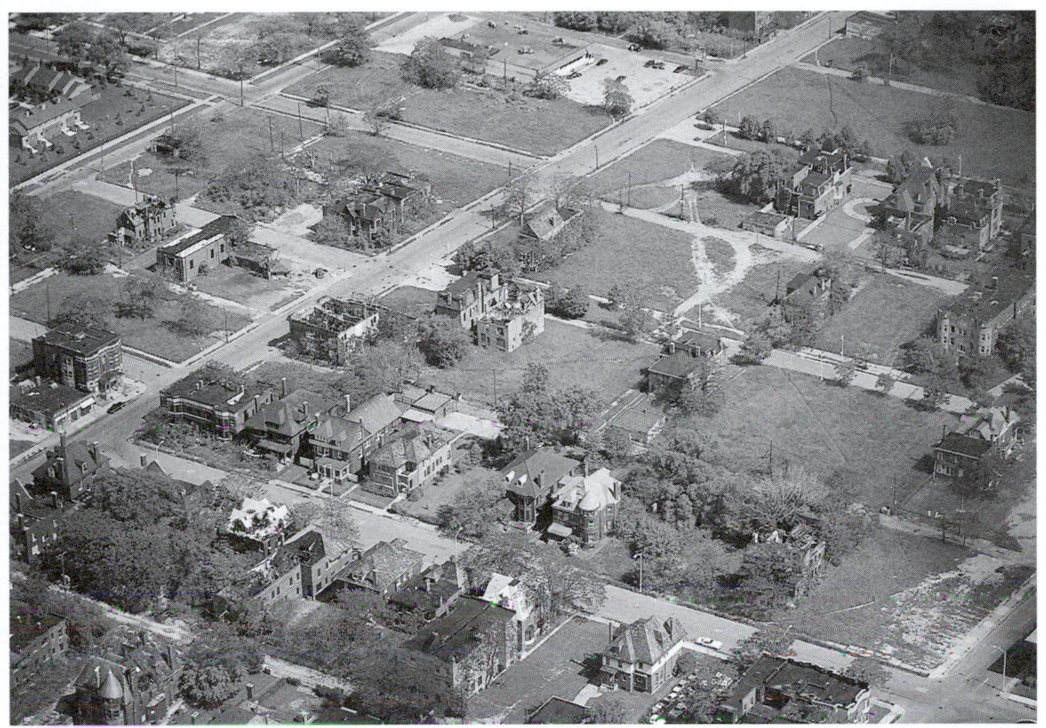

6.2
Brush Park, aerial photograph courtesy Alex MacLean/ Landslides

> The city's ombudsman . . . is essentially suggesting that the most blighted bits of the city should be closed down. Residents would be relocated from dying areas to those that still had life in them. The empty houses would be demolished and empty areas fenced off; they would either be landscaped, or allowed to return to "nature."[6]

Until the public release of the survey, the depopulation of Detroit was largely accomplished without the endorsement of, or meaningful acknowledgement by, the architectural and planning professions. What was remarkable about Detroit's 1990 *Vacant Land Survey* was its unsentimental and surprisingly clear-sighted acknowledgement of a process of post-industrial de-densification that continues to this day in cities produced by modern industrialization. Equally striking was how quickly the report's recommendations were angrily dismissed in spite of the fact that they corroborated a practice of urban erasure that was already well underway (Figures 6.3–6.6).

While European proponents of modernist planning had originally imported Fordism and Taylorism from American industry and applied them to city planning, it was the American city (and Detroit in particular) that offered the fullest embodiment of those principles in spatial terms. Ironically, while the American planning profession ultimately embraced the virtues of Fordist

6.3
Motor City, photographs courtesy Jordi Bernado

urbanism in the middle of the twentieth century, it was ill-prepared for the impact those ongoing processes would have on forms of urban arrangement as evidenced by the condition of Detroit at the end of that century. Among those impacts were the utter abandonment of traditional European models of urban density in favor of impermanent, *ad hoc* arrangements of temporary utility and steadily decreasing density.

While flexibility, mobility, and speed made Detroit an international model for industrial urbanism, those very qualities rendered the city disposable. Traditional models of dense urban arrangement were quite literally abandoned

6.4
Motor City, photographs courtesy Jordi Bernado

6.5
Motor City, photographs courtesy Jordi Bernado

6.6
Detroit's Vacancy, photographs courtesy Jordi Bernado

in favor of escalating profits, accelerating accumulation and a culture of consumption. This of course was the genius of Ford's conception: a culture that consumes the products of its own labor while consistently creating a surplus of demand, ensuring a nomadic, operational, and ceaselessly reiterated model of ex-urban arrangement. That ongoing provisional work of rearrangement is the very model of American urbanism that Detroit offers.

Typical of their peers in other American cities, Detroit's city planners, architects, and urban design professionals clinicalized the dying industrial city to the extent that Detroit came to represent an *urban* failure, as though the

responsibility for its viability rested with the techniques of modernist urbanism that shaped its development. This was to mistake effect for cause. As a product of mobile capital and speculative development practices in the service of evolving models of production, Detroit was a clear and unmistakable success. As promoted internationally by the proponents of Fordism, Detroit served as a model of urbanism placed in the service of optimized industrial production. With each successive transformation in production paradigms, Detroit re-tooled itself more completely and more quickly than virtually any other city in history.

What was remarkable about the *Detroit Vacant Land Survey* and the City of Detroit's plan to decommission parts of itself was not its impossibility, but rather the simple fact that it dared articulate for public consumption the fact that the city was already abandoning itself. This fact alone did not make Detroit unique. In the 1990s, Detroit ranked a distant twenty-second nationally in the percent of its population lost compared with other metropolitan centers, having already surrendered the majority of its citizenry over the previous four decades.[7] The original abandonment and subsequent suburban annexation of central Detroit began well before similar conditions emerged in other major cities. Unlike other cities, however, Detroit began its process of decentralization and urban abandonment sooner and pursued it more completely than any other city in the modern world. Perhaps more importantly, Detroit was the only city that dared publicly to articulate a plan for its own abandonment and conceive of organizing the process of decommissioning itself as a legitimate problem requiring the attention of design professionals. In a graphically spare document featuring maps blacked-out with marker to indicate areas of vacant land, Detroit's planners rendered an image of a previously unimaginable urbanism of erasure that was already a material fact (Figure 6.7).[4]

> One last question must now be asked: during a crisis period, will the demolition of cities replace the major public works of traditional politics? If so, it would no longer be possible to distinguish between the nature of recessions (economic, industrial) and the nature of war.[8]

Over the course of the 1990s, the City of Detroit lost approximately 1 percent of its housing stock annually to arson, primarily due to "Devil's Night" vandalism.[9] Publicly, the city administration decried this astonishingly direct and specific critique of the city's rapidly deteriorating social conditions. Simultaneously, the city privately corroborated the arsonists' illegal intent by developing, funding, and implementing one of the largest and most sweeping demolition programs in the history of American urbanism. This program continued throughout the 1990s, largely supported by the city's real estate, busi-

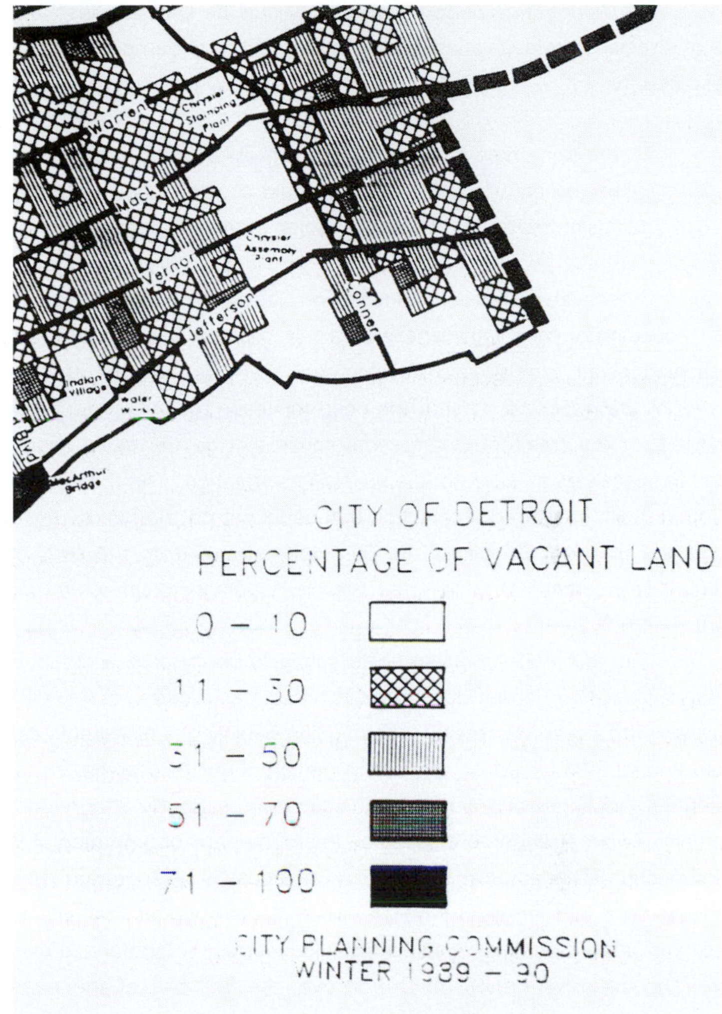

6.7
City of Detroit City Planning Commission Vacant Land Survey

ness, and civic communities. This curious arrangement allowed both the disenfranchized and the propertied interests publicly to blame each other for the city's problems while providing a legal and economic framework within which to carry out an ongoing process of urban erasure. Ironically, this "solution" to Detroit's image problems completed the unsanctioned process of erasure begun illegally by the populations left in the wake of de-industrialization. Vast portions of Detroit were erased through this combination of unsanctioned burning and subsequently legitimized demolition.[10] The combined impact of these two activities, each deemed illicit by differing interests, was to coordinate the public display of social unrest with administration attempts to erase the visual residue of Detroit's ongoing demise.

In *The Practice of Everyday Life*, Michel de Certeau describes the limits of disciplinary relevance absent the human subjects demanded by professional authority:

> . . . the dying man falls outside the thinkable, which is identified with what one can do. In leaving the field circumscribed by the possibilities of treatment, it enters a region of meaninglessness.[11]

For the architectural profession, the city of Detroit in the 1990s entered a similar condition of meaninglessness precisely because it no longer required the techniques of growth and development that had become the modus operandi of the discipline. Absent the need for these tools, Detroit became a "non-site" for the architect in the same sense that de Certeau's dead body ceased to operate as a "site" for the physician's attention.[11] As the city decommissioned itself, it entered a condition that could not be *thought* by the architectural and planning disciplines. As Dan Hoffman put it, in the early 1990s ". . . unbuilding surpassed building as the city's primary architectural activity (Figures 6.8, 6.9)."[12]

The fact that American cities began to dissolve as a result of the pressures of mature Fordist decentralization came as a surprise only to those disciplines with a vested interest in the ongoing viability of a nineteenth-century model of urbanism based on increasing density. Free of that prejudice, the development of American industrial cities can more easily be understood as a temporary, *ad hoc* arrangement based on the momentary optimization of industrial production. The astonishing pliability of industrial arrangement and the increasing pace of change in production paradigms suggest that any understanding of American cities must acknowledge their temporary, provisional nature. The explosive growth of Detroit over the first half of the twentieth century, rather than constructing an expectation of enduring urbanism, must be understood as one-half of an ongoing process of urban arrangement that ultimately rendered its previous forms redundant.[13] Detroit can be seen as nothing more than the most recent idea about production as manifest in spatial terms. The fact that American industrial urbanism would decreasingly resemble its European and pre-Fordist precedents should come as no surprise. Rather than a permanent construction, one must take American urbanism as an essentially temporary, provisional, and continuously revised articulation of property ownership, speculative development, and mobile capital.[14]

6.8
Erasing Detroit, **courtesy Dan Hoffman**

Especially for those modernists interested in mobility and new models of social arrangement, the flexibility and increasing pace of technological change associated with Fordist production served as models for an increasingly temporary urbanism. The most obvious model for this iterative and

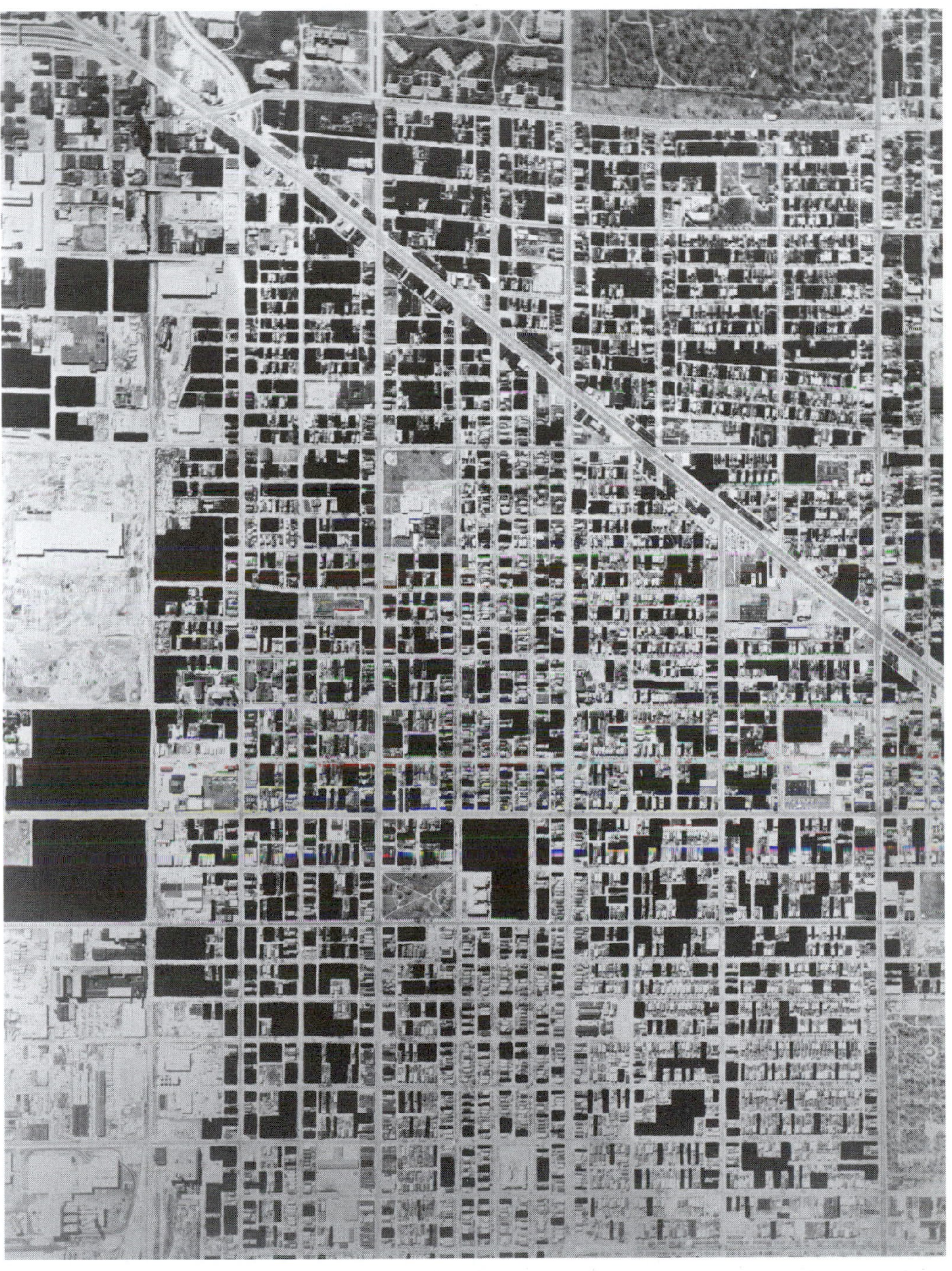

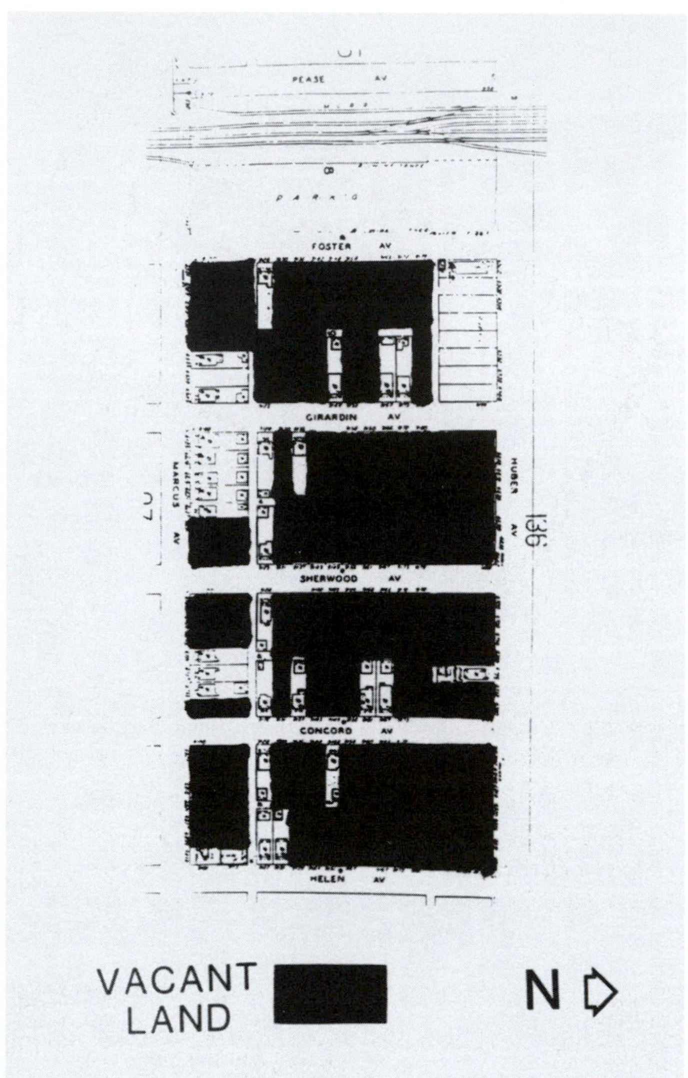

6.9
Detroit Vacant Land Maps, City of Detroit

responsive urbanism could be found at the intersection of industrial production and military infrastructure.[15] For Le Corbusier, the origins of the city itself could be found in the urbanism of the military encampment. Commenting on the architectural myths of the primitive hut, this drawing of a circumscribed martial precinct reveals the essentially nomadic pre-history of urban arrangement in European culture (Figure 6.10). Ancient rites for the founding of Roman cities were essentially symmetrical with those for the founding of military encampments. In *The Idea of a Town*, Joseph Rykwert describes how performing the precise reverse of those founding rites was used to signify the decommissioning or abandonment of an encampment, thus corroborating their essentially

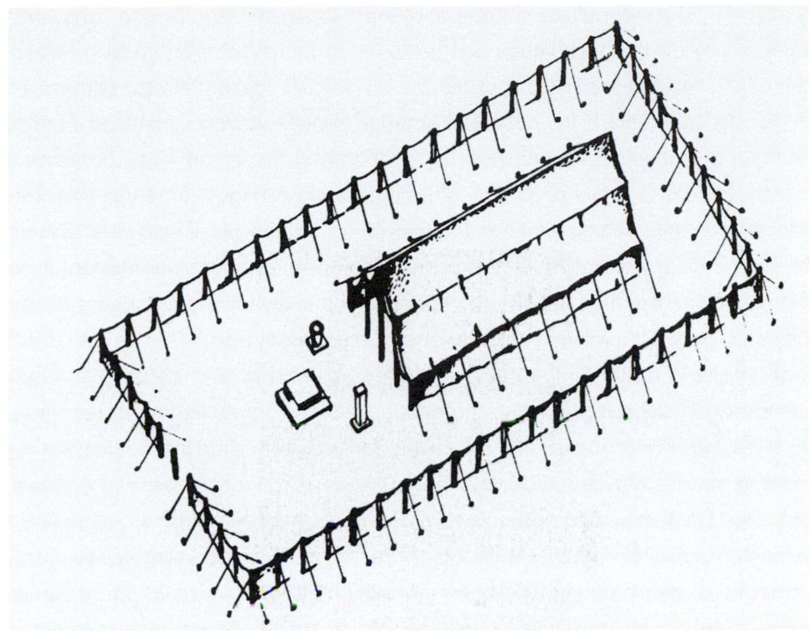

6.10
Military Encampment as Primitive Hut

symmetrical status.[16] With his Coop Zimmer project, Hannes Meyer commented on the collusion between the mass consumer products of Fordist production and their replication in the miscellany of modern military nomadism.[17] Meyer's project arranged a *petit-bourgeois* domestic ensemble of semi-disposable consumer furnishings as the interior of an equally transportable military accommodation (Figure 6.11).

6.11
Hannes Meyer's *Coop Zimmer*

The most direct critique of modern urbanism as informed by twentieth-century military techniques can be found in the projects of Ludwig Hilberseimer.[18] Hilberseimer's proposals for a radically decentralized pattern of regional infrastructure for post-war America simultaneously optimized Fordist models of decentralized industrial production and dispersed large population concentrations that had become increasingly obvious targets for aerial attack in the atomic age. Hilberseimer's drawing of an atomic blast in central Illinois renders a clear imperative for the construction of a civil defense infrastructure capable of transporting dense urban populations away from the dangers of the city and toward the relative security of suburban dissolution.[1] This model of the highway as a military infrastructure afforded a form of civil defense through camouflage. Not coincidentally, the depopulation of urban centers in response to the Cold War argues quite effectively for precisely the kind of decreasing density that his previous work had been predicated on in the name of efficient industrial production and optimized arrangement. In both modalities, as military encampment and industrial ensemble, the vision of a nationally scaled infrastructure of transportation and communication networks revealed a fundamental sympathy between Fordist models of industrial production and military models of spatial projection.

Much has been written on the military origins of the modern interstate highway system in the US, and the impact of military policy on post-war American settlement patterns has been well documented. While the highway is arguably the clearest evidence of Fordism's impact on post-war urban arrangement in America, it is also clear that this most Fordist network is itself an essentially military technology. Given Ford's well-documented sympathy to Nazism, the infrastructural and logistical logics of the German war machine provided an essential case study in the virtues of Fordist mobility.[19] Not simply a model of production, but an essential Fordist precept, mobilization was understood as a preparation for not only the projection of military power but also the retooling of the very industrial process itself toward martial ends. It should come as no surprise that the modern interstate highway, the very invention Ford's success postulated, was itself first proven necessary through German military engineering. By witnessing the logistical superiority and civil defense potential of the autobahns, the American military industrial complex was able to articulate the need for the highway as an increasingly urgent matter of national security.

Not coincidentally, Detroit has the dubious honor of being the only American city to be occupied three times by Federal troops.[20] Another evidence of the parallels to be drawn between military encampments and Detroit's temporary urbanism can be found in the symmetrical techniques employed to enforce social order amidst the dense concentration of heterogeneous populations. The history of Detroit's labor unrest documents the various quasi-military techniques employed to render a suitably compliant labor pool to serve the needs of the production line. Detroit's social history has oscillated between periods of peacefully coerced consumption (fueled by advertising and increasing wages) and periods of profound social unrest, largely based on the desire for collective bargaining, improvements in economic conditions, and to redress racial and ethnic inequities.[21]

Ford's famous *five-dollar day* and *five-day workweek* were quite calculated levers intended to fuel the consumption of mass products by the working classes themselves. The volatile concentration of diverse populations of laborers in dense urban centers was among the factors that led Ford to begin decentralizing production as early as the 1920s.[14] The combination of decentralized pools of workers each with sufficient income to consume the products of their own labors produced a new economic paradigm in the twentieth century, and also helped to fuel the rapid depopulation of post-industrial urban centers in post-war America.

In 1955, at the height of post-war emigration from the city, a uniquely talented team was assembled to renovate one of the city's "failing" downtown neighborhoods.[22] A federally underwritten Title I FHA urban renewal project, which would come to be known as Lafayette Park, the work of this interdisciplinary team offers a unique case study in a continuously viable and vibrant mixed income community occupying a modernist superblock scheme. In light of recently renewed interest in the problems of modernist planning principles, and the continual demolition of many publicly subsidized modernist housing projects nationally, Lafayette Park offers a unique counterpoint, arguing precisely in favor of modern principles of urban planning, and recommending a thoughtful revision of the perceived failures of modern architecture and planning *vis-à-vis* the city (Figures 6.12–6.14).

Led by the developer Herbert Greenwald (until his untimely death in a 1959 airplane crash) and a team of real-estate professionals, the financial underpinnings of the project included $7.5 million in FHA loan guarantees (out of a total construction budget of $35 million) as well as a substantial federal subsidy toward the cost of the land. Originally planned as a mixed-income and mixed-race development, Lafayette Park continues to this day to enjoy multiple original family residents, high relative market value, and greater racial, ethnic, and class diversity than both the city and suburbs that surround it. Greenwald's original conception of the neighborhood remains remarkably viable today, as the site continues to provide central city housing to a middle-class group of residents with the perceived amenities of the suburbs, including decreased density, extensive landscaping and public parks, easy access by automobile, and safe places for children to play.

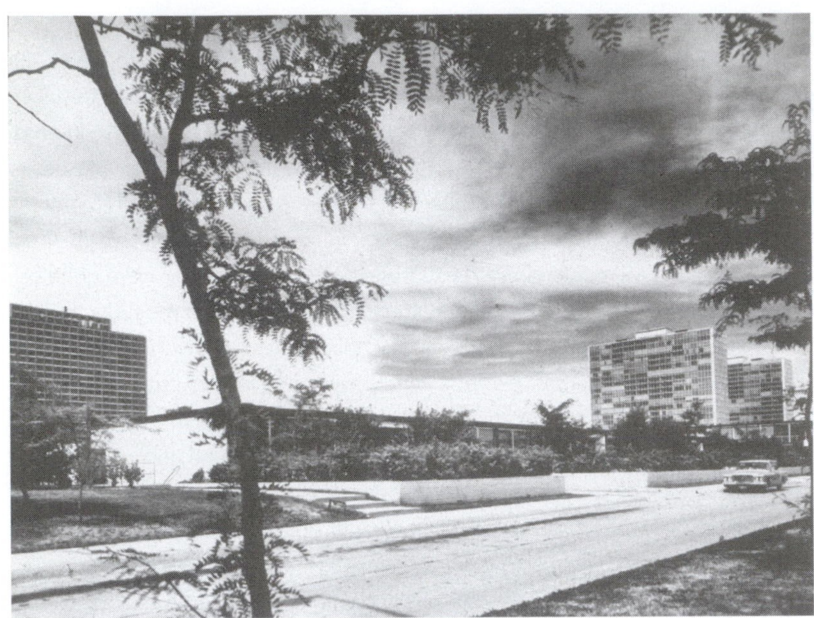

6.12
Lafayette Park, Hedrich Blessing Photographs courtesy Chicago Historical Society

6.13
Lafayette Park, Hedrich Blessing Photographs courtesy Chicago Historical Society

6.14
Lafayette Park, Hedrich Blessing Photographs courtesy Chicago Historical Society

Greenwald enlisted the professional services of architect Ludwig Mies van der Rohe for the design of the project, with whom he had previously worked on the development of the 860–880 Lake Shore Drive Apartments in Chicago. Mies brought to the team Ludwig Hilberseimer, to plan the site, and Alfred Caldwell, to execute the landscape design. Based largely on his previous academic projects in Germany and the US, Lafayette Park provided the most significant application of Hilberseimer's conception of the "settlement unit" as well as the most important commission of his career. Hilbs' settlement unit was particularly apt as an aggregation of planning principals and types appropriate to the decentralizing North American city.[22] Best known for his un-built urban design projects from the 1920s (e.g. Hochhausstadt, 1924), Hilbs began to work on the notion of landscape as the primary medium for a horizontal and radically decentralized post-urban landscape as early as the 1930s. First evidenced in mid-1930s' projects for mixed-height housing schemes and the University of Berlin campus, these tendencies toward an idea of landscape *as* urbanism are immediately evident in Hilb's plans for the Lafayette Park site, a portion of the city of Detroit that decentralized first, fastest, and most fully.

Hilberseimer's plans for the site proposed landscape as its primary material element, the commission offering both sufficient acreage as well as budget for what could have otherwise been an uninspired urban void. Central to this was Greenwald's finance and marketing scheme, which positioned landscape as the central amenity in the form of an eighteen-acre park bisecting the site and providing a much sought-after social and environmental amenity in the midst of Detroit. Lafayette Park removed the vestiges of the obsolete nineteenth-century street grid, in favor of a lush verdant and extensive green *tabula verde*. By doing this, Hilberseimer accommodated the automobile completely at Lafayette Park yet rendered it secondary to the primary exterior spaces of the site, as the parking is in proximity to units while zoned to the perimeter of the site and dropped by approximately one meter below grade. To the extent that landscape can be seen as a primary ordering element (in lieu of architecture) for the urbanization of the site, Hilbs' collaboration with Mies at Lafayette Park provides a unique case study for examining the role of landscape in post-war modernist planning more generally.

At the end of the twentieth century, at least 70 urban centers in the US were engaged in an ongoing process of abandonment, disinvestment, and decay.[23] While most Americans for the first time in history now live in suburban proximity to a metropolitan center, this fact is mitigated by the steadily decreasing physical density in most North American cities. Rather than taking the abandonment of these previously industrial urban centers as an indicator of the so-called "failure" of the design disciplines to create a meaningful or coherent public realm, these trends must be understood as the rational end game of industrial urbanism itself, rendering legible a mobility of capital and dispersion of infrastructure that characterize mature Fordist urbanism as prophesied by Ford himself.[14] In spite of a decade-long attempt to "revitalize" the city of Detroit with the construction of theaters, sports stadia, casinos and other publicly subsidized, privately owned, for-profit destination entertainment, Detroit continues steadily to lose population and building stock. These latest architectural attempts to proclaim Detroit "back" have effectively committed the city to a future as a destination entertainment theme park for its wealthy suburban ex-patriots. Rather than signaling a renewed "vitality" or life for the post-industrial city, these projects continue to mine the brand name of Detroit, while the city continues to abandon itself to a decentralized post-industrial future. In spite of a massive federally funded advertising campaign and a small army of census takers, the 2000 US census showed Detroit's population continuing to shrink (Figure 6.15).[24]

As Detroit decamps it constructs immense empty spaces – tracts of land that are essentially void spaces. These areas are not being "returned to nature," but are curious landscapes of indeterminate status. In this context, landscape is the only medium capable of dealing with simultaneously decreasing densities and indeterminate futures. The conditions recommending an urbanism of landscape can be found both in the abandoned central city and on the periphery of the still spreading suburbs. Ironically, the ongoing process of green-field development at the perimeter of Detroit's metropolitan region

6.15
Destination tourism, stadia and casinos trade in the brand "Detroit," aerial photograph courtesy Alex MacLean/ Landslides

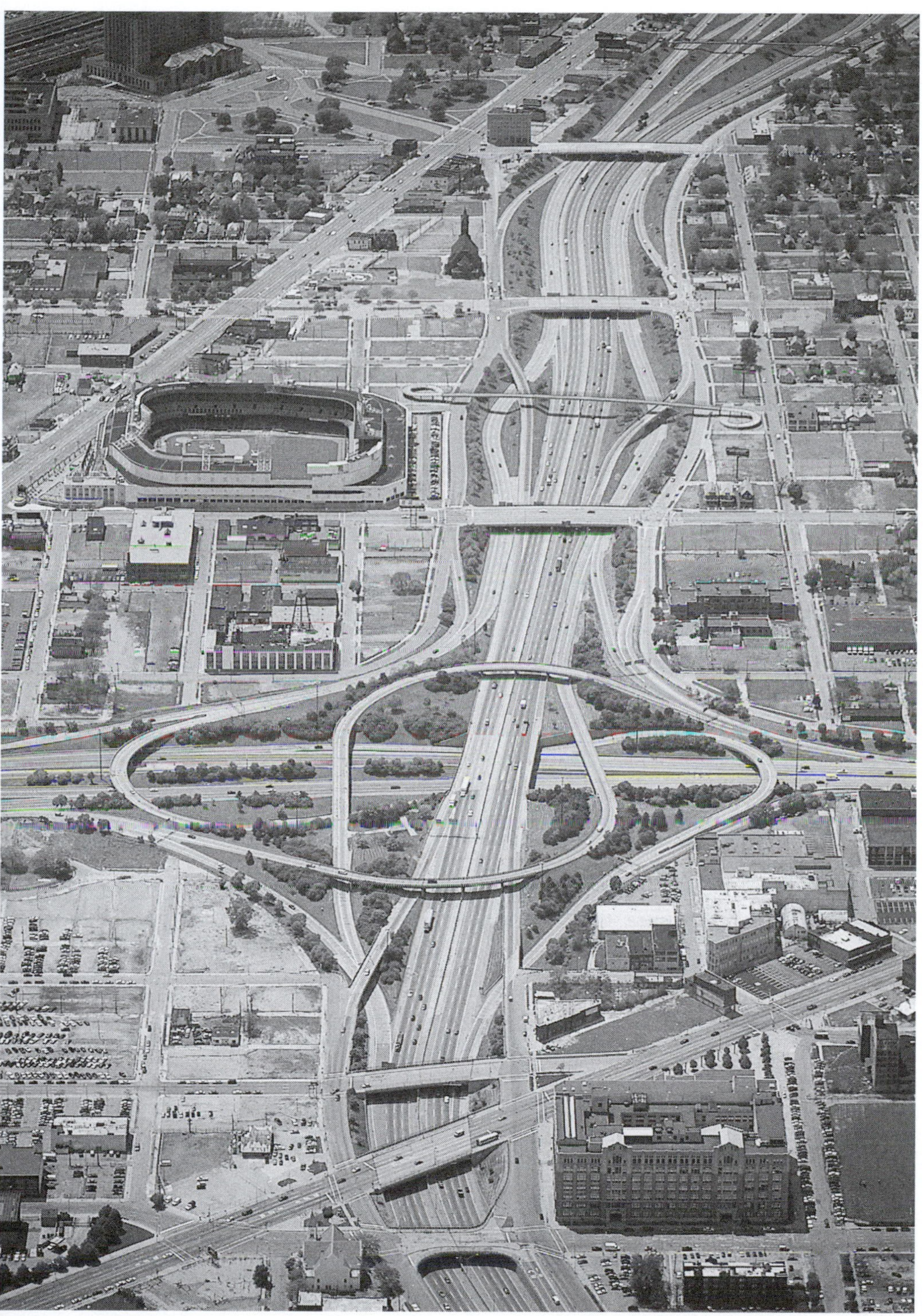

brings up similar questions posed by the incursion of opportunistic natural environmental systems into areas of post-urban abandonment. For these sites, both brownfield and greenfield, what is demanded is a strategy of landscape *as* urbanism, a *landscape urbanism* for Detroit's post-industrial territories.[25]

The decommissioning of Detroit's vacant lands recommends strategies for staging or setting-up reserves of open land of indeterminate status. These reserves of open space necessitate infrastructural strategies for social and ecological arrangement in the context of an indeterminate future. Also needed are collective conceptions of these spaces that are capable of rendering Detroit's post-industrial territories legible to various populations and constituencies. Rather than allowing these spaces to be legislated by brand naming and destination tourism, their future viability as true void spaces depends upon the imaginary and mythic conditions of their founding. Toward this end, the decommissioning of these territories requires the same kind of public participation and rites that attended to their original annexation and incorporation.

One of the more compelling cultural images for these deterritorialized "zones" can be found in Andrey Tarkovsky's film *Stalker*.[26] Tarkovsky's film constructs a decommissioned post-industrial wilderness in which the causality, linearity, and temporal organization of Fordist space are inverted. In the place of a recently and catastrophically absent Fordist/militarist control, *Stalker* presents a uniquely imaginative view of a post-industrial future in the aftermath of Chernobyl, Three Mile Island, and Bhopal (Figures 6.16–6.18).

Tarkovsky's protagonist, the Stalker himself, displays a post-urban intelligence capable of divining a trajectory across an otherwise inhospitable and foreboding landscape. At once both more ominous and more inspiring than the primordial European wilderness that serves as its inverted other, Tarkovsky's "Zone" conflates the worst of post-industrial contamination, invisible toxicity and entropic decay. Occasionally offering a deceptively beautiful impression of a seemingly pastoral and benign nature, Tarkovsky's Zone represents the overlay of a primordial and abundant natural environment, an aging and abandoned industrial infrastructure, and an increasingly opportunistic set of mutating ecological conditions. The Zone's cessation of Fordist/Taylorist imperatives in lieu of a post-modern conflation of infrastructure and ecology recommends it as an image of Detroit's not too distant future.

Acknowledgments

Work on this essay has benefited greatly from the support and advice of others, particularly Rodolphe el-Khoury, whose generosity and insight were abundantly apparent at all stages of the work. This work has particularly been informed by numerous conversations with Jason Young and Georgia

6.16
Andrey Tarkovsky's *Stalker*

6.17
Andrey Tarkovsky's *Stalker*

6.18
Andrey Tarkovsky's *Stalker*

Daskalakis, with whom I co-edited *Stalking Detroit* (Barcelona: ACTAR, 2001). Contributors to that anthology, Jerry Herron, Patrick Schumacher, Dan Hoffman, and Kent Kleinman, have each helped to clarify my interests in Detroit in particular ways. The origins of this essay can be found in the research and design project "Decamping Detroit," co-authored with Marili Santos-Munne in *Stalking Detroit* (Barcelona: ACTAR, 2001), 104–121.

Notes

1 Henry Ford as quoted in Ludwig Hilberseimer, 1945, pp. 89–93.

2 In the first half of the twentieth century, the population of Detroit grew from under 285,700 in 1900 to over 1,849,500 in 1950. That number dropped steadily in the second half of the century to 951,270 at the 2000 Census. For more on Detroit's declining population, see Rybczynski, 1995, pp. 14–17, 19.

3 See Herron, 1993.

4 *Detroit Vacant Land Survey*, 1990.

5 *Detroit Vacant Land Survey*, 1990, pp. 3–5.

6 *The Economist*, 1993, pp. 33–34.

7 US Census Bureau figures for Detroit indicate that the populations of 21 metropolitan areas in the United States, including St Louis, Washington DC, and Philadelphia, were shrinking at a faster rate than Detroit's during the decade of the 1990s.

8 Virilio, 1986. In 1998, Detroit's Mayor Dennis Archer secured $60 million in loan guarantees

from the US Department of Housing and Urban Development to finance the demolition of every abandoned residential building in the city. See *Metropolis*, 1998, p. 33.

9 See Chafets, 1990, pp. 3–16. While precise numbers of houses lost to arson are hard to quantify, local myth places the figure at a conservative 1 percent annually. On media coverage of arson in Detroit, see Herron, 1993.

10 On the urban impact of Detroit's massive demolition program, see Hoffman's, 2001.

11 De Certeau, 1984, p. 190.

12 See Hoffman, 2001a. According to research by Sanford Kwinter and Daniela Fabricius, between 1978 and 1998 approximately 9000 building permits were issued for new houses in Detroit, while over 108,000 demolition permits were issued. See Kwinter and Fabricius, 2000, p. 600.

13 Hoffman, 2001b.

14 Schumacher and Rogner, 2001.

15 Paul Virilio has commented on the fundamentally warlike conditions of Fordist urbanism. See Virilio, 1986.

16 Rykwert, 1988.

17 Hays, 1995, pp. 54–81.

18 Hilberseimer, 1949; Pommer *et al.*, 1988.

19 For a discussion of the military imperatives of modernist urbanism, see Kwinter, 1994, pp. 84–95.

20 For a description of the martial enforcement of civil order in the context of race relations in Detroit, see Sugrue, 1996.

21 Sugrue, 1996, pp. 259–271.

22 For an excellent overview of Lafayette Park, see Pommer *et al.*, 1988, pp. 89–93.

23 Alan Plattus "Undercrowding and the American City: A Position Paper and a Proposal for Action," unpublished manuscript, pp. 1–8.

24 The aggressive and unsuccessful federally funded campaign to count Detroit's citizens for the 2000 census was aimed in part at maintaining Detroit's eligibility for certain federally funded programs available only to cities with a population of one million or more. See *Chicago Tribune*, 2000.

25 Waldheim coined the term "landscape urbanism" in 1996 to describe the emergence of landscape as the most relevant medium for the production and representation of contemporary urbanism.

26 For a more complete description of the Stalker's subjectivity, see Andrey Tarkovsky, 1986.

Chapter 7

Los Angeles – Between Cognitive Mapping and Dirty Realism

Paulette Singley

> The Los Angeles region is increasingly held up as a prototype (for good or ill) of our collective urban future. Yet it is probably the least understood, most understudied major city in the United States.[1]

> A Metropolis that exists in semidesert, imports water three hundred miles, has inveterate flash floods, is at the grinding edges of two tectonic plates, and has a microclimate tenacious of noxious oxides will have its priorities among the aspects of its environment that it attempts to control.[2]

Define *postmodernism*. Or more specifically, define *Los Angeles*. These two terms – which resist the limitations of conventional definition – act as accomplices in discussions about the contemporary city. If postmodernism (PM) in architecture and urban design implies the indiscriminant application of historical references to the production of space, resulting in superficial layers of pastiche, then the stylistic diversity and commercial noise of Los Angeles – a city of back lots within an urbanism of set design – certainly fits this model *avante lettre*. If postmodernism, conversely, works within literary theory as a set of operations that expand upon and transform the canons of high modernism into an empty chain of signifiers, imploding vertiginously upon an illegible hyperreality, then again Los Angeles – and its postindustrial landscape of late capitalism – might offer a different model of this same term.[3] The unclean alliance between PM and LA begs the following questions. Is Los Angeles superficial or is postmodernism? If the city cannot be read is this because it is illegible or because many of its interpreters are casual readers? We know that a frontal attack on the slippery practices of postmodern theory and its concomitant libidinal freedoms proves unwise and that nostalgia – worse yet – contaminates any possible return to history. Wresting an image of the city, therefore, from the mythology that has placed it within the crosshairs of such theorizing, proves challenging if not entirely Utopian. In other words, Los Angeles is bigger than *postmodernism* and yet, has been defined by it.

Admittedly, several other pivotal moments in Los Angeles's urban history and theory would provide rewarding areas of inquiry to the extent that focusing on the so-called postmodern moment of the city, at a certain level, risks further shoring up the same rhetoric. Regarding in particular the impact of what has come to be known as the "LA School" of thought on configuring the city, Kazys Varnelis writes the obituary for this phase of Los Angeles's urban history, arguing that:

> the 1992 riots and 1994 Northridge Earthquake validated the L.A. School's predictions, but, they were also the end of its relevance. Unable to propose any intervention and unable to offer an insight into the recovery of the late 1990's, the L.A. School seems spent, the fatalism of the program having inevitably undermined it.[4]

Varnelis's indictment likewise verifies a need to examine the city with different criteria and to focus our attention on different sites. Included in such research might be approaching the city as it has been rendered in film, beyond the discussion of *noir* and the later interpretations of this genre, such as Roman Polanski's *Chinatown* (1974) or Ridley Scott's *Bladerunner* (1982). The influence of various waves of European immigration upon the city, ranging from the arrival of Rudolf Schindler and Richard Neutra to Theodor Adorno and Bertolt Brecht, might form another locus of inquiry. Another compelling study of the city might consider shifting patterns of diversity, density, and ethnicity through an analysis of emigration and demography that examines physical rather than cultural geography. Or one might explicate Los Angeles with equal success by examining infrastructural matrices such as those formed by the Pacific Electric Railway, oil wells, freeways, the Metro Transit Authority, the Department of Transportation, or the Department of Water and Power.

Although a number of scholars have initiated or completed some of the projects outlined above, establishing a substantial bibliography about Los Angeles, the work of contemporary theorists has absorbed this often conventional research into a larger and more exciting fiction of postmodernism that reaches a wider audience than that of a simple architecture or urban design readership.[5] As proffered by Jean Baudrillard in "The Precession of the Simulacra" (1983), Fredric Jameson in "Postmodernism or, The Cultural Logic of Late Capitalism" (1984), Umberto Eco in *Travels in Hyperreality* (1986), Edward Soja in *Postmodern Geographies: The Reassertion of Space in Critical Social Theory* (1989), and Mike Davis in *City of Quartz: Excavating the Future in Los Angeles* (1990) – to name the most conspicuous examples – the geopolitical imaginary of Los Angeles remains coincident with the writings of these thinkers. Soja summarizes Jameson's take on the Westin Bonaventure Hotel in downtown Los Angeles as emblematic of the larger city:

> For Jameson, this "populist insertion into the city's fabric" has become a "hyperspace" of both illusion and compensation, a new kind of cultural colony and brothel (my combining of Foucault's separate allusions) that exposes many of the archetypal "performative" conditions of contemporary postmodernity: depthlessness, fragmentation, the reduction of history to nostalgia, and, underlying it all, the programmatic decentering of the subordinated subject and the rattling awareness that the individual human body has been losing the capacity "to locate itself, to organize its immediate surroundings perceptually, and cognitively map its position . . ."[6]

Back and forth, these scholars have invested a certain amount of intellectual capital debating whose interpretation of John Portman's design for this hotel is the most prescient to the extent that ever since Baudrillard, Jameson, Soja, and Davis have had their way with the city, little, one might think, is left to be said about LA.

Jameson's essay, both for its clarity and its chronological position in the debate, is the definitive starting point for explicating the conditions of postmodernity. He outlines the following attributes that Soja began to enumerate above: (1) a lack of depth, center, or thematic coherence; (2) the death of the author, the subject, and the grand narrative; (3) history as pastiche, *la mode rétro* (4) "the spatial logic of the simulacra"; and (5) fragmentation or random heterogeneity – terms that he conveniently exports into LA urbanism. If, as Jameson asserts, architecture remains "the privileged esthetic language" of postmodernist culture, then Los Angeles, too, remains the privileged city for describing such an urbanism.[7] In the approximate decade spanning from the early 1980s to the early 1990s, Los Angeles served as a model site for discussions surrounding the loss of a center, fragmentation, uncritical paranoia, the lack of a master narrative, etc., that collectively stood in for a larger notion of postmodern urbanism.

However, rather than serving as an exemplar of these terms, Los Angeles has been buried, somewhat paradoxically, under the weight of a surplus of the rhetoric that initially made this city a subject of interest. One method – to borrow a phrase from Davis – for "excavating the future" of Los Angeles involves reinterpreting the past with the very terms that provoked its inhumation. Or to put it in yet another way, and borrow instead from Catherine Ingraham in *Architecture and the Burdens of Linearity*, is to claim:

> What is not so clear – what is here in a state of suspension and suggestion – is how architecture and cities are built at the crossroads of their own lines (urban and architectural) and the lines of writing. This is ultimately related to the question of how the violence of spacing (urbanism and architecture) occurs before or at the same time as the violence of writing.[8]

Ingraham offers an understanding of urbanism wherein metropolitan parietals emerge from a drive toward a singular, pre-Euclidean assessment of space and from a point of view that acknowledges the violence of the critical project as much as that of the design of cities – a warning against the hypostatization of research into urban design.

Instead of dismissing either historical research or postmodern theory *tout court*, conjoining these unwilling twins allows students of the city to return to the scene of the crime with the same tools, applied to different subjects, and yielding – one might suppose – alternative results. Given that *Heterotopia* or its feeble counterpart of *Heteropolis* is a compelling yet dangerous (or compelling because it is dangerous) condition to which any city might aspire, the proximity of these terms to the contemporary condition of Los Angeles should be treated neither as fact nor as fiction but certainly as both.[9] Thus it is that occasionally approbative words such as fragmentation, heterogeneity or incommensurability become positive when examined with the slightly different critical view of multiplicity, diversity, or even sublimity. A subtle shift in emphasis portrays Los Angeles as a diverse urban milieu of intense and, at times, profound spatial experiences, instead of as a city where generic spaces produce bland experiences.

In what follows I will arrest Los Angeles through the flipside of these terms, through "Lefebvre's concept of abstract space as what is simultaneously homogeneous and fragmented."[10] I will respond to Jameson's challenge that it is impossible "to draw the boundary lines in which we ourselves are contained" and argue that, unlike the Bonaventure Hotel, it is possible to produce a cognitive map of the city by using the very critical tools implemented to congeal it in an unmappable state.[11] Based upon Jameson's idea of the "cognitive map," Los Angeles emerges through a series of archaeological sondages – or probes – as sharply delineated by borders, centers, lines, and networks etched upon the landscape of Southern California and brought into relief by the most ordinary of analytical tools – plan, section, and perspective. Based upon Jameson's explication of "dirty realism," these maps ultimately play upon a critical field of urbanity described by the factual, if at times brutal, exigencies of the city.

In this discussion about cognitive cartographies, one of the more lasting perceptions of Los Angeles is that it lacks a center – hence the neat lamination of postmodern theory onto this supposed urban prototype. But where lacking a center certainly implies that the center is lacking – as with LA's rather anemic downtown core – we cannot claim that the city lacks centers.[12] Even the most orthodox studies of Los Angeles conclude that its growth followed the pattern of mulitcentered or polynucleated cities, of villages loosely grouped around a downtown core. Perhaps the indefinite center suggests instead a deeper lack, a more problematic loss, or a similar absence of any attributes with which either to identify or to empathize. In response to this, one could convincingly argue that the various centers dotted throughout the city define specific urban territories that offer mythological, psychological, and libidinal pressure points. Such is the organization of the balance of this chapter in which I will examine the quasi-mythological origins and psychological trajectories of the city at Olvera Street, the La Brea tar pits, and Griffith Park. Taking one small step at a time, my strategy here is modestly to add more dimension to debates about the city by examining three specific sites as they might relate to the research of Elizabeth Moule and Stefanos Polyzoides, Mario Gandelsonas, Douglas Suisman, William Fain, and Dagmar Richter. That the earth is moving under the city while I write is one of the more reliable determinates of the city, adding to the discussion of an unstable and shifting terrain where fault lines lie hidden both below and above ground.

Cognitive map

Where Jameson will mention urban cartography In "Postmodernism or, The Cultural Logic of Late Capitalism," asserting that Los Angeles is an unmappable product of postmodernity, indeed of the "dirty realism" he eventually will describe in *The Seeds of Time*, he sets forth the principles of his psychological geography in a later, 1988 essay titled "Cognitive Mapping" – explaining that this "slogan," as he calls it, is a "synthesis between Althusser and Kevin Lynch."[13] Jameson proposes that the processes Lynch describes in constructing a mental map of the city might also apply to the construction of a mental map of the "social and global totalities we all carry in our heads." As Jameson puts it, "Lynch suggests that urban alienation is directly proportional to the mental unmappability of local landscapes."[14] Jameson's earlier visit to the Bonaventure – with its vertical elevators accelerating spectacularly upward through a glass atrium, jetting along the exterior mirrored skin, and finally landing its captive audience next to a rotating cocktail lounge – provoked him to argue that:

> this latest mutation in space – postmodern hyperspace – has finally succeeded in transcending the capacities of the individual human body to locate itself, to organize its immediate surroundings perceptually, and cognitively to map its position in a mappable external world.[15]

Despite Jameson's forceful erudition and the depth of his analysis, the more interesting question is not whether it is possible to produce a map of the city cognitively – we all navigate to a greater or lesser extent through some crude understanding of our geopolitical coordinates – but instead, to interrogate the quality of that map, to ask what the map indicates *vis-à-vis* the subject's apprehension of ideological and representational space.

The publications from the 1980s and 1990s succeeded in reducing Los Angeles's image into that of an urban *enfant terrible* thrashing about destructively, and in telescoping its history into a timeline beginning with the 1965 riots, concluding with 1992 rebellion, and leaving the 1781 Spanish foundation, the 1848 USA conquest, or even the 1943 Zoot Suit Riots to mere historical miscellany.[16] For a theory seeking a subject without a history, without depth, Los Angeles's own history had to be erased in order to tell the story. Likewise, its unique silhouette necessarily disappeared into an amorphous layer of form-eradicating smog that dispersed itself uncontrollably into an arid infinity of sprawl. Yes, marathon commutes occur in the larger metropolitan area, and the city, especially around late August, appears as vast and as ugly as Adorno described the products of the culture industry "whose monuments are a mass of gloomy houses and business premises in grimy, spiritless cities."[17] As with Richter, who clearly understands the aerial view of "Euclidian fields woven together by threads of moving red and white lights, the larger metropolitan area of Los Angeles should be measured by the speed of jet planes descending into LAX" (Figure 7.1).[18] This, alas, is to agree with Suisman and others who claim that Los Angeles is "the manifestation of forty years of investment in suburbanization, sustained by the automobile industry."[19]

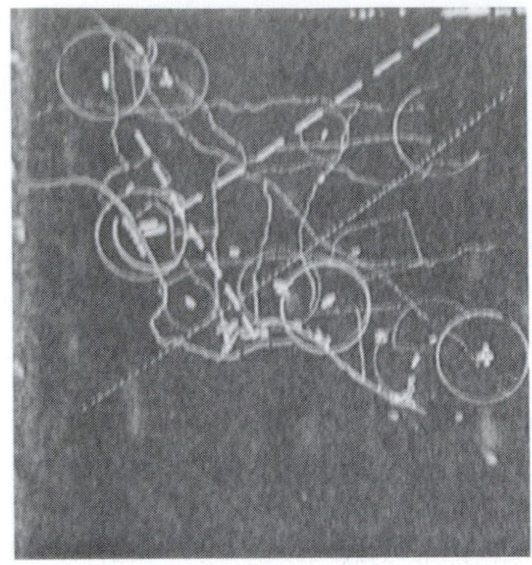

7.1
Study of arrival and departure patterns of planes above Los Angeles by Dagmar Richter

Where Los Angeles does not exhibit the rigid boundaries of Manhattan, the strict planning of Savannah, or the scenic texture of New Orleans, it does display definitive and unimpeachable geographies that both enable navigation and fix the city's physiognomy within a precise cartographic imaginary (Figure 7.2). To the north, the Angeles National Forest and the San Gabriel Mountains separate the city from the desert and form a natural boundary of open space set against expansion in this direction. These mountains delimit a symbolic section in which it is possible, quite literally, to stand above the refreshing (though highly polluted) ocean surf in 80-degree weather while looking directly at snowcapped peaks that, at Mount Baldy, rise to a height of more than 10,000 feet above sea level. When the city does leak between the San Gabriels and the eastern edge of the Santa Monica Mountains into the San Fernando Valley, the Santa Susanna Mountains ultimately bound this edge. Expansion to the east is more vulnerable to the encroachment of sprawl, with the first formidable natural boundaries located as far out as Palm Springs and the San Andreas fault line, the Joshua Tree National Park and, ultimately, the Mojave Desert. Where Los Angeles struggles to engulf the city of San Diego to the south, the naval base of Camp Pendelton separates these two metropolises with 28 miles of raw coastline and scattered war games. The Inland Empire, a euphemism for an area of unplanned expansion and rampant growth, accommodates the momentum growing between San Diego and LA to merge with development sneaking behind Camp Pendelton.

And further south still to the definitive Mexican–American border, if any distinction between these two cities will perhaps blur with reciprocal growth, more permeable walls, and the progressive urbanization of Tijuana, it will remain nonetheless a symbolic separation between Los Angeles, North America, and Mexico. To the west, where the Pacific Ocean functions as

7.2
Satellite view of Los Angeles

another permeable boundary for Asian immigration, it nonetheless forms an acute physical edge to the city as well as to the United States. In comparison with the size of other metropolitan areas – such as New York City – Los Angeles's urban dimensions and concomitant tensions dwarf Manhattan and the combined other four boroughs of Brooklyn, Queens, Staten Island, and the Bronx (see Figure 7.3). A comparative view of Los Angeles might place it in proximity to a reverse Manhattan; an oasis surrounded by desert, rather than an island bounded by water; a city wrestling with an expansive and irregular natural terrain, rather than a city boxing a highly regular park; a city where rabid land speculation promoted horizontal rather than vertical expansion. The city's physical geography alone offers striking coordinates with which to begin constructing a cognitive map.

Rotated grid

In their important essay "The Five Los Angeleses," Elizabeth Moule and Stefanos Polyzoides document the urban history of the city from its origins to their prognosis for its future. "The Five Los Angeleses," for these authors, are "The Pueblo" (1781–1880; Figure 7.4) and its siting near the river; "The Town" (1880–1900; Figure 7.5) which coincides with the transcontinental railroad reaching LA in 1876; "The City" (1900–1940; Figure 7.6) which expanded

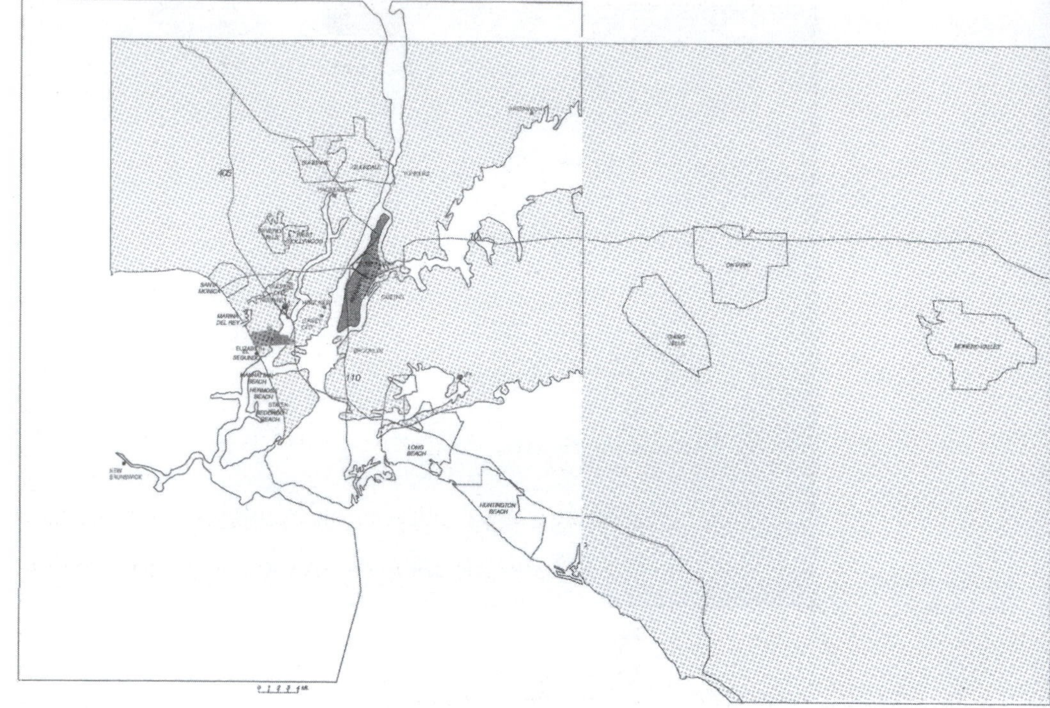

7.3
New York City superimposed upon Los Angeles by Paul Wysocan

proportionally with the 1913 aqueduct importing water from the Owen's river valley, "The Metropolis" (1940–1990; Figure 7.7) which emerged with the ground breaking of the Pasadena Freeway in 1938; and finally "Region/State" (1990–), a Los Angeles that dominates an increasingly expansive geopolitical position and faces numerous but not necessarily abject circumstances.[20] Along with analyzing and diagramming the growth of the city in a series of diachronic maps of the first four Los Angeleses, Moule and Polyzoides also rail against the pernicious topos that the city has no history. They present a compelling critique of the more renowned interpreters of the city for having set agendas that disadvantaged the development of Los Angeles to the extent that "the romance of a *tabula rasa* to be redeemed through modern form was irresistible to the cultural protagonists of the last era and still persists today."[21] Moule and Polyzoides point out that Reyner Banham – author of *Los Angeles: The Architecture of Four Ecologies* – exhibits a "particular fixation on freeways," and indulges his desire to promote the agenda of the post-CIAM generation that "caricatured Southern California as the epitome of a futurist paradise in our midst." "The gap between the myth and the facts," according to the authors, may be explained by: (1) a rapid speed of building that promoted urban clearance and "collective memory lapses"; (2) a cultural heterogeneity and mass immigration that underestimated the traditions of a "common, native past" and; (3) an

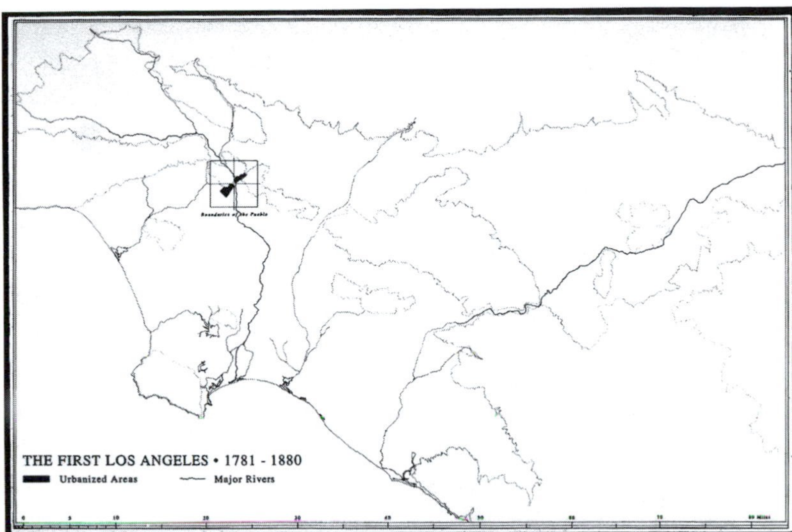

7.4
First Los Angeles by Moule and Polyzoides

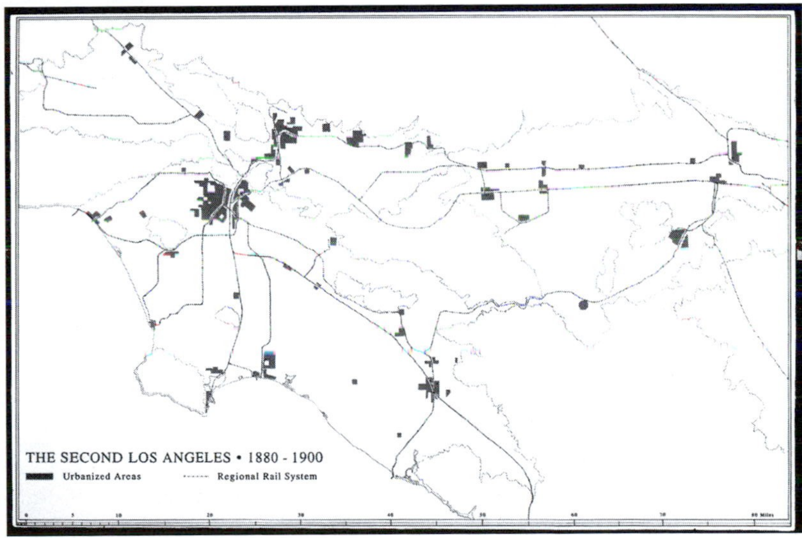

7.5
Second Los Angeles by Moule and Polyzoides

emphasis on progress that deprecated the "value of the existing city and its natural setting."[21]

As they describe the 1781 foundation of *El Pueblo de Nuestra Señora La Reina de Los Angeles de Porciuncula*, Los Angeles

> was afforded the rare civic destiny of being settled by decree of the Spanish Crown. On September 4, 1781 Governor Felipe de Neve, having laid out the pueblo based on the guidelines for site selection and urbanization coded in the Laws of the Indies, led a procession

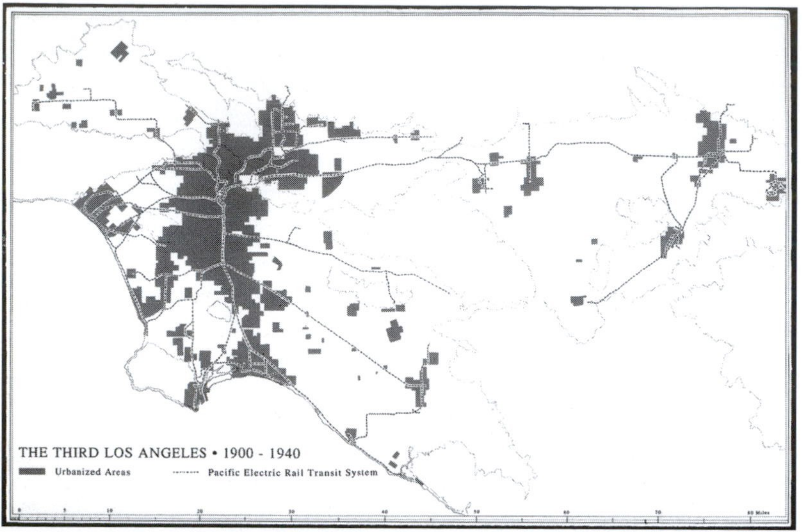

7.6
Third Los Angeles by Moule and Polyzoides

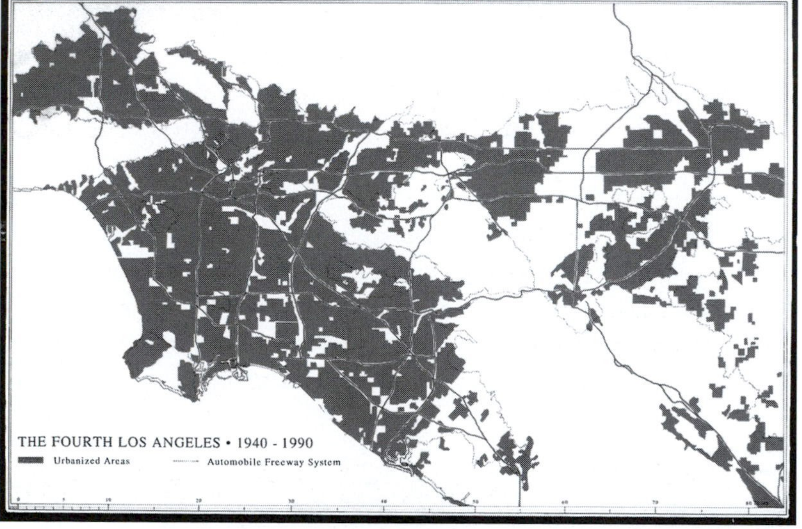

7.7
Fourth Los Angeles by Moule and Polyzoides

> of other soldiers, eleven families of forty-four individual settlers, mission priests and some natives marching slowly around the pueblo site. They invoked the blessing of the new community. Los Angeles became one of the few cities in the North American continent deliberately planned in advance and ceremoniously inaugurated for and by its new settlers.[22]

What is most significant about their description of the city's inauguration, for the purposes of this discussion, is the tenacity of this story and its replication at the site of Olvera Street – a "colorful Mexican-style marketplace" and "part of the city-owned *Pueblo de Los Angeles* Historic Monument."[23] As Moule, Polyzoides, and others have written, the original pueblo was founded on a site closer to the river, but owing to flooding was relocated to the higher site of the present plaza, the legendary location of the city's founding. Not unlike the supposed hut of Romulus on the Palatine in Rome, the Olvera Street plaza and its little rustic shops provide physical evidence for the equivalent of Los Angeles's *roma quadrata* – a cosmic urban axis established by locating polar coordinates of the city through the use of a templum. Where the 1573 Laws of the Indies required the pueblo grid to be rotated at the compass corner points rather than on a strict north–south axis as in ancient Rome, the precedence of such a rotation nonetheless refers to Roman planning techniques.

The plaza has been constructed and reconstructed as an idealized reflection of the ranchero life of Spanish aristocracy and the pastoral landscape Helen Hunt Jackson extolled in her novel *Ramona*.[24] Even more than Pershing Square, the putative heart of the central business district, Olvera Street functions as an active and vital component of public life. The visual corridor created by the Hollywood Freeway makes visible an important urban twist in José Rafael Moneo's design of the Cathedral of Our Lady of the Angels (see Figure 7.8). If only by the accident of Los Angeles's grid shifts and the architect's overt gesture to the 101 freeway that borders the site, the cathedral's façade faces east toward the Plaza of Olvera Street, turns its back on the cultural corridor of Bunker Hill, and shifts the urban focus from downtown to the pueblo – from the last cathedral to the first church of the city. More than a tourist attraction for those unwilling or unable actually to travel to Mexico, more than a state park preserving the pseudohistory of Los Angeles, Olvera Street provides physical space (albeit severed from downtown by the 101) for the city's Hispanic

7.8
View of Los Angeles Cathedral by Nicholas Roberts

community to congregate in proximity to the governmental center. Considering Olvera Street's inclusion in the cultural menagerie created by its proximity on the east side to Chinatown, and on the west to Little Tokyo, it nonetheless performs successfully as part of a series of cultural centers dedicated to LA's diverse ethnic communities.

In spite of (or perhaps because of) the overly scripted narrative of the Spanish revival architecture, the street and plaza preserve, mark, and provide a center for the original geometry of the city, the point where the Spanish grid begins its 45-degree rotation off of true north to eventually collide – after one or two significant metamorphoses developed through the surveying of Ord (1848) and Hancock (1853) – with Jefferson's mile-by-mile grid on Hoover Boulevard (Figure 7.9). These laws required a church and a government house to be built at the edge of a central plaza. The Laws also established sophisticated parameters for expansion so that "a roughly orthogonal grid of streets" could spread, as Suisman explains, "outward from the plaza and a square pueblo boundary of two leagues (=5.25 miles) per side." Outward further from the Pueblo, the Ranchos established a system of land division that allowed the Spanish to "carve up and distribute the lands of greater Los Angeles under a system of public and private land ownership," the traces of

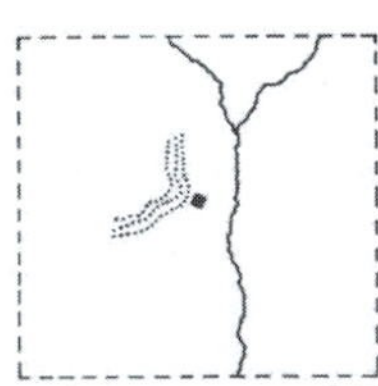

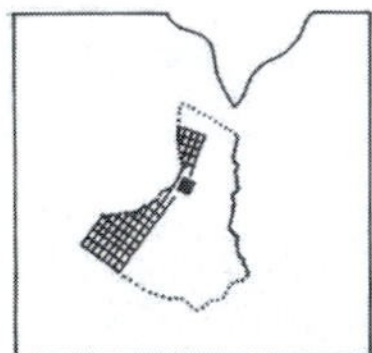

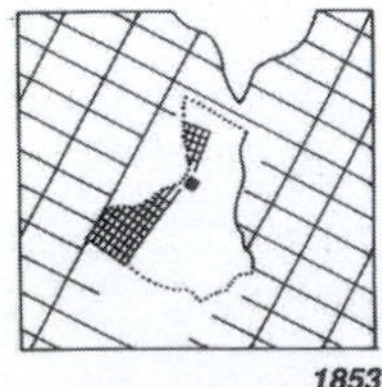

7.9
Douglas Suisman's diagrams of the Ord and Hancock surveys

which may be seen in many of the city's boulevards.[25] Finally, Suisman writes, in an argument that places Los Angeles once again upon a rotated *roma quadrata*, "the original plaza's diagonal orientation – prescribed by the 1573 Laws as a Vitruvian technique for breaking prevailing winds – set into motion the sequence of diagonal grid planning efforts."[25]

In contrast to Moule and Polyzoides, who generate a series of diachronic studies of the city, in *X-Urbanism* Mario Gandelsonas draws a self-described "synchronic cut" through Los Angeles.[26] Such a move from chronological to formal analysis works well with Richard Lehan's understanding of postmodern literature as a kind of writing wherein "synchronic time replaces diachronic time."[27] Gandelsonas's postmodern cut through Los Angeles asserts a combined reading of the "specific *formal armature* of the city" with the "local *sociopolitical* and *economic* forces."[28] In "Plan 1: The Territorial Grid" he describes this work as documenting "the perceived chaos of the Los Angeles plan" which "obscures a complex system combining city grids as colossal city fabrics as objects (laid out at different angles) with the one-mile grid as background (acting as a "glue" between the different cities)" (see Figure 7.10).[31]

Gandelsonas analyzes the geometries of Santa Monica, Beverly Hills, the megacity, the boulevards, intersections, grids shifts and more in a cartography that, in fact, describes an architectural cognition of the city (see Figure 7.11). Indeed Gandelsonas specifically contextualizes his work in opposition to the *Image of the City*, explaining that his "object is the architecture of the city," which he describes with "two- or three-dimensional drawings based upon plans, as opposed to the phenomenological mapping suggested by Kevin

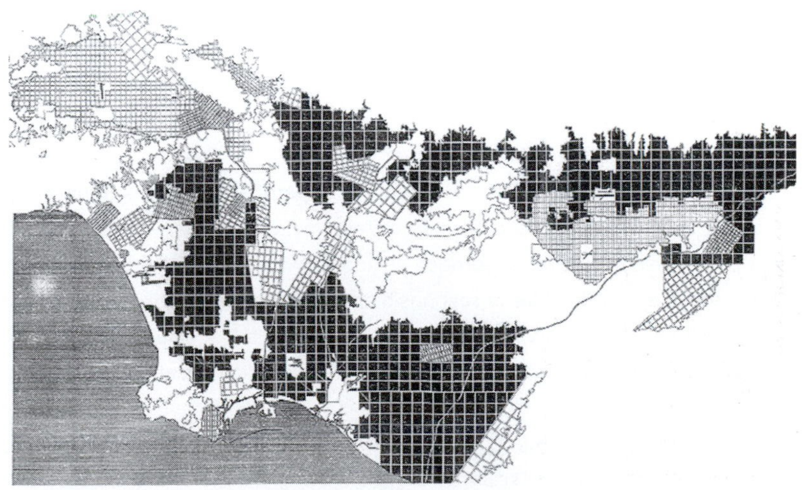

7.10
Mario Gandelsonas' "Territorial Grid" of Los Angeles

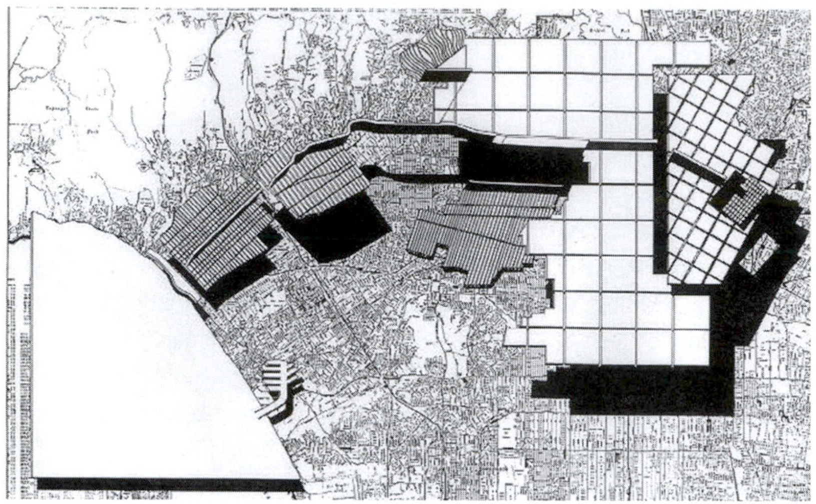

7.11
Mario Gandelsonas' Grid Puzzle

Lynch." Gandelsonas defends this position by arguing that "the urban drawings are conceived as part of a practice with the potential to transform or mutate the city and not the city as a place for the development of everyday tactics."[28] That Lynch attempts to test the urban alienation of a region as a direct index of its mental mappabililty by no means suggests that Gandelsonas's cartography is any less cognitive, but rather that it is a form of mapping that might be included in a more ecumenical or even more precise understanding of the techniques available in such an exercise.

Linear city

In describing his drawing titled "The Boulevards," Gandelsonas writes that, because flows of energy "act as connectors between the different elements of the Los Angeles plan," he depicts them as linear walls channeled through "both the explicit and the absent city grids" (Figure 7.12).[30]

Here Gandelsonas draws upon the armature of Wilshire Boulevard, the single most dominant and forceful street in Los Angeles, created by a seventeen-mile-long business corridor linking downtown with Santa Monica and the sea. Gaylord Wilshire is responsible for completing the four-block-long link connecting two separate streets at Westlake Park – one leading from downtown to the ocean, and the other from the ocean to downtown – thereby creating a complete boulevard.

This second sondage into Los Angeles's "deep structure" proposes to excavate the undiggable terrain of the archaeological site at the La Brea tar

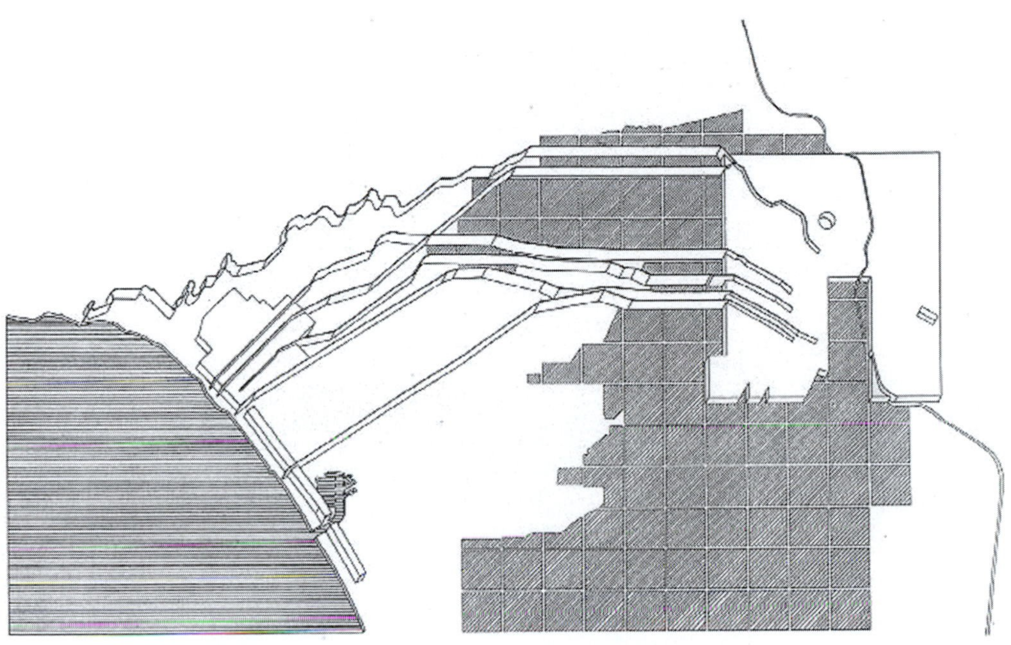

7.12
Mario Gandelsonas' The Boulevards

pits on Wilshire Boulevard. The largest of the pits is an open lake of bitumen, mistakenly referred to as tar, out of which bubbles up the bones of mastodons, saber-toothed tigers, and other fossils dating back 40,000 years (Figure 7.13). Between the destabilizing tar and the promised demolition of the museum to make way for Rem Koolhaas's winning design for an extension to Los Angeles County Museum of Art, Ed Rushca's 1965–1968 painting, titled "The Los Angeles County Museum on Fire," is more than a vivid portrait of the city's cultural center, it is also portentous of the museum's proposed demise (see Figure 7.14). The gaseous, viscous liquid of ur-suppe underneath the surface is a reminder of the hundreds of oil wells that once dotted the city and the vestiges of these landmarks found at sites such as the Beverly Hills High School and the Beverly Center. The conflation of such images was not lost on Mick Jackson, who directed *Volcano* (1997), or Steve De Jarnatt, who directed *Miracle Mile* (1989) – films that portray the mass urban destruction of Los Angeles either with lava flowing through shopping malls (The Beverly Center in fact) or the ubiquitous helicopter (also see *Boys N the Hood*) sinking into the tar pits after a nuclear attack destroys the city.

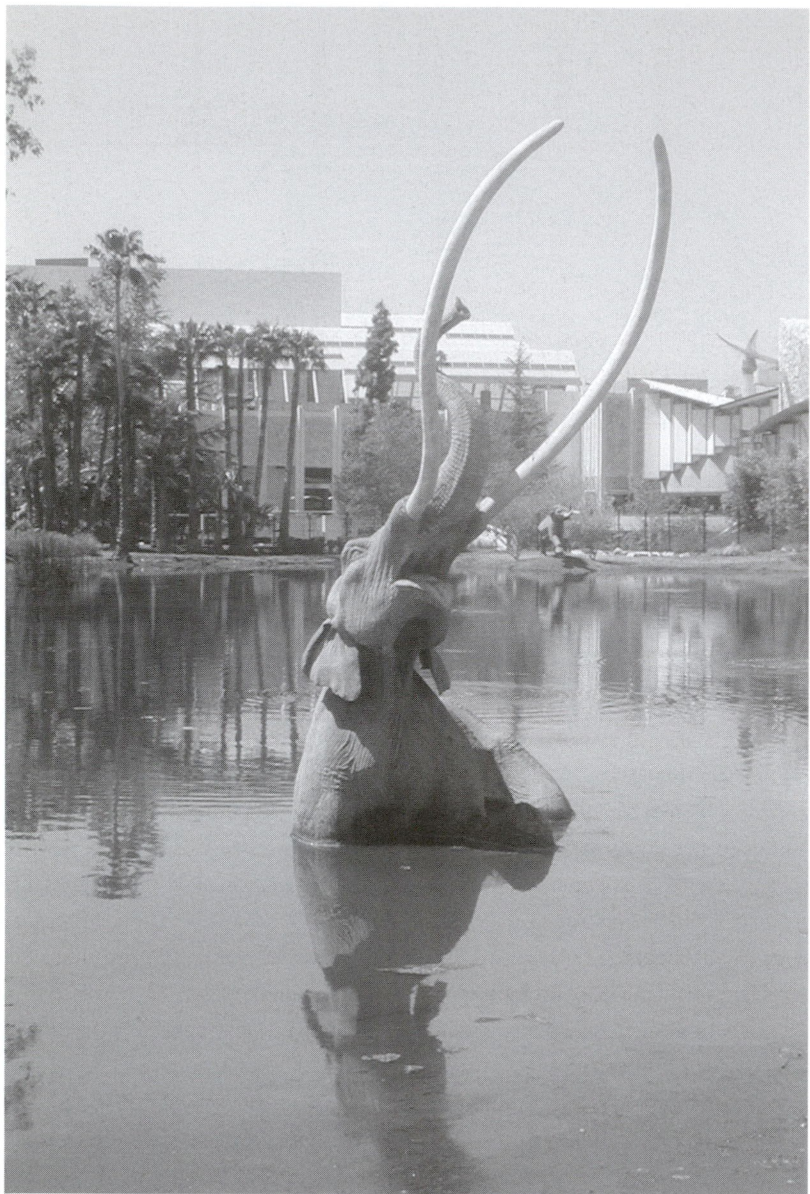

7.13
View of La Brea tar pits and the Los Angeles County Museum of Art photographed by author

In Jackson's film:

A volcano appears in Los Angeles and sends lava flowing towards houses. There are minor complications, such as a stranded subway car, but essentially this one situation sustains the movie. In 1991, Jackson directed Steve Martin's hilarious *L.A. Story*, a film that

7.14
Ed Ruscha, the Los Angeles County Museum on fire 1965–1968

painted (admittedly with some sense of irony) a picture of L.A. as an idyllic wonderland for the rich. Riots, fires and mudslides dated that one fast, and Jackson seems intent on making amends with this slow motion L.A. demolition job. As the sky rains fireballs and the ground spouts flame and molten rock, it's hard not to read a judgement day subtext to the whole thing.[31]

As Mike Davis points out, Los Angeles is one of those cities that cinema takes pleasure in destroying. While Park La Brea contains a version of the "psychological lava" that Colin Rowe finds bubbling underneath the contemporary city, it locates Los Angeles's cultural center at the County Museum of Art.[32] The museum, the mastodons, and the ongoing excavation fuse the urbane and the fantastic, the cultural and the prehistorical. While the staged prehistory undoubtedly bears a striking resemblance to Baudrillard's concept of the *simulacra*, "the generation of models of a real without origin or reality," this site also describes a deeper umbilicus leading from Los Angeles, quite allegorically, to the center of the earth.[33]

Inscribed, then, on an infinite "Y" axis of the city, the tar pits operate on an infinite "X" axis as the symbolic midpoint along Wilshire between downtown LA and the Pacific Ocean. In *Los Angeles Boulevard: Eight X-rays of the Body Public*, Suisman (1989) researches the symbolic and spatial implications of linear public spaces such as Wilshire Boulevard and Sunset Boulevard, concluding that, in Los Angeles, a boulevard "makes arterial connections on a metropolitan scale," "provides a framework for civic and commercial destinations," and "acts as a filter to adjacent residential neighborhoods."[34] We might note, as a compelling aside, Suisman reported on a panorama built on Main Street that depicted the 1870 Battle of Paris. He speculates that "through the smoke and the cannon fire," this attraction

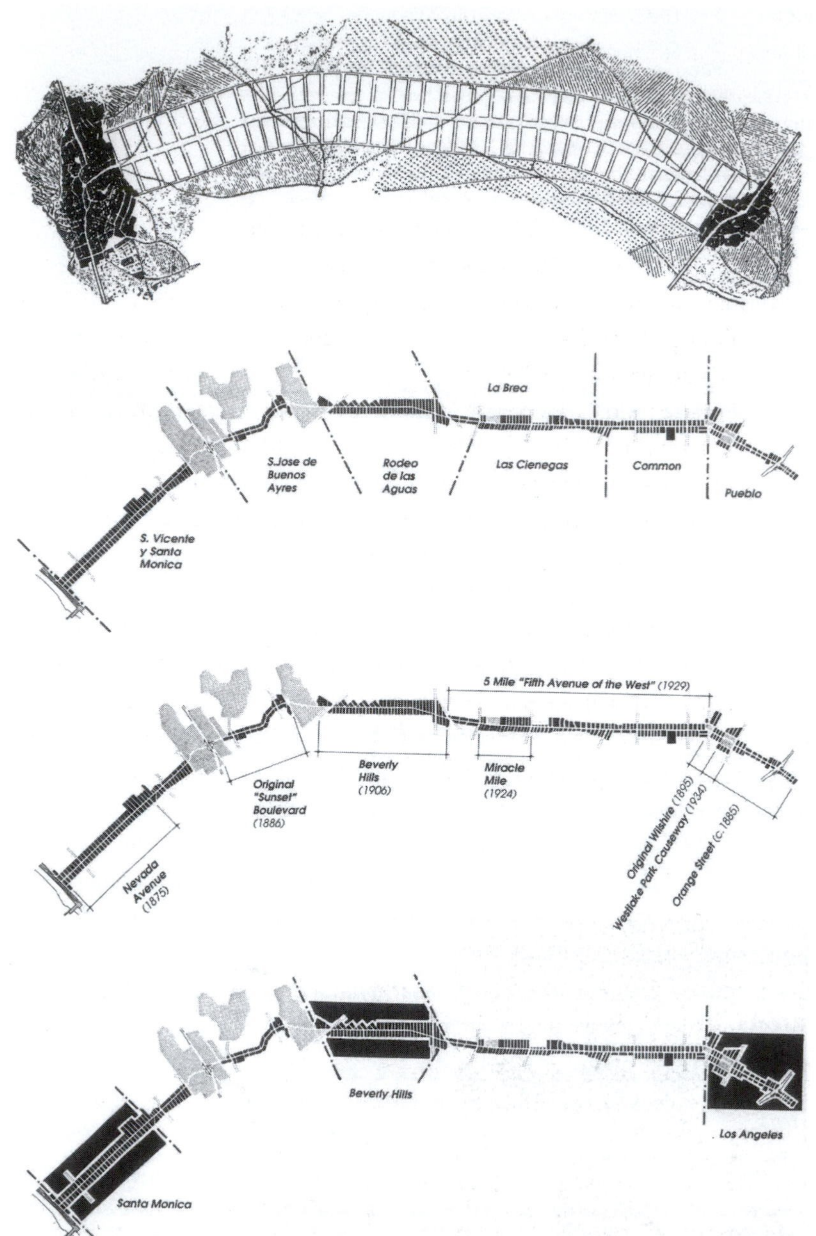

7.15
Douglas Suisman's "Comparison between Wilshire Boulevard and the Linear City"

presented to the populace "a vivid image of Haussmann's Paris."[35] The density and urban disposition of Wilshire supports Suisman's explication of this boulevard as a nascent "linear city" after Arturo Soria y Mata's 1886 plans for Madrid (Figure 7.15).[36] Indeed, Suisman tells us that "Reyner Banham would dub it the world's first linear downtown."[37] Wilshire, of course, is not a linear city and although the many other satellite downtowns that have sprung up throughout LA – in places like Glendale, Century City, and Universal City – have rendered this morphology a remote possibility, they do not take away from the significance of Suisman's perceptual cartography.

As listed in his table of contents, Suisman's eight "X-rays" divide the city into the colorful allegorical sections of: (1) Suture: The Pueblo/Rancho Landscars; (2) Umbilical: The Spawning of Sunset Boulevards; (3) Spine: Piecemeal Grandeur on Wilshire Boulevard; (4) Girdle: The Studios Face the Boulevards; (5) Phosphors: Day for Night on Hollywood Boulevard; (6) Torrent: The Boulevards Accelerate; (7) Pathogen: Signs and Symbols on the Boulevards; and (8) Fuselage: Cross-sections of the Public Realm. His work contributes to a larger understanding of the city both through his careful analyses and through the visual imagery he deploys to elicit meaning from the maps he describes. His mapping, while perhaps more playful than Moule, Polyzoides, or Gandelsonas, arrives at a cognition of the city based upon highly imagistic formal comparisons that serve as visual shifters whose value it is to explain the city through comprehensible analogies. Thus, where his comparison between the Discobolus and the boulevard is glib, it also serves visually to reinforce the notion that Wilshire is the city's spine – bending and flexing at the will of its burden to link downtown with the ocean (Figure 7.16). For this comparison alone, Suisman has created a lyrical cartography of Los Angeles's geopolitical form.

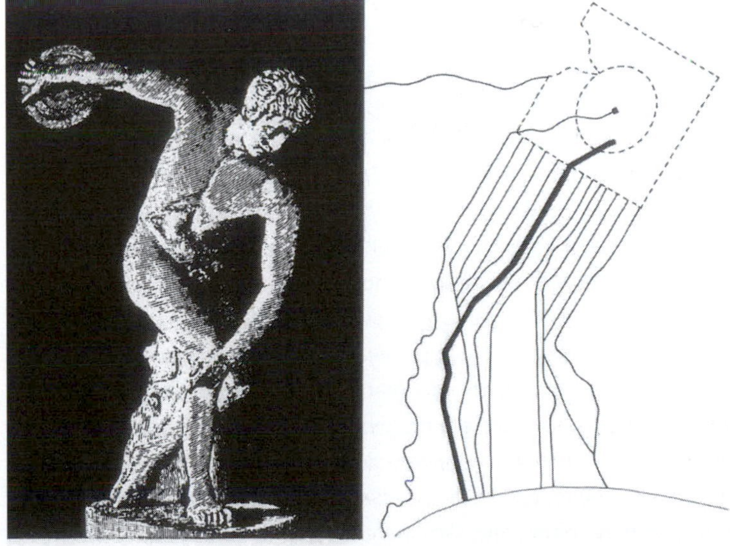

7.16
Douglas Suisman's comparison of Wilshire Boulevard and the Discobolus

An urban wilderness

A third and final site for probing the city centers on the observatory, an astronomical museum located in Griffith Park that offers a panoramic view of LA from the San Gabriel to the Santa Monica Mountains. Built in 1935 according to the designs of John C. Austin and F. M. Ashley, the various domes shelter a solar telescope, a refractor telescope, and a planetarium – equipment dedicated to surveying and studying the universe. The most facile reading of the observatory would be to interpret it as a Panopticon, as a structuring system of surveillance that the Scottish social engineer Jeremy Bentham designed and that Michel Foucault made indelible in the memory of architects and urban designers with his publication of *Discipline and Punish: The Birth of the Prison*. Wim Wender's depicted this site as a remarkably similar space of social reform in his 1997 film *The End of Violence*, by transforming the observatory into the headquarters for a secret government plot to eliminate criminal activity through satellite surveillance and instant execution.[38] Under the large rotunda that some might describe as Foucault's Panoptican we find not a gaoler but, instead, Foucault's Pendulum, a moving sphere that swings reliably from a suspending cable, marks the earth's rotation, and acts as a metronome, keeping time with the urban pulse.

The observatory – inhabited by the citizenry of the city rather than by prison wardens – is the single most pivotal location from which to comprehend and observe Los Angeles (Figure 7.17). On a necessary but not infrequent clear day it is possible to absorb the city, see the 45-degree rotation of downtown in comparison with the Jeffersonian grid, witness the geographic boundaries of the mountains and the ocean, see the saucer-shaped outline of the Santa Monica bay extend from Point Dume to Palos Verdes, and understand the arching movements of the boulevards – scar tissue from the ranchos acting as subcutaneous ripples beneath the more recent surface of the mile-wide grid. For those who do not respond well to a printed map, the Griffith Park Observatory transforms Los Angeles into a version of Jorge Luis Borges's "Map of the Empire," a map that is drawn at the same scale and is coexistent with the city it describes. Conversely, the observatory also works as a focal point for navigation in which, from distant points and among random hills, the white domes appear and disappear with the curves and swells of the urban topography.

One of the paradoxes of urbanity is its reliance upon its opposite, the condition of coarse activity in unprogramed spaces that approximates Foucault's idea of *heterotopia*. Such are the pleasures of tracking and hunting in a dangerous built domain as if it were raw wilderness. Contrary to the expectations of order and culture, part of the *jouissance* of urbanism is the proximity to lawlessness, wild abandon, and illicit behavior. Undomesticated and feral, a

7.17
View of the Griffith Park Observatory at night

large part of urbanity derives from those pockets of space that provide for these desires – such as *Club Silencio*, a locus of sortilege and sexuality in David Lynch's 2001 film *Mulholland Drive*. These terms are more than "desires" in Los Angeles; they are physical components of the city that drives its unconscious narrative.

Griffith Park dominates the center of the larger metropolitan area stretching from the San Pedro Harbor to the San Fernando Valley sprawl: a 4,000 acre parcel of land – "the largest municipal park in the nation" – donated to the city in 1896 by Mr. Griffith J. Griffith as a "place of recreation and rest for the masses, a resort for the rank and file."[39] According to Greg Hise and William Deverell, Mr. Griffith – "a Progressive reformer interested in issues of social hygiene and the influence of the environment over the individual" – believed that integrated parks and boulevards could "do the work of deep reform." For Griffith, "park space could be the lungs of the city; parks would relieve class tensions; parks could be tied directly to Comprehensive City planning."[40] Griffith Park features 53 miles of hiking trails, two open-air theaters (the Greek Theater and the Hollywood Bowl), tennis courts, golf courses, and the Los Angeles Zoo – caged animals dwelling within a larger field of liberated predators. As the literature warns, "hikers should approach the park with caution; Griffith Park is a wilderness area with wild quail, rodents, foxes, coyotes, rattlesnakes and deer."[41]

In Los Angeles, the ever-present markers of the park, the

observatory, Mt. Hollywood, and the Hollywood sign stand as reminders that wild abandon and atavistic urges dwell in the heart of the city. The Griffith Park acreage provides pathways for imagined and real predators to find their way from the wilderness directly into the city proper. In Los Angeles, the presence of lions on city hall – Terry Gilliam's image of Philadelphia in *12 Monkeys* (1995) – is something of a possibility. Mike Davis has made much of the predatory persona of Los Angeles in his *Ecology of Fear: Los Angeles and the Imagination of Disaster* (1998), writing a series of essays which also portray wild fires, liquefaction zones, drought, and earthquakes with such convincing detail that he provokes even semi-rational citizens to question the sanity of living in Los Angeles.[42] Ten years earlier, John McPhee's "Los Angeles Against the Mountains," in *The Control of Nature* (1989), similarly terrified readers learning about the near-death experiences caused by flows of rock and mud trapping people perilously in their homes. As McPhee demonstrates, to understand Los Angeles is to know its precise geography; the natural environment provides the significant window onto the urban landscape.

Mulholland Drive runs through Griffith Park as a narrow, winding artery of fairly high-speed traffic that Lynch fuses into the opening scenes of his film as a ribbon of road slipping up and down, in and around the crest of the Hollywood Hills and the Santa Monica Mountains. Operating as a boundary between the Los Angeles basin and the San Fernando Valley, the 21-mile-long highway connects the Cahuenga Pass in Hollywood with Leo Carillo State Beach at the Venture–Los Angeles county line. The name of the highway, of course, memorializes William Mulholland (1855–1935), the founder and head of Los Angeles's Department of Water and Power, who in 1913 and with a 233-mile-long network of channels and aqueduct, brought water to the arid ground of the valley and, with it, the possibility of suburban morass. Mulholland Drive, less for the lore that surrounds car chases and more for its physical condition as a hinge between the city and the valley, dwells in the work of David Hockney, an avid interpreter of both the city and complex visual fields. In his 1980 painting "Mulholland Drive: The Road to the Studio," Hockney develops a definitive cognitive cartography based upon shifting perspectives and simultaneous spatial moments, offering specific strategies for documenting the city that merge plan and perspective into an interpretive and analytical representation of space (Figure 7.18). The tools Hockney develops offer a unique understanding of the city, one that he spatializes as the interpenetration of flat grids and curving mountain roads in order to reveal a cognitive map created by the superimposition of perspectival vignettes upon a city map.

In fact, Richter documents the area of Century City as a series of cartographic exercises that offer an architectural response to Hockney's spatial lesson of hybrid drawing. Richter "studied and overlapped maps from various

7.18
David Hockney Mulholland Drive: The Road to the Studio

moments in the history of Century city" producing documents that marked "forgotten landscapes" and displayed the "apparatus of dislocated film towns, as well as oil fields, orange groves, and single-family bungalows." She then, in a second reading of the city, transformed the shadows cast by the skyscrapers into an "axonometrical collapse of the vertical object onto the projection screen," and in a third, studied the skyscraper façades as folded and layered surfaces.[43] Richter's analyses, in which she ultimately collapses these various cartographies upon each other, emerges as a simultaneous map, urban analysis, and building design (Figures 7.19, 7.20).

The views from Griffith Park evoke such cartographic potential. The park also serves as a gigantic, almost incomprehensible example of the many smaller open spaces that can be found throughout the city with the major difference being less about size than about a persistent state of dilapidation. Much of Los Angeles is filled with what Norman Klein refers to as empty dirt patches – patches of raw nature filled with the foundations of recently demolished homes or the debris of illicit activities.[44] As far back as the early 1930s,

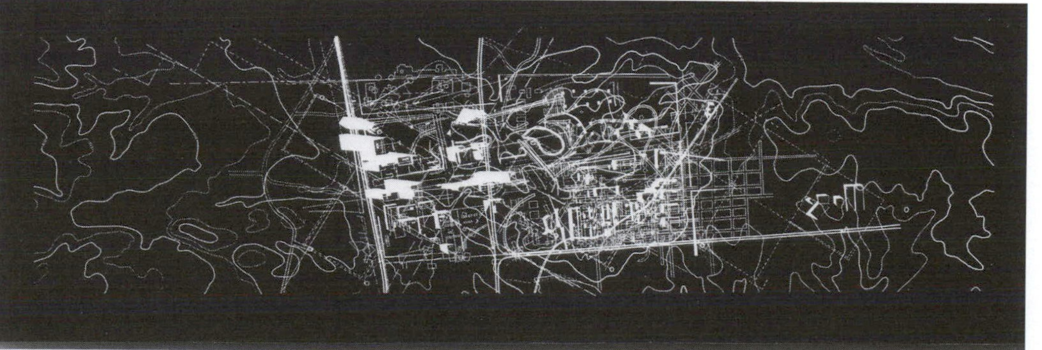

7.19
Collected Traces and Shadows of Century City

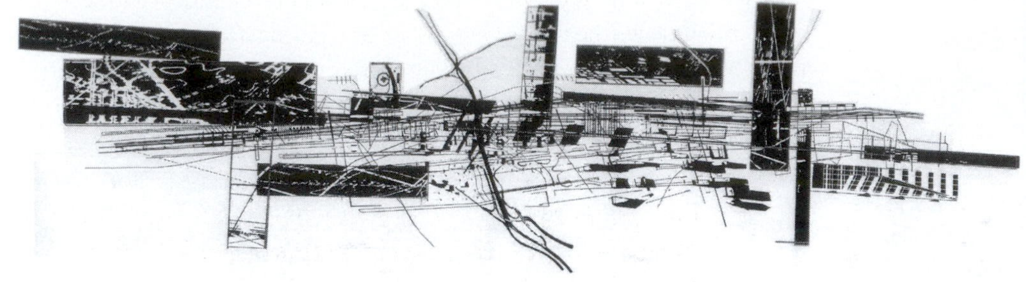

7.20
Working Diagram A: Layered Traces and Shadows

when members of the Los Angeles business community observed that a shortage of open space in the city would act as a possible hindrance to tourism, citizens employed the firms of Olmsted Brothers in Brookline Massachusetts and Harland Bartholomew and Associates of St. Louis to propose a solution to the problem. Through this initiative emerged the "178-page, clothbound document, *Parks, Playgrounds and Beaches for the Los Angeles Region*" (1930). The Olmsted–Bartholomew plan demonstrates the significance the authors placed on the natural environment of the city. As Hise and Deverell also write, their "focus is resolutely on systems – the robust but ultimately endangered systems of nature in the mountains, high desert, the basin, and the Pacific coastline – and the ways these might be integrated with urban systems, especially the infrastructure necessary for expanding the metropolitan region."[45] Conflicting interests would see to it that little direct transformation of the city based upon the recommendations of the report would occur, given that it "garnered almost no public attention" and the response was a "resounding silence."[46]

Many of the neglected patches of open space that can be found in the contemporary city run along abandoned rights of way or next to property owned by governmental services. In 1994 the architectural firm of Johnson Fain Partners, in collaboration with Beth Rogers of Pacific Earth Resources (California's largest grower of turf), addressed the problem of open space in the city when William Fain observed that Los Angeles devotes only 4 percent of its area to open space – in contrast to Boston and New York, which maintain 9 percent and 17 percent respectively. Fain devoted unreimbursed office time to creating the award-winning "Greenway Plan for Metropolitan Los Angeles."[47] He and his team of architects and urban designers completed a series of close analyses of the city, drawing layer upon mylar layer of separate infrastructures, systems, networks, and demographics in order to arrive at the last map, the "closest to a polemic," they developed into a plan for open space that takes advantage of these overlapping systems and networks.[48] Given that this was primarily a self-sponsored project, the Johnson–Fain research remains an attempt to offer guidelines for the city's development, some of which are being realized with plans to transform the Los Angeles river from a concrete-lined flood control basin filled with waste water into a viable riparian landscape. The firm describes this research with the following words:

> The Los Angeles Open Space concept provides a substantial increase in public open space by using available land resources such as transit lines, bikeways, rail rights-of-way, rivers, flood control channels, and powerline encasements. The plan links a number of these land resources to existing town centers, schools, libraries, post offices, and senior centers while providing new sites for other uses. The concept can be the catalyst for the establishment of additional public parks, squares, and plazas, increasing the amount of open space available for public use and enjoyment.[49]

The design team attempted to study the "unnoticed network of connective tissue" that forms the city of Los Angeles and derives from rights of way, interstices, networks, and parallel activities.[48] The various layers include: (1) an analysis of the over 50 various "centers" that can be identified throughout the metropolitan area; (2) independent jurisdictions with their own city halls; and (3) an existing greenways map (Figures 7.21, 7.22). As with the Olmsted–Bartholomew report, the Johnson–Fain analysis focuses on open space, geography, infrastructure and demographic data in order to form a stratified but nonetheless cognitive map of the city wherein nature and natural elements frame and define Los Angeles.

The dirty real

Writing in his 1965 novel, *The Crying of Lot 49*, Thomas Pynchon delineates what could be the landscape of LA:

> Like many name places in California it was less an identifiable city than a grouping of concepts – census tracts, special purpose bond-issue districts, shopping nuclei, all over laid with access roads to its own freeway. . . . She [Oedipa Maas] looked down a slope, needing to squint for the sunlight, onto a vast sprawl of houses which had grown up all together, like a well-tended crop, from the dull brown earth; and she thought of the time she'd opened a transistor radio to replace a battery and seen her first printed circuit. The ordered

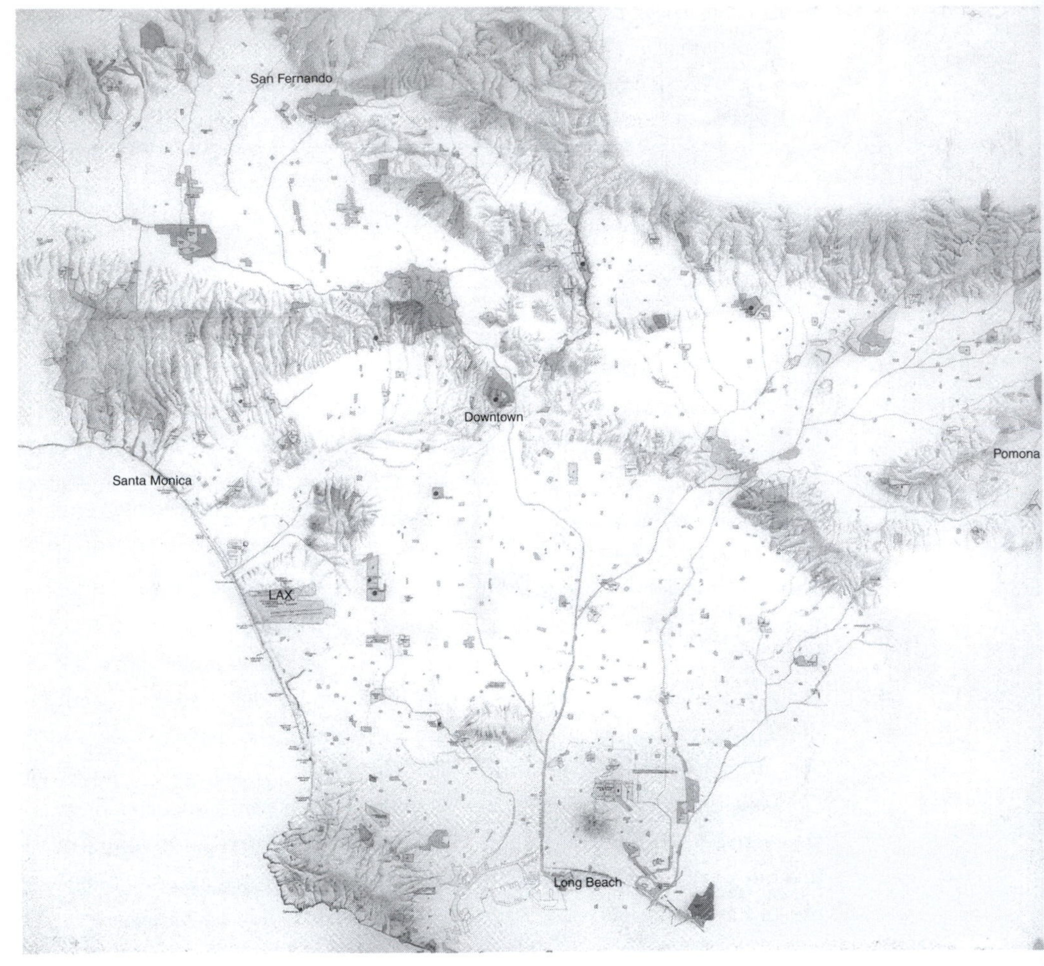

7.21
Johnson Fain, Los Angeles Open Space

> swirl of houses and streets, from this high angle, sprang at her now with the same unexpected, astonishing clarity as the circuit card had. Though she knew even less about radios than about Southern Californians, there were to both outward patterns a hieroglyphic sense of concealed meaning, of an intent to communicate.[50]

An urban *roman à clef* in which both real and fictional place names merge into a composite portrait of LA urbanism, Pynchon weaves a detective story concerning the spatial narratives of paranoia, entropy, and aporia into Southern California's physiognomy. Pynchon's novel serves as a pivotal location for concluding this discussion about Los Angeles as a quintessential PM city. Underscoring

7.22
Johnson Fain, Greenway Developments

this assessment of LA, Lehan summarizes the conclusion to *The Crying of Lot 49* with the following observation:

> At the end of the novel, she is left at the edge of the ocean, a rented car between her and the lifeless continent, holding a dead phone. She has come to land's end in the machine society, dependent on technological forms of communication that constantly fail her. What she gets back, as with a computer, is what she brings to it. All of Los Angeles has become an Echo Court, as the motel where she is staying is called. By the end of the novel the world is breaking down into solipsism.[51]

In Lehan's distinction between modern and postmodern writing about the city, once urban signification breaks down into an unstable system of signs, into solipsism, then the city no longer holds claim to being "real."[27] Lehan's use of the term *real*, in specific connection with a more recent kind of fashioning of this term – see, for example, Rodolfo Machado and Jorge Silvetti's *Unprecedented Realism*, Hal Foster's *Return of the Real*, Baudrillard's and Eco's "Hyperreal," or the spate of publications on the "Surreal," – when taken in combination with Jameson's deployment of "dirty realism," marks a moment of potential insight into the enigmatic and shifting cartographies that constitute Los Angeles.

For Baudrillard it is not that, in "the precession of the simulacra" the map "engenders the territory" rather than the other way around, but that "it is no longer a question of maps and territory" – hence the insignificance of cognitive navigation when faced with a more overwhelming inability to break free from ideological constructs. "Something has disappeared" and this is the possibility of perceiving reality:

> Disneyland is there to conceal the fact that it is the "real" country, of all "real" America, which *is* Disneyland (just as prisons are there to conceal the fact that it is the social in its entirety, in its banal omnipresence, which is carceral). Disneyland is presented as imaginary in order to make us believe that the rest is real, when in fact all of Los Angeles and the America surrounding it are no longer real, but of the order of the hyperreal and of simulation. It is no longer a question of a false representation of reality (ideology), but of concealing the fact that the real is no longer real, and thus of saving the reality principle.[52]

While an initial rejoinder to Baudrillard's assessment of LA might be to suggest a similar comparison with, say, Paris, Norman Klein would argue that indeed postmodernism hazards superficial and casual readings of LA, that this "theory has probably devoted too much energy to looking at corporate simulation – engaged too much disengaged gawking at expensive hyper-real spaces, and not done enough digging into the political contradictions of local culture step by step."[53] Step-by-step, Disneyland offers a peek at the evil genius behind its curtains, step-by-step LA is neither monolithic nor homogeneous, and step-by-step the notion of the *simulacra* has been displaced by the actuality of the "pure event," to pit Baudrillard against himself, "an event that can no longer be manipulated, interpreted, or deciphered by any historical subjectivity" – earthquakes, fires, floods, uprisings, terrorism.[54] Any reading of LA must go beyond

Baudrillard's idea of an "operational negativity" in which the fake serves the utilitarian purpose of making real.

As a cautionary note, the notion of *realism* pulls upon certain semantic threads that become Gordian knots when placed in an urban or architectural context. Unlike literature, cinema, or painting, that arguably maintain an explicitly representational modality in contrast to an external or "real" space, architecture and urbanism exist as both representational and inhabited domains. Thus when we describe a city such as Los Angeles through a term such as *realism*, this critique necessarily suggests that other stylistic motifs – "Noir," "Tech," "Futuristic," "Jungle," "Frontier," or "Glam," for example – may apply. My interest here, instead, is to examine *realism* in opposition to *idealism* as a philosophical construct that critiques the Utopian with the quotidian, and the theoretical with the absurd. As the sondage into Griffith Park presupposes, Los Angeles's urbanity dwells in both the real and ideal, the planned and accidental, the cultivated and fallow; it exists as much in the topiary, the floral, and the perfumed as in the patches of dirt, the dirty, the trashy, the seamy, and the real. Thus, in addition to Lehan's tempting assertion that the postmodern city ceases to be real, the other way of looking at this is that the city also becomes all too real, "dirty real." If a city ceases to be understood as artificial, that is, as a construct, then is it part of the natural order, a brute fact of some deterministic principle, lacking design and, most necessary of all, artifice?

Jameson takes the idea of "dirty realism" from Liane Lefaivre, who in turn appropriates it from the literary critic, Bill Buford. Buford's realism concerns the "unadorned, unfurnished, low-rent tragedies about people who watch day-time television, read cheap romances, or listen to country and western music," focusing on "drifters in a world cluttered with junk food and the oppressive details of modern consumerism."[55] The condition of dirty realism describes a world in which mass culture penetrates the "utmost recesses and crannies" of everyday life, with a resulting colonization of any "residual enclaves that had hitherto remained exempt," enclaves as diverse as those instituted through farming, high culture, ghettos, traditional villages, or "classical urban forms of collective living." Finally, Jameson presents this concept as "the passage from the amusement park to the mall," a world in which a "new type of closure simulates all the chaotic libidinal freedom of the now dangerous world outside."[56] In order to exemplify this condition of the "fallen real," he seeks allegories of the "intestinal necessity of the modern building." He finds them in Rem Koolhaas's Zeebrugge Terminal, which includes "whole former structures, such as a hotel and an office building" along with on- and off-ramps, which he compares to the "delicately interlaced" ramps at the "Figueroa grade crossing in downtown Los Angeles"[57] If not precisely the Phalanstery Jameson alludes to in his description of this "new type of closure," then at least LA appears to be the archetypal city for this anti-urban urban form. And while comparing the landscape of Los Angeles to the detritus of consumer culture unleashed within these novels may further liberate a field of reductive cliches into the city, it also brackets the infrastructure of transportation, complex spaces, hybrid programs, and parasitical structures proliferating LA as significant conditions of urbanity.

Jameson turns to *Blade Runner* and cyberpunk, to megastructures and OMA's Piranesian spaces, spaces that blur the distinction between inside and outside. But the more recent depiction of Los Angeles in films such as *Pulp Fiction* (1994, Quentin Tarantino) or *Boogie Nights* (1997, Paul Thomas Anderson) more closely approximates Buford's original thesis – the Big Mac cum *Royale* with cheese and the beverage choice of beer, the blandness of the San Fernando Valley and the malaise of living on the extremity of the so-called city of LA. This is the genre that compels Roemer Van Toorn to question and to answer:

> To what extent does Tarantino enable us to read reality more perceptively? In *Pulp Fiction*, it is not so much the filmic montage of sound and image, but the *mise en scène* that induces us to comprehend everyday reality as a "dirty realism." The film is set in the city periphery. It is a pulp movie with an architecture without architects. It tells strange stories that come across as completely realistic.[58]

Ironically or pathetically, Tarantino's filmic perspective reterritorializes the grim condition, the infinite acreage of sheer architectural sludge in Los Angeles that so depressed Adorno, through the very medium of mass culture that Adorno condemned. This is the aspect of the dirty real found in "supermarkets, roadside cafes, cheap hotels."[55] It is the sectional cut through the city described by Michael Douglas's walk through the film *Falling Down*, or by the sectional slice of Sunset Boulevard as it winds its way from downtown, past flop houses, billboards, cafes, hotels, motels, mansions and murders in the neighborhoods of Echo Park, Silverlake, West Hollywood, Westwood, Brentwood, and the Pacific Palisades, only to end unceremoniously at the sea. Through cinema these subgenres of LA's urban milieu proliferate, reframed and distilled into a series of infinite jump cuts. In this respect, cinema operates in Los Angeles at the intersection of the cognitive map and the dirty real. If it anticipates its subject, as Baudrillard argues, the deformations and excrescencies of its subject anticipate cinema.

While eschewing any ethical imperative, the postmodern sublime successfully colonizes the uncultured, feral, filthy, and raw as viable design terrain responding to the libidinal play of city pleasures. The "dirty real" clearly differs from "popular culture and the everyday," as an urbanism predicated upon conditions in the city that, while undesigned, is also incomplete, ruinous, fragmented, or unsupervised. As the title of Michael Sorkin's collection of essays verifies – *Variations on a Theme Park: The New American City and the End of Public Space* – Jameson's trajectory from amusement park to mall is an apt description of LA, but one that should not exclude the city's omnipresent and equally apt persona of a working town.

While the socioeconomic axis from Malibu Beach to Beverly Hills describes one dimension of the city, other dimensions pertain to the axes from Central America to MacArthur Park, the Greyhound bus terminal to skid row, or San Pedro to the sweatshops of downtown. Each manicured lawn presupposes the dirt lots and hovels that occupy much of the city. From the depths of despair to the height of affluence, the dirt of LA provides fertile ground not only for prosperous residents within the city, but also for the rest of the United States. To place the possibility of the cognitive map onto the field of the real, the fallen, or even the execrable is to adopt what the editors of the *Assemblage* understand to be Richter's approach to LA, "a belief in the transmutative effect of formal operations and a conviction that a critical reading of the negative characteristics of Los Angeles might generate new, constructive principles."[59] All of this protective apparati I have marshaled in depicting the city ultimately has very little to do with realism – a Hollywood term after all – but does attempt to displace the rather uninteresting "precession of the simulacra" from its position of authority in defining LA as a theme park. Which all goes to say that Los Angeles is a living breathing entity, an organism, an object of love and hate, a serpent of highways, an ocean of asphalt, a monster, a war zone, a playground, a flowering garden, a map – a city.

Epilogue

Walking in LA
Look ahead as we pass, try to focus on it
I won't be fooled by a cheap cinematic trick
It must have been just cardboard cut out of a man
Top forty cast off from a record stand
Walkin' in LA
Walkin' in LA
Nobody walks in LA
I don't know, could've been a lame jogger maybe
Or someone just about to do the freeway strangler baby
Shopping cart pusher or maybe someone groovie

One thing's for sure he isn't starring in the movies
'Cause he's walkin' in LA
Walkin' in LA
Only a nobody walks in LA
You won't see a cop walkin' on the beat
You only see 'em drivin' cars out on the street
You won't see a kid walkin' home from school
Their mothers pick 'em up in a car pool
Could it be that smog's playing tricks on my eyes
Or it's a rollerskater in some kind of headphone disguise
Maybe somebody who just ran out of gas, making his way
Back to the pumps the best way he can

Missing Persons
Spring Session M
1982 One Way Records Inc.

Notes

1 Dew *et al.*, 1996, p. ix.
2 McPhee, 1989, p. 191.
3 See Jameson, 1991, p. 3, originally published in the *New Left Review* (1984) 146, 53–92. I have, in this phrase, conflated two terms Jameson discusses in this essay: Daniel Bell's "postindustrial society" and Ernest Mandel's book title of *Late Capitalism*. "Postindustrial society" refers to consumer, media, information, electronic, or high-tech societies, while "late capitalism" refers to a "third stage or movement in the evolution of capital." Later in this essay Jameson further explains that, according to Mandel, the three phases of capitalism are: "market capitalism, the monopoly stage or the stage of imperialism, and our own, wrongly called postindustrial, but what might be better termed multinational capital" (p. 35). Also see Lyotard (1984), where Jameson explains that Daniel Bell and others have argued in for the concept of a "postindustrial society" in which "science, knowledge, technological research, rather than industrial production and the extraction of surplus value," are the determining factors.
4 See Varnelis, 2003. Special thanks are owed to Dr. Varnelis for his generosity in sharing his unpublished manuscript with me as well as several bibliographical references. On the ascendancy of the LA School see Marco Cenzatti, 2003. According to Cenzatti "the name 'Los Angeles School' identifies the work of a group of local researchers who, from the early '80's onwards, discovered in Los Angeles a series of social, economic, and spatial trends symptomatic of a general transformation currently taking place in the entire U.S. urban and social structure" (p. 5). The inherent assumption in this loose collection of thinkers from UC Irvine, UCLA, USC, and SCIARC is that "Los Angeles is exemplary of the new urban model currently emerging from a new round of economic and social changes taking place across the country" (p. 6).
5 Along with the authors mentioned in elsewhere throughout this text the following publications have contributed substantially to the bibliography on Los Angeles: McWilliams,

1946; Fogelson, 1967; Hayden, 1995; Barron and Eckmann, 1997; Hall, 1998; Heilbut, 1998; Cuff, 2000; Fulton, 2001; Salas and Roth, 2001.

6 Soja, 1996, p. 196. Soja writes the following about Jameson's essay "Postmodernism or, the Logic of Late Capitalism": "In 1984, while the article was in press, Jameson, Lefebvre, and I wandered through the Bonaventure, rode its glass-encased elevators, and had some refreshments in the rooftop revolving restaurant overlooking downtown. In 1989, I took much the same trip with Robert Manaquis and Jean Baudrillard, when Baudrillard was participating in the revolutionary bicentennial."

7 Jameson, 1991, p. 37. For alternative interpretations of postmodern cities, see Ellin, 1999.

8 Ingraham, 1998, p. 86.

9 My reference to *heterotopia* alludes to Michel Foucault's nomenclature (see Foucault, 1993, pp. 420–426). *Heteropolis* refers to Jencks, 1993.

10 Jameson, 1988, p. 351.

11 Jameson, 1994, p. 130. I am indebted to Michael Speaks for directing me to the publication where Jameson outlines his idea of "dirty realism." On "dirty realism" also see Office for Metropolitan Architecture, Rem Koolhaas, and Bruce Mau, 1995.

12 We might recall that Gertrude Stein's famous 1935 quip that "there is no there there," refers not to Los Angeles, but rather to Oakland, California.

13 Jameson, 1998, p. 353. While the *psychogeography* of Situationism comes to mind here, this act of urbanism is perhaps too vague and imprecise a term upon which to develop an apprehension of LA.

14 Fredric Jameson, 1998, p. 353. Jameson explains these authors with the following: "you know that Kevin Lynch is the author of the classic work, *The Image of the City*, which in its turn spawned a whole low-level subdiscipline that today takes the phrase 'cognitive mapping' as its own designation" and Althusser's "great formulation of ideology itself" as "the Imaginary representation of the subject's relationship to his or her Real conditions of existence."

15 Jameson, 1991, p. 44.

16 For example, Suisman (1992, pp. 586–587) writes: "Per come appariva dopo la seconda guerra mondiale, Los Angeles fu a lungo trattat da *enfant terrible* delle città americane."

17 Adorno and Horkheimer, 1994, p. 120.

18 Richter, p. 69. Her description merits quoting at length:

> "When one arrives in Los Angeles by plane at night, the city appears as fragments of Euclidian fields woven together by threads of moving red and white lights. From the air, these threads, interconnected at geometrically unpredictable points, superimpose a fluid order over a basin of pixels. They sponsor the illusion of effortless movement from point to point on this urban screen of light. But the lack of congruity among the different layers of spatial orders in Los Angeles in fact emphasizes a reading of fragmentation, rupture, and localization. On closer inspection, the nighttime city reveals itself to be a giant shantytown on a desert ground; the lights illuminate the spaces in between, a no-man's land of parking lots, roads, and industrial yards."

Also see Dagmar Richter *XYZ: The Architecture of Dagmar Richter* (New York: Princeton Architectural Press, 2001).

19 Suisman (1992, p. 52) writes: "Questa città è la manifestazione estrema d'una quarantina d'anni di investimenti nazionali nella suburbanizzazione, sostenuta dalle industrie automobilistiche, bancarie, ed edilizie, e dalle linee programmatiche governative."

20 Soja and Scott (1996) similarly divide LA's history into chronological "surges." Surge I (1870

to 1900) "created a regional economy based in agriculture, land speculation, real estate boosterism, and the provision of specialized health and leisure services particularly to white retirees" (p. 5). During Surge II (1900–1920) "the private and public promoters of Los Angeles turned increasingly to industrial development and succeeded in plugging the city into the dynamo of the American manufacturing belt in the northeastern states" (p. 5). Surge III (1920–1940) experienced a "renewed land boom, petroleum production and refining experienced a resurgences," as well as growth of the motion picture and the air craft industries. During Surge IV (1940–1970) the region tripled in size to nearly 10 million, mass suburbanization emerged "on a scale never before encountered" (p. 8). Finally, Surge V (1970–1990) led to the development of an "extremely varied economy based on a diversity of high- and low-technology industries, as well as a thriving business and financial services sector" (p. 12).

21 Moule and Polyzoides, 1994, p. 9.

22 Moule and Polyzoides (1994, p. 10) also explain that "the *Laws of the Indies* was a very sophisticated set of urbanizing rules propagated by decree of King Philip II in 1573 and used extensively in the process of Spanish colonization in America. The Pueblo's location near a river and not near the ocean was deliberate, protecting the settlement from the unhealthy effects of swamps and from pirating. Two separate precincts were delineated for each settler: a lot for the construction of an urban house and a plot of land in the adjacent countryside for farming. The residences encircled the plaza along with royal public buildings, the granary and a guardhouse lining the southern edge. The plaza was rectangular with corner streets heading straight into the square. It was oriented at the compass quarter-points in order to protect the streets from the wind . . . in 1815 the pueblo was washed away by floods and its site was subsequently moved to its present location."

23 Pitt and Pitt (1997, p. 366). The authors also write:

> A powerful tourist magnet since its opening in 1930, Olvera Street now attracts 2 million visitors yearly. The street's original name, Winde Street, reflected the vineyards and wineries one located nearby. It was renamed in honor of Mexican judge Agustín Olvera, a prominent Mexican who once lived there. In the 1920's when Christine Sterling organized a campaign to save its brick and adobe structures from destruction, the street was a back alley for machine shops. Out of whole cloth she created a lively Mexican *mercado*, closed to cars and open to tourists . . . counts among its other attractions the Avila Adobe and the Sepulveda House . . ."

24 Thanks to Diane Ghirardo and a lecture she gave at the regional ACSA conference in St. Louis, Missouri for directing my attention to the staging of Olvera Street. Pitt and Pitt (1997, p. 227) note:

> Although Jackson's novel, about a part-Indian orphan raised in Spanish society and her Indian husband, achieved almost instant success, it failed to arouse public concern for the treatment of local Native Americans. Instead, readers accepted the sentimentalized Spanish aristocracy that was portrayed, and the Ramona myth was born. Jackson died a year after her novel was published, never knowing the impact her book made on the Southern California heritage. The novel *Ramona* has inspired films [the first directed by D. W. Griffith], songs [the 1920s hit "Ramona"], and a long-running pageant in Hemet . . .

25 Suisman (1989, p. 12) also mentions that the colonists "generally ignored the territorial claims of the Native American tribes."

26 From a telephone interview with Mario Gandelsonas conducted during the writing of this essay.
27 Lehan, 1998, p. 266.
28 Gandelsonas, 1996, p. 6.
29 Gandelsonas, 1996, p. 101.
30 Gandelsonas, 1996, p. 104.
31 Stephen Rowley, from http://home.mira.net/~satadaca/v.htm.
32 Rowe and Koetter, 1975, p. 11.
33 Baudrillard, 1984, p. 253.
34 Suisman, 1989, p. 6.
35 Suisman, 1989, p. 21.
36 Suisman, 1989, p. 23.
37 Suisman, 1989, p. 29.
38 Conversely Baudrillard (1984, p. 273) claims that "We are witnessing the end of perspective and panoptic space . . ." A perhaps more noteworthy film that features this site is the 1955 *Rebel Without a Cause*, with performances by James Dean and Natalie Wood.
39 Pitt and Pitt, 1997, p. 183.
40 Hise and Deverell, 2000.
41 See: http://www.laparks.org/grifmet/gp/test/main_hiking.htm.
42 Davis, 1998, pp. 1, 2, 108.
43 Richter, 74–75. Joshua Levine, Theodore Zoumboulakis, Anna Bolneset, Mark Donnahue, Rick Mascia, Cordell Steinmetz, and Robert Thibodeau assisted Richter on this project.
44 Klein, 1997, p. 1.
45 Hise and Deverell, 2000, p. 8.
46 Hise and Deverell, 2000, p. 4.
47 The firm received a citation in the January, 1994 41st Annual P/A Awards. The office team consisted of William H. Fain Jr., Robert P. Shaffer, Patric B. Dawe, Donna L. Vaccarino, John C. Begazo, Neil Kritzinger, Mark R. Gershen, Katherine W. Rinne, and Lori Gates. Cf. *Progressive Architecture* (January 1994). Thanks to Alan Loomis and Vinayak Bharne of Moule and Polyzoides for pointing this work out to me.
48 From an interview Mr. Robert P. Shaffer, Senior Associate at the Johnson–Fain Partnership, generously offered me during the course of writing this chapter.
49 Dobney, 1997, p. 88.
50 Pynchon, 1965, p. 49.
51 Lehan, 1998, p. 273.
52 Baudrillard, 1984, p. 262. He continues:

> Los Angeles is encircled by these "imaginary stations" which feed reality, reality-energy, to a town whose mystery is precisely that it is nothing more than a network of endless, unreal circulation – a town of fabulous proportions, but without space or dimensions. As much as electrical and nuclear power stations, as much as film studios, this town, which is nothing more than an immense script and a perpetual motion picture, needs the old imaginary made up of childhood signals and faked phantasms for its synthetic nervous system.

53 Klein, 1997, p. 140.
54 Baudrillard, 1987, p. 70.
55 Jameson, 1994, p. 145.
56 Jameson, 1994, p. 144.

57 Jameson, 1994, p. 138.
58 Van Toorn, 1997.
59 Preface to *Assemblage* 14, p. 68.

Chapter 8

Philadelphia – The Urban Design of Philadelphia: Taking the Towne for the City

Richard M. Sommer

William Penn developed the plan of what is now known as center-city Philadelphia in the middle of the seventeenth century. Penn's plan for Philadelphia, an alloy of Quaker Utopianism and colonial real-estate speculation, is distinguished not only for its influence as a prototype in the founding of subsequent American cities, but for the ways in which its basic outlines have continued to endure in the form of the city's historical center. Although not unique among North American cities for having been established with a deliberate plan, Philadelphia's evolution over the past three centuries presents an singularly important case through which to examine the interplay between the concepts embodied in an originating plan, the material characteristics of the plan itself, and the historical circumstances that transform, usurp or supersede that plan.

Prescribing a precise layout of streets, squares and boundaries, Penn's scheme sought, but fell short of achieving, an ideal combination of the pastoral order of a seventeenth-century English gentleman's country farm with the market and communal functions of a town. The anomalies and omissions found in Penn's plan may be explained by the conflicts of use and spatial incompatibilities that arise from this somewhat unique attempt at a hybrid urban settlement. In what follows, the fate of both the ideas and the forms that have endured from Penn's plan are taken as a synecdoche for the larger conditions and urban geographies that have come to characterize Philadelphia today. Several issues are at play in such a reading. Foremost among these are questions concerning the interplay between so-called planned and un-planned aspects of cities; that is to say, the very usefulness of distinguishing between conscious, comprehensive efforts to project or reform the layout of a city, and the effects of more piecemeal forms of land development. Also at play is the recurring appeal, within American culture, of a pre-industrial, pastoral vision of the city.

Two moments stand out as examples of deliberate planning and design in Philadelphia: the crafting of Penn's original plan, and planning efforts undertaken three centuries later that came to fruition in redevelopment projects led by the city planner Edmund Bacon. In between these two moments, and during the period of its greatest expansion, Philadelphia grew primarily by means of *laissez-faire* commercial development. Along with the extension of existing suburban patterns, new territories were surveyed and platted in an entirely perfunctory way. Pressure to plan and manage unbridled growth built up towards the end of the nineteenth century, following the city's incorporation of all of the surrounding county's townships in 1854. This incorporation made Penn's "walking city" just one-tenth of an emerging metropolis.

This study of Philadelphia will concentrate on the symbolic and functional role that its historical core has come to play within a city whose physical extents have grown well beyond its original boundaries. For aging industrial cities such as Philadelphia, whose populations and economic fortunes have been in steadily decline since the 1950s, the fate of the historical core is especially important. Such a reading of Philadelphia necessitates retracing the assumptions and critically accessing the planning and urban design efforts led by Edmund Bacon during three decades of major transformations in the middle of the twentieth century. Harking back to the authority of William Penn's vision for the city – and the city's colonial prominence as the "cradle of liberty" – Bacon's efforts focused on reinvigorating the historical core by using new projects and infrastructure to recast implicitly the original figures and boundaries of William Penn's plan.

In weighing the hegemony of schemes orchestrated by Bacon in Philadelphia against both Penn's founding principles and 250 intervening years of "un-planned" changes to the form of the city, I hope to explore two interconnected dilemmas which generally plague the professional practice of urban design. The first concerns how the goals of urban design are established relative to the question of what distinguishes a metropolis from a town.[1] The second concerns the analytical means used to establish a methodological ground to justify such goals, including the ways in which a city's historical and contemporary form are framed, evaluated and characterized in the urban design process. To examine Philadelphia in this context will require a short historical survey of its founding plan and evolution, an analysis of some of the projects that prefigured Bacon's work in the early twentieth century and a rehearsal of the background, intentions and outcome of Bacon's work itself.

Philadelphia's propitious beginning: William Penn's plan

In exchange for the settlement of a debt with the estate of Admiral Penn, in 1670 Charles II of England established a charter granting his son William Penn as proprietor and governor of 26,000,000 acres in the American Colonies. Named Pennsylvania, the territories granted were in the mid-Atlantic region of the colonies bordered by Delaware and New Jersey on the eastern coast. Penn had already gained experience in the planning, development and governance of colonial cities in the region, having participated in establishing the provincial capitals of Burlington and Amboy (later Perth-Amboy) in New Jersey.[2] The plan of Burlington presages the general disposition of Philadelphia, but without its innovations or distinct gridiron. At Burlington Penn employed the most fundamental of town-making devices, which he would later repeat at Philadelphia; the establishment of two main crossing roads – in this case a "high" street and a "broad" street.

While the form of these earlier cities in which Penn participated provides some insight into the later planning of Philadelphia, they are perhaps more indicative of Penn's entrepreneurial skill. He was adroit at establishing colonial settlements that would attract his fellow Quakers with the combined promise of commercial opportunity and freedom from religious persecution in England.

Seven months after he received the charter from Charles II, Penn selected three commissioners to accompany the first group of settlers to Pennsylvania. Drawing on his previous experience with colonial towns, Penn drew up an elaborate memorandum for the commissioners that included detailed and pragmatic directives on how to select a site for the city, taking into consideration the acreage needed. Penn asked that a site be chosen along the Delaware River where the rivers and creeks are "sounded" (long and broad) on his side and where "it is most navigable, high, dry, and healthy; that is, where most ships may best ride, of deepest draught of water . . ."[3]

He then instructed that (my italics):

> 3d: Such a place being found out, for navigation, healthy situation and good soil for provision, *lay out ten thousand acres contiguous to*

> *it in the best manner you can, as the bounds and extent of the liberties* of the said town.[4]

After the selection of a proper site, Penn also specified the uniform way in which the streets, parcels and buildings would need to be disposed, asking the commissioners to "12th: Be sure to settle the figure of the town so as that the streets hereafter may be uniform down to the water from the country bounds . . ."[5]

Penn's instructions concerning the placement of houses is perhaps the most revealing of his intentions for the character of the town:

> 15th: Let every house be placed, if the person pleases, in the middle of it plat, as to the breadth way of it, so that there may be ground on each side for gardens or orchards, or fields, that it may be a green county town, which will never be burnt, and always be wholesome."[6]

Following Penn's instructions, the commissioners selected a "high and dry" site where the bank of the Delaware River ran closest and parallel to the banks of Skulkill River, the main inland tributary in the area. A few Dutch and Swedish settlers had already established themselves in the area. There is some ambiguity as to the sequence of events that led up to the completion of a formal plan for the city in 1683. Penn appointed Captain Thomas Holme as surveyor general, but he did not arrive until June of 1682, after the site for the city had already been selected. Holme worked with the commissioners on a plan, of which no record survives, but it is understood to have only covered an area extending halfway from the Delaware Bank towards the banks of the Skulkill. What is now understood as the original plan did not emerge until Penn joined Holme four months later. Anticipating the success of Philadelphia and "future comers," Penn had the city extended to the banks of the Skulkill, allowing for a front on each river. In a short time Penn and Holme finalized the plans. A survey was prepared and lots were sold. A year later Holmes published *A Portraiture of the City of Philadelphia* with a written narrative and "Plat-form" meant to draw new settlers (Figure 8.1). Holme's drawing and narrative describes the pattern of streets and public squares that still define central Philadelphia:

> the City of Philadelphia now extends in Length from River to River, two Miles and in Breadth near a Mile . . .
>
> The City (as the model shews) consists of a large Front-street to each River and a High-street (near the middle) from Front (or River)

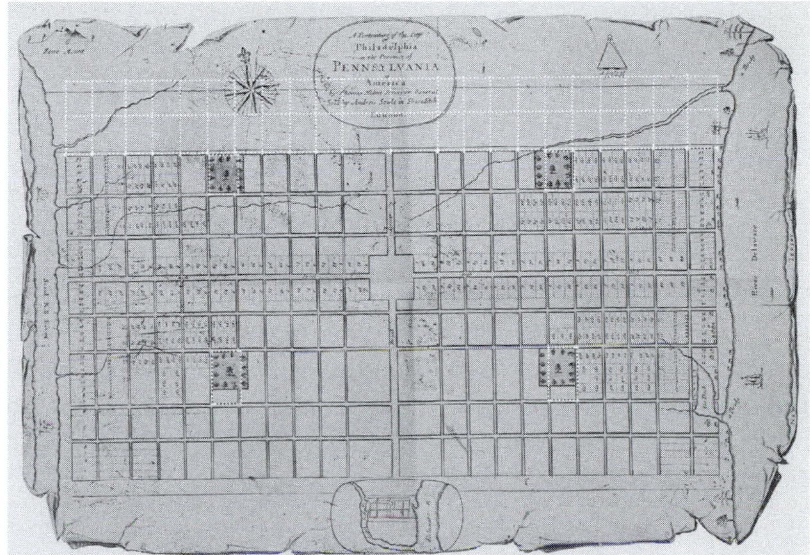

8.1
Plat-form (plan) of Philadelphia in 1682, after Thomas Holme, surveyor (Olin Library, Cornell University)
Source: As published in John W. Reps, *The Making of Urban America: A History of City Planning in the United States* (Princeton, NJ: Princeton University Press, 1965)

> to front, of one hundred Foot broad, and a Broad-street in the middle of the City, form side to side, of the like breadth. In the center of the City is a Square of ten Acres; at each Angle there are to be Houses for Public Affairs, as a Meeting House, Assembly or State-House, Market-House and several other buildings for Publick Concerns. There is also in each Quarter of the city a Square of eight Acres, to be for like Uses, as the Moore-fields in London; and eight Streets, (besides the High-street), that run from Front to Front, and twenty Streets, (besides the Broad-street) that run cross the City, from side to side; all these Streets are of Fifty Foot breadth[7]

The creation of a great "city or town" was central to Penn's plans for a "Holy experiment" in the colonies. "Holy experiment" refers to the then novel idea that adherents of differing religious faiths and political convictions would be free to settle and live side by side in these new territories. Thus the use of the name Philadelphia, borrowed from the name of the ancient city in Asia Minor and the Greek term for "city of brotherly love."

Penn's scheme for Philadelphia was founded on the proposition that each investor in a large rural parcel in Pennsylvania would also receive a "bonus" plot within a large, new capital city.

> "I.: That as soon as it pleaseth God . . . a certain quantity of land shall be laid out for a large town or city . . . and every purchaser shall, by lot, have so much land therein as will answer to the

> proportion which he hath bought or taken up upon rent. But it is to be noted that the surveyor shall consider what roads or highways will be necessary to the cities, towns, or through the lands . . . and V.: That the proportion of lands that shall be laid out in the first great city or town, for every purchaser, shall be after the proportion of ten acres for every five hundred acres purchased, if the place will allow it."[8]

The linking of large rural tracts to plots in a planned town quickly – and artificially – established European settlement patterns in Pennsylvania that might have otherwise taken a century or more to achieve. Unlike earlier (and some later) colonial settlers, who had to build homes, locate ports, and found markets in essentially wilderness conditions, investors in Pennsylvania could anticipate a settlement plot in a well-planned community.

The fate of Penn's colonial plan

Foreshadowing Thomas Jefferson's agrarian vision for the United States, Penn sought to create, through a highly speculative real-estate venture, a pastoral yet culturally and economically pluralistic town that would balance the effects of trade with the civilizing effects of a landed gentry. Philadelphia would be a "wholesome," "green country town," serving the ideals of religious freedom while tempering the barbarous effects of trade. Although many of Penn's investors were involved in maritime-based trade, and his instructions for the selection of a site gave priority to the founding of a port, Penn believed that profits made from the ownership and management of land were morally more defensible than those made from trade.

Penn's original 1683 Plan is consistent with this desire, as it fluctuates between an ideal "checkerboard" geometry, the accommodation of local geographic circumstance and the anticipation of future extensions into, and annexations of, the surrounding countryside.

The city's gridiron layout, subdivided into four quadrants by a "broad" and a "high" street, was fairly typical for colonial towns and had numerous Spanish and English precedents. Penn and Holmes' subtle innovation was the placement of a large, open public square at the crossing of the two main streets, and one additional square within each of the four quadrants. John Reps has conjectured that Penn or Holme may have been inspired by Richard Newcourt's 1666 plan for the reconstruction of London, which also contains an equal distribution of five open spaces within a field of regular, rectangular blocks.[9] Yet the difference between these two plans may be as

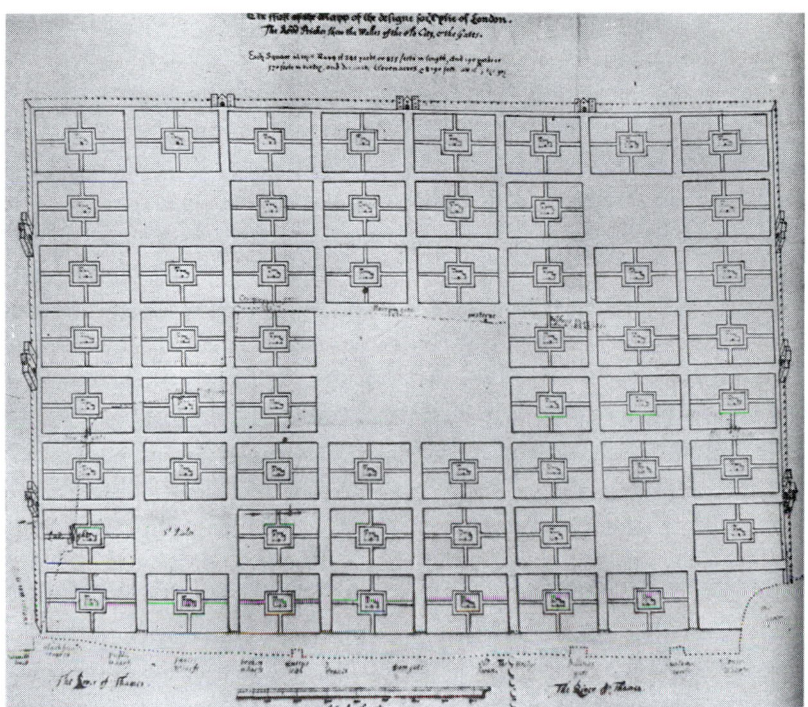

8.2
Design for the rebuilding of London, Richard Newcourt, 1666 (retouched by John W. Reps, from a reproduction in Towne Planning Review, Vol. 18, No. 3 (1939))
Source: As published in John W. Reps, *The Making of Urban America: A History of City Planning in the United States* (Princeton, NJ: Princeton University Press, 1965)

illuminating as their similarities. Despite being conceived to reorganize both existing areas and the parts of London destroyed by the great fire in 1666, the Newcourt plan is entirely symmetrical, with an equal number of blocks emanating from the central square in each direction. Newcourt also maximized the value of each of the quadrant's public squares by surrounding them on all sides with developable frontage (Figure 8.2).

In contrast to Newcourt's London plan, the Philadelphia plan exhibits some striking anomalies. The southern half of the Philadelphia plan is similar to the London plan: platting five blocks to the south of the east–west High (now Market) Street divide allowed public squares to be positioned at roughly the center of their quadrants. Yet only three blocks to north of High Street were platted, leaving the northern boundary of the public squares exposed. There was also great variation in the size of the rectangular blocks, and their geometry was at odds with that of the squares. The plan pragmatically places rectangular blocks with their long face oriented along the north–south streets, maximizing potential access to daylight. Yet despite the prevailing rectangular geometry, the public squares are projected as absolutely "square." The mismatch between the geometry of the squares and the blocks produces a set of irregular spaces around more than half the frontages of the squares, without planning for any public streets between the squares and the parcels (see dashed overlay on Figure 8.1).

The anomalies in the Philadelphia plan aptly illustrate Penn's struggle to balance Utopian ideals with the exigencies of real estate and land governance. At stake was a legal and symbolic connection between the city and its outlying districts, and the authority of the plan itself to maintain the projected boundaries and disposition of blocks, parcels and set-aside public squares.

A vast amount of Pennsylvania land was already under contract prior to the platting of Philadelphia. The promise of a 2 percent bonus city plot would have been impossible to accommodate within the scale of a sixteenth-century colonial city (or any city at that time). The planned city, at 1280 acres, would have provided roughly less than one-fifth of the needed parcels, all of which would have exceeded the average seven-acre size of the city blocks. Penn's first ideas for Philadelphia included surrounding a compact rectangular town between the rivers with gentlemanly estates of 80 acres, with the house at the center of each plot separated by at least 800 feet (Figure 8.3). When the geography of the surrounding areas made this pattern of development a difficult prospect, Penn instead, through a questionably legal sleight-of-hand, met his promise to investors by offering land in the 10,000 acres of "Liberty" lands laid out by his surveyors adjacent to the city's northern border. Penn then

8.3
Map of the improved part of Pennsylvania, including Philadelphia and vicinity, with an inset plan of Philadelphia. Drawn by Thomas Holme, published 1720 (US Library of Congress, Map Division)
Source: As published in John W. Reps, *The Making of Urban America: A History of City Planning in the United States* (Princeton, NJ: Princeton University Press, 1965)

attempted to incorporate some of the estate planning principles planned for the outskirts into the city center, showing many of the blocks as subdivided into regular acre or half-acre parcels.[10] As the recent history of Philadelphia reveals, the perceived northern boundary of the city continued to be in play well into the twentieth century. By leaving the northern edge of the city incomplete, it is likely that Penn sought ambiguously to associate the undeveloped areas of the Liberty lands with the city proper.[11]

The platting of the parcels in 1683 plan reflects Penn's belief that the city would grow simultaneously from its two river frontages in towards the center. The city did not comply. Rather, following convention, the city grew into unplanned areas to the north and south, extending in a low-slung, crowded pattern parallel to its busy eastern port on the Delaware. During Philadelphia's storied period as the American Revolution's "cradle of liberty," Penn's checkerboard plan could in fact hardly be discerned (Figure 8.4). The broad city blocks with large parcels that were meant to accommodate large, free-standing town homes in a green, leafy setting also succumbed to the conventions of the colonial period. The original 425 by 570 (or 675) foot blocks were subdivided with narrow alleys within which emerged a dense city fabric of rowhouses.

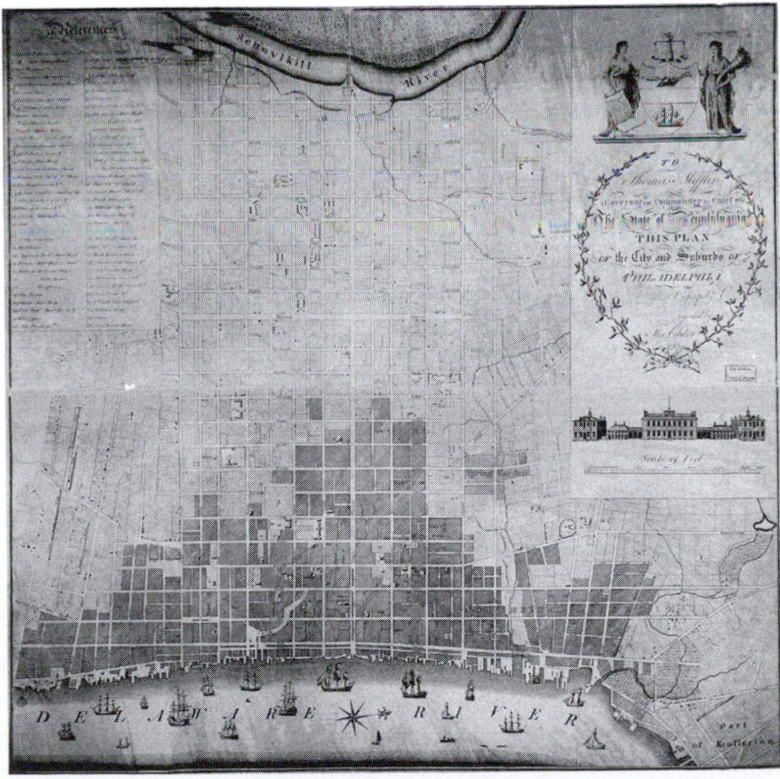

8.4
Plan of the city and suburbs of Philadelphia, drawn by A.P. Folie in 1994 (US Library of Congress, Map Division)
As published in John W. Reps, *The Making of Urban America: A History of City Planning in the United States* (Princeton, NJ: Princeton University Press, 1965)

The planned public squares suffered a better fate, and bear out the utility of Penn's scheme. After being obscured by eighteenth-century surveys which document the shifting of Broad Street two blocks west, better to straddle the highest ridge between the two rivers, the central and two western squares reappear in altered locations by the early nineteenth century. All five squares were made subject to new city ordinances, banning their use as dumping grounds. These new ordinances designated the squares as civic open spaces in perpetuity, providing financial support for their improvement.[12]

What logic can be gleaned from the uncoupling, by means of geometry and placement, of the idealized public squares from the rectangular gridiron of private development? Perhaps, because of their ideal geometry, the squares were able to endure (or at least recover) as an idea uncontaminated by the evolving, speculative form of the grid. The recovered squares were eventually able to provide relief from a scale and density of development never anticipated by William Penn. Philadelphia is credited – and blamed – for introducing the gridiron plan with a main square at its center as a model for establishing cities throughout the United States. The scheme was duplicated *ad infinitum*, often on hilly, less appropriate sites. Nevertheless, the public squares establish an important precedent for the concept of neighborhood parks taken up by city planners more than two centuries later. Likewise, the annexing of the northern liberties, as a semi-planned green buffer zone, anticipated the greenbelt and garden city concepts.

Nineteenth-century expansion: from town to metropolis

Philadelphia's premiere status during the revolutionary period grew out of its dominance of the political and commercial activities of the day. The city hosted the Continental Congress, it was the site of both the signing of the Declaration of Independence and the drafting of the Constitution, and served as the nation's first capital after independence was won. During the latter half of the eighteenth century Philadelphia contained the largest port in the western hemisphere; it was the largest city in the English-speaking world after London, to which it was often compared. Penn's vision of the city as a marketplace and symbolic center for the vast agricultural production of Pennsylvania, Southern New Jersey and Delaware had been achieved.

Yet the city did not achieve its iconic form until the middle of the nineteenth century. Paradoxically, the full realization of the city platted by Penn, stretching from river to river, coincided with a consolidation of the various townships in Philadelphia County under one municipality in 1854. Though still the core, "Old" Philadelphia was now just one-tenth of a vast, expanding metropolis. Until that time the city had been steadily increasing in population by an average of 25 percent per decade, growing from 41,000 inhabitants in 1800 to 121,000 in 1850. The incorporation increased the city's official population fivefold, to about a half-a-million residents. By 1900 the population had increased another two-and-a-half times, to 1.25 million.

If the explosive growth spurred by the industrial revolution had multiplied Philadelphia's population by 30 times over the course of the nineteenth century, New York City had grown at twice that rate. Upon the completion of the Erie Canal in 1825, New York City became the dominant port and commercial center on the eastern seaboard. In addition to New York City's geographic advantage for trade, Manhattan's linear form, clearly delimited boundaries and industrial-scale grid all helped to organize and discipline new growth, making it a highly propitious site for the formation of a distinctive, modern city. The Philadelphia gridiron laid out by Penn, on the other hand, was not large enough to contain the amount of new growth in the city. Moreover there was little impetus to physically integrate, by means of planning, the various adjacent townships that had been legally consolidated in 1854. In Philadelphia, as in much of the US during this period, the rush of industrial expansion and the *laissez-faire* attitude towards commerce allowed little municipal control over – or even reflection on – civic planning and land development.

In the period of Philadelphia's greatest growth and expansion, from the years 1850 to 1950, existing suburban patterns were extended, roadways were improved, and new turnpikes and train lines were built. Outside the center, a robust, but haphazard gridiron pattern of industrial plants and speculative residential blocks eroded formerly agricultural tracts. Though often containing the ubiquitous Philadelphia rowhouse, most of these new areas possessed neither the grandeur of the old downtown, nor its pedestrian scale (Figure 8.5). Though still prosperous, by 1900 Philadelphia trailed New York and Chicago in size. New York, by virtue of its physical layout, and Chicago, by virtue of the "The Great Fire" of 1871, had had the opportunity to expand the physical plan and profile of their central areas.

The form of Philadelphia's center continued to evolve well into the early decades of the twentieth century. At the turn of the century, projects were undertaken to update the downtown. But it was not until faced with loss of population and the decaying of historic districts as the city declined in the wake of the Second World War that the city's leaders and citizens attempted a wholesale remaking of was by then simply referred to as "Center-City."

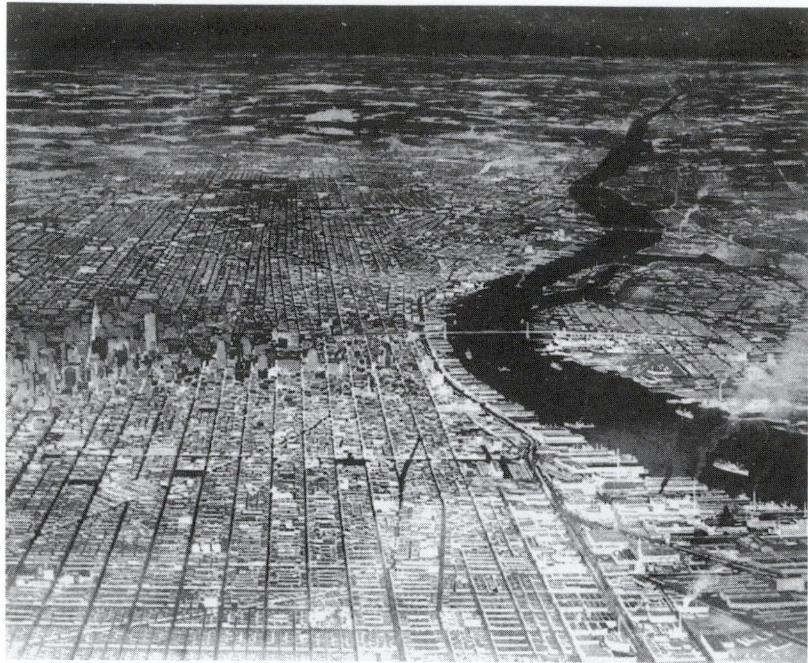

8.5
Philadelphia, aerial photograph looking north, 1951

The declining fate of the central city

The narrative of stagnation and decline that defines the recent history of Philadelphia is shared by a number of other aging industrial cities in the United States, including Baltimore, Detroit, St Louis and Pittsburgh. Maritime trade and, later, the railroads necessitated compact, concentrated cities during the period in which these cities were established and grew. With the advent of the automobile, mass suburbanization became a possible and often preferred form of land development. The very highways that planners and engineers promised would make physical travel between the old city centers and their outlying regions faster and more convenient facilitated the creation of whole new urban sub-centers that replaced the goods and services formerly only available in the old centers. Via FHA mortgages and highway construction, a new, federally subsidized suburban arcadia of single-family homes also drew business and industry, eager to shed their old plants and avoid the costs of organized labor and higher taxes that faced them in the old city centers.

Industrial plants built to support the war effort during the 1940s temporarily stayed the rates of decline in cities like Philadelphia. These facilities stimulated, for a time, the city's economies, levels of employment and population that had already begun to drop in the 1930s, but following the War the downward trend resumed. By the 1960s, the desegregation of ethnic minorities within the city also played a decisive role in the decline of urban centers such as Philadelphia. Large segments of the white middle-class population had already left the city. Threatened by the changing (read: "ethnic") public face of the city they fled further, a phenomenon that came to be known as "white flight." Once ensconced in new, more homogeneous communities, their xenophobia only increased, further reducing their desire to interact with the old centers.

Although the events that caused a decline in the fortunes of many American cities in the post-industrial era can be generalized as above, the effects of these commonly-shared events upon the physical form of the city in each case varied. Corresponding attempts at redevelopment and revitalization often met with limited success. Unlike many of the other US cities that have suffered decline, Philadelphia eventually managed to reinvent its downtown. The very area platted by William Penn was arguably more vital at the beginning of the twenty-first century than it was before the loss of population and industry began 50 years previously. What actions, if any, on the part of citizens, politicians and designers, contributed to the revitalization of the historic core? How was the transformation achieved, and at what cost to the rest of the city?

Three phases in the remaking of Philadelphia

I. Public works inspired by the City Beautiful movement

Anticipating the sesquicentennial of the American Revolution in 1926, and spurred on by the Columbian Worlds Exposition and the City Beautiful movement, Philadelphia undertook a series of ambitious plans beginning in about 1904. These included two major projects, the Fairmont (now Benjamin Franklin) Parkway and the Delaware (now Benjamin Franklin) Bridge. These projects, while essentially transportation-driven, had the effect of creating two new monumental entries into the city. Located to the northwest of the city along the Skulkill River and containing the city's nineteenth-century quasi-Greek Revival waterworks at its base, the promontory at Fairmount was already noted on Penn's 1683 plan.[13] The new parkway was to function as both a traffic artery and a civic center, with a plaza at its southern edge acting as a gateway from Fairmount Park and the expanding northern and western suburbs to the heart of the city. Fairmount itself was to be occupied by an elaborate art museum complex and linked by a grand diagonal axis slashing through one of the city's original squares (now Logan Circle) to Center Square, where the city had built a new, gargantuan, Second Empire style City Hall, completed in 1901.

The Benjamin Franklin Parkway and Philadelphia Art Museum were complete by the 1930s. As with many City Beautiful schemes, the full realization of the Parkway as a civic center was primarily undermined by the lack of centralized authority to plan, finance and develop urban land. The economic challenges of the Great Depression and then the Second World War contributed as well. The *beaux arts* parkway scheme had been part of a larger study by Jacques Greber, a French landscape architect. Greber was the primary designer in charge of the Parkway and the urban planning related to it. He proposed a network of diagonal avenues bisecting the city's original squares, attempting to conjoin them with the city's new train stations, cultural institutions and government buildings in the Parisian manner made popular in the nineteenth century.

While Greber's city-wide proposal was not as visionary or comprehensive as Burnham's plans for San Francisco and Chicago, it does propose a reading and layout of the city that is provocative in the light of urban design and planning projects implemented several decades later. Greber's 1917 "Partial Plan of the City Shewing the New Civic Centre . . ." played down the original northern and southern borders of Penn's plan, placing particular emphasis on integrating built-out areas of the Northern Liberties and Spring Garden Districts into the old downtown (Figure 8.6). The plan projected new development

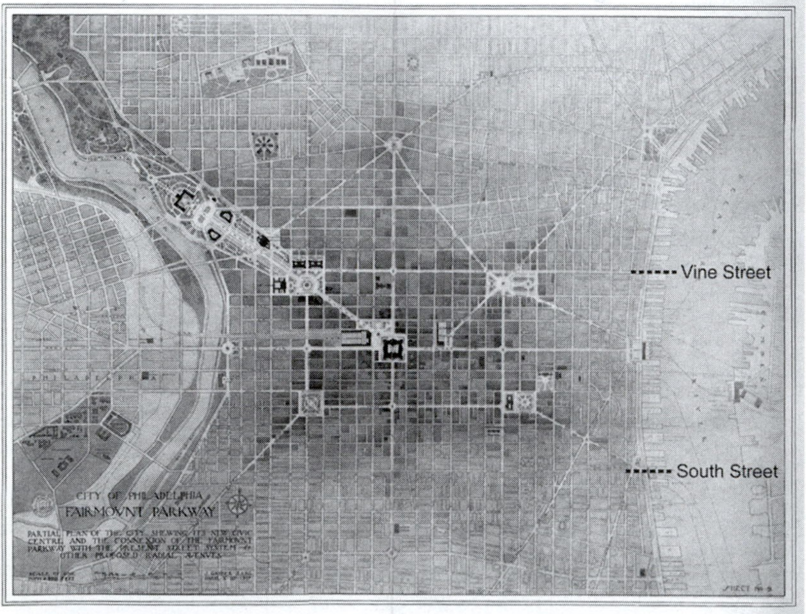

8.6
Partial plan of the city showing the new civic center and the connection of the Fairmount Parkway with the present street system and other proposed radial avenues, Jacques Greber, 1917
Source: From Folio, *The Fairmount Parkway* (Philadelphia: Fairmount Park Association, 1919)

around the two northern squares, Franklin Square to the east and Logan Square to the west, fulfilling their potential as open spaces central to their quadrants. Vine Street was no longer understood as the edge of the city, but as another main east–west avenue running between Squares, akin to Locust Street on the south side. The way in which the plan was framed suggested that the city's center was shifting north towards Vine Street, a reorientation confirmed shortly after by the building of the Benjamin Franklin Bridge, the second monumental entry into the city.

After more than 100 years of failed attempts to build a bridge that would span the Delaware River from Camden, New Jersey to Philadelphia, the growing use of the automobile precipitated the construction of the Benjamin Franklin Bridge, completed in 1928. Drawing twice as much traffic as anticipated, the suspension bridge created a sweeping panorama into the early, eastern districts of the city. The Bridge's massive landing fell between Race and Vine Street, ending in a plaza fronting Franklin Square.

Although a movement devoted to the stewardship of the city's colonial past had begun to emerge almost 100 years prior to the construction of the Benjamin Franklin Bridge, completion of the bridge and the celebration of the sesquicentennial in 1926 brought a new set of concerns to light about the "Old (re: eastern, colonial) City." Commercial and business interests that had once thrived in these areas began to move westward with the construction of the new city hall at Center Square. The area experienced a slow but steady decline. Although there were still many buildings of historical value from the Philadelphia's colonial period, much of the built fabric had been transformed during the nineteenth century. Recognition of past and possible future losses promoted the appreciation of older structures from the colonial period, and in particular the veneration of the Old Pennsylvania State House. The State House became the catalyst for a series of projects and studies that eventually led to the construction of the Independence National Park – and, arguably, to the wholesale transformation of the "Old City."

II. Independence Mall: William Penn's greene country towne writ large

The most hallowed shrine in Philadelphia, perhaps in the United States, is the site of what has come to be known as Independence Hall and Independence Square (not one of the original squares laid out by Penn). Originally the Pennsylvania State House, Independence Hall is the site where the terms of the American Revolution were forged. The first Continental Congress met at the State House in 1776, and subsequently drafted, signed and publicly read the American Declaration of Independence there. Upon winning the War for Independence, the Second Continental Congress met again there and framed the

Constitution of the United States. Philadelphia and its State House served as the United States Capitol in the first, formative decade of the county's existence, during which the Bill of Rights was amended to the Constitution. Following the move of the federal government to Washington, DC and the simultaneous transfer of Pennsylvania's capital to Harrisburg, the State House housed a changing series of functions throughout the nineteenth century. These included Philadelphia's city government, federal courts and, from 1802 to 1828, the first public museum of natural history in the United States, formed by the painter Charles Willson Peale.[14] Already in the early 1800s, Peale stated that Independence Hall would be "a building more interesting in the history of the world, than any of the celebrated fabrics of Greece and Rome!"[15]

Only after the much-heralded visit of the Marquis de Lafayette to Philadelphia in 1824, during which he was received in the State House's assembly room redecorated as a "Hall of Independence," did the site emerge as a shrine. The re-naming of the State House as Independence Hall precipitated a series of projects to "restore" the Hall, along with its outbuildings and Square, to their condition at the time of the American Revolution. The first of these projects began to mark the centennial of American Independence in 1876. The Daughters of the American Revolution and the American Institute of Architects undertook later renovation projects.[16]

The veneration of the Hall was furthered by the enshrinement of another relic of perhaps greater symbolic value than the building itself: the old state house bell, inscribed with the Old Testament words "proclaim liberty throughout the land, unto all the inhabitants thereof." While no historical records exist to confirm the Bell's connection with any of the great events surrounding the Revolution, its value as a symbol was nonetheless taken up by the abolitionists, who first coined the term "The Liberty Bell" in the title of an anti-slavery pamphlet. Only later, through popular songs, children's books, and extensive national railroad tours, was the Liberty Bell appropriated as a more generalized patriotic symbol.

Following the First World War, the surge in patriotism only increased the status and veneration of the Independence Hall complex and the Liberty Bell enshrined therein. Temporary viewing stands were often constructed adjacent to Independence Hall on Chestnut Street to serve the frequent patriotic parades, pageants and rallies held there. Many found the eclectic language, workaday uses and decaying condition of the older buildings facing the hall on Chestnut Street distasteful, and hoped to replace them with a plaza that would more permanently serve patriotic events.[17] Jacques Greber, the designer of the Parkway, and many of his collaborators and professional colleagues that taught at the University of Pennsylvania (including the prominent architect Paul Cret) made proposals for the site over a 30-year period.[18]

The scheme that most influenced the remaking of this area was not conceived by an architect, politician or civic leader, but rather by a Professor of Hygiene at the University of Pennsylvania named Dr Seneca Egbert. His 1928 proposal was apparently a response to a 1925 Philadelphia City Council proposal to abate traffic congestion at the Benjamin Franklin Bridge Plaza by diverting traffic from the Plaza to Market Street, through the creation of a grand boulevard mid-block between Fifth and Sixth Streets. Egbert instead proposed "the development of a Concourse or Esplanade between Independence Hall and the plaza at the west end of the Delaware bridge that should serve as a permanent and impressive Sesquicentennial memorial of the historic events incident to the founding of the nation."[19]

No drawing is known to exist of this scheme, but Egbert did draft an elaborate report outlining his proposals. Several aspects of the scheme he outlined were present in the plan finally implemented in the late 1940s. Egbert justified his boldest proposition, the demolishing of three city blocks stretching from Independence Hall on Chestnut Street to the Bridge plaza on Race Street – over 20 acres – by citing a widely-held fear that a fire could at any time consume one of the area's abandoned or dilapidated buildings and spread to Independence Hall or another cherished colonial edifice. His other influential proposals included the widening of Fifth and Sixth Streets to accommodate increased traffic from the Bridge, the creation of a central pedestrian esplanade "possibly as broad as Broad Street," the creation of a plaza for events fronting Independence Hall, the accommodation of underground parking, and the building of a new subway stop.

Most of his proposals for the surface development of individual blocks were not adopted. Egbert envisioned a scheme in which a building representing the Pennsylvania Commonwealth would cap the first block at the far end of the Mall at the bridge plaza. The Pennsylvania building was to be symmetrically flanked on the next block south by replicas of colonial buildings representing the other original twelve states of the union. The final block fronting Independence Hall was to house memorials and a plaza for celebrations.

Perhaps even more influential than the physical proposals made was Egbert's supposition that the new Mall would increase tax revenues by increasing the assessed value of the three cleared blocks – and, ultimately, increase the perceived value of adjacent properties and the district as a whole. Egbert chided the city for narrowly promoting development around Center (now Penn) Square to the west at the expense of the area of the city most associated with its illustrious history. He also implied that the historical value of the Old City could be mined to commercial advantage. To achieve a project of this magnitude, Egbert also foresaw the need for a structure of cooperation between various federal, city and state agencies. Egbert's scheme remained unrealized until world events prompted a reconsideration of his proposal for the Mall.

The bombing of Pearl Harbor and the outbreak of the Second World War brought a renewed resolve to protect Independence Hall and the Liberty Bell. Starting in 1941, Edwin O'Lewis, a charismatic, highly persuasive and well-connected judge, and president of the Pennsylvania Society of the Sons of the Revolution, mounted a campaign to build the three-block long Independence Mall. Mindful of the potential for federal support for the construction and management of the Mall, the project was conceived as a National Park that would eventually include the entire complex of buildings associated with Independence Hall. Roy Larson, a partner of Paul Cret's who made a proposal for the site in 1937, prior to the war, which drew liberally on Egbert's scheme, was asked to develop a plan for the Mall. It was Larson's revised plan from 1937, extending three blocks north of Independence Square and two partial blocks to the east, that was eventually implemented after the National Park was approved by the US Congress in 1949[20] (Figure 8.7).

8.7a
Looking east from "Independence Hall" towards the future site of Independence Mall

8.7b
Adopted proposal for Independence Mall, Roy Larson, 1937
Source: From pamphlet, *Independence Hall and Adjacent Buildings, A Plan for their Preservation and the Improvement of their Surroundings* (Philadelphia: Fairmount Park Art Association in collaboration with the Independence Hall Association, 1944)

The construction of the Mall, eventually part of a larger entity known as Independence National Park, did not proceed without resistance and controversy. Three blocks of businesses, many of which were (despite statements to the contrary) still active, were taken by eminent domain. Many fine nineteenth-century buildings were destroyed, including Frank Furness's magnificent polychrome Guarantee Trust Company and the Provident Life & Trust Company Bank and Office Building. Gaining governmental approval for the project hinged on the landmark status of the colonial buildings, and having the Park Service manage the site. Nevertheless, architects, preservationists and historians associated with the Park Service were critical of the effect the wholesale clearance of the site would have on the colonial monuments entrusted to them.[21]

Linking a memorial dedicated to a patriotic theme to an infrastructure-driven urban renewal project was not unique in the early decades of the twentieth century, or in previous eras; the roughly concurrent Jefferson National Expansion Memorial in St Louis was a prime example of the type. However, the sheer degree to which the Independence Mall and National Historic Park of which it is part combined an anachronistic, if not reactionary, esthetic project with a somewhat progressive economic planning model warrants further examination.

One could simply reduce the esthetic proposition of Independence Mall to a matter of stylistic fashion, expressive of its historical moment, but this reading would not fully embrace the profound irony and implications of the project. Here a crude imitation of eighteenth-century European classicism was deployed in a plan to transform a once discreet set of colonial buildings and artifacts, prized for the way their modest form and casual arrangement connoted the humble beginnings of the American democracy, into a National Historic Park. In the process, a large piece of the city's actual history, a dense but often architecturally rich urban fabric built up over three centuries, was destroyed.

The Mall itself was considered a failure almost from the start. Too vast to frame the diminutive Independence Hall and too formal to serve as an active city park, the Mall's most lauded purpose was as an underground garage serving the adjacent businesses and institutions in the bureaucratically designed office buildings that eventually lined it. The necessity of a mall of this size in this part of Philadelphia is itself questionable, but its form was disastrous. Looking north but cut off from the northern areas of the city by the landing of the bridge and later a highway, the mall's orientation represents a profound misreading of city's original morphology; a rectangular grid with its major streets stretching between two rivers. If interested in celebrating the city's history with a mall, it would have had to be positioned east–west, parallel to (or along) Market Street. An east–west link would have tied Independence Square to the city's true beginning point, a landing at the Delaware River, and better articulated a spatial narrative of the city's history.[22]

More connected to the national network of historic parks and related tourist sites than to the history of Philadelphia, Independence Mall indicates how, at a time when metropolitan areas like Philadelphia were dissipating into the suburbs, the esthetic chosen for the symbolic areas at the center was one that put a premium on cleanliness, easy automobile access and open, verdant vistas. It was as if Penn's Greene Country Towne was finally going to be realized with a vengeance, but at a scale that could only be appreciated from a moving automobile or as part of a larger tourist's itinerary.

The Mall's misguided form follows from the order of priorities that established it, from the pragmatic to the ambiguously altruistic – that is, first traffic abatement, then the framing of hallowed shrines, and finally "urban renewal." In hindsight, it seems that the radical transformation of this urban site into a pastoral park was mired in mid-century American politics of national mythmaking and a seemingly symbiotic relationship between urban divestment, the restoration of historic structures and re-gentrification.

More generally, the Mall suggested processes by which the city's historical form and stock of historic buildings could be leveraged to stimulate both public and private reinvestment in the old heart of the city. It is in this sense – as an amalgam of transportation planning, historic "preservation" and commercial redevelopment, conceived to restore the symbolic capital of a decaying city – that the plan for Independence Mall presaged not only the larger redevelopment of Philadelphia's downtown but also the post-War focus of urban design in general.

The completion of the three-block Mall took twenty years, from 1949 to 1969, years that almost directly correspond to Edmund Bacon's highly influential tenure as Executive Director of Philadelphia's Planning Commission. Considering himself a modernist, Bacon was never comfortable with the anachronistic character of the Mall's design, which he had inherited, but he supported the larger planning goals it represented. The massive clearing and highlighting of colonial architecture set the stage for many initiatives later facilitated by Bacon, including the gentrification of the surrounding Old City and its "Society Hill."

III. The urban design of "Better Philadelphia" under Edmund Bacon

In 1964, a heroic portrait of Edmund Bacon was featured on the cover of Time magazine, under the banner "Urban Renewal: Remaking the American City" (Figure 8.8). Now, half a century after Bacon's planning efforts were initiated, perhaps it is possible to evaluate his role in the vaunted renaissance of Philadelphia's downtown. However, a full evaluation of Bacon's theories and work in Philadelphia would not be possible here. Instead I will focus on the question of

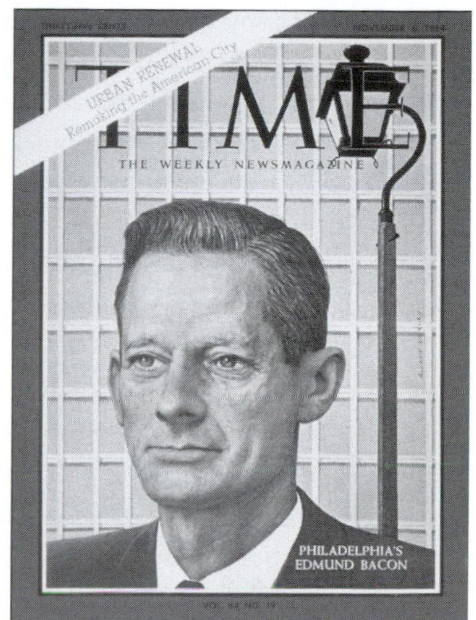

8.8
Portrait of Edmund Bacon, cover: *Time* Magazine, November 9, 1964
Source: *Time* Magazine Archive

how interventions undertaken by the city under Bacon's direction can be read, relative to both William Penn's founding principles and the multitude of historical forces acting on the form of the city subsequent to its founding. This will bring to light several interrelated questions. First, for what purpose were the boundaries of the old, central portion of the city re-inscribed and what have been the consequences of focusing so much economic, political and intellectual resources on those areas? Second, how central was the leveraging of the city's historical form and stock of colonial buildings to the downtown's redevelopment? Third, as urban design did not exist as a distinct professional activity prior to Bacon's work – Bacon was essentially an architect who became a city planner – in what ways can his work in Philadelphia be seen as constituting urban design practice as it exists today? This last question raises the issue of the degree to which urban design practice is too much invested in an historical rather than a contemporary idea of the city – that is, designing for the town rather than the metropolis.

John F. Bauman has written an account of an ideological struggle that occurred during the early 1940s among planners and others concerned with urban policies that would guide the post-War years. Bauman describes a clash between those who placed a priority on replacing slums through the rebuilding of communities spread throughout a metropolitan region, and those who stressed the remaking of the downtown and central areas of the city. The first group, emphasizing new housing as the most basic building block of a more humane city, grew out of the communitarian and reformist politics of the

1930s. Their position was that the government's resources should be focused on producing a variety of housing of a kind and quality that would, through controls over land use, zoning and utilities, spread density in a planned manner throughout the city, providing communities that could successfully compete with what was already being offered in the new suburbs. Fearful that the artificially overvalued cost of land in the most inner-city areas would undermine programs dedicated to distributing resources equitably to the greatest number of people, they warned against an overemphasis on rebuilding the centers.[23]

The second group, which Bauman called the "houser-redevelopers," viewed the provision of new housing as "the handmaiden of downtown renewal." This new breed of urbanists put great stock on the symbolic and strategic value of restoring the vitality of the downtown. They were also more aligned with the emerging federal policy and housing bureaucracy of the Cold War years, which resisted any planning policies with socialistic overtones – that is, any policies that might overly limit or compete with private commercial enterprise.

Although Bauman considered Edmund Bacon to be one of the new breed, Bacon had at the outset of his career embraced initiatives related to both the regionalist and downtown-centered positions in Philadelphia. The experiences of his early career may help to explain both his espousal of design as a tool for building consensus and the ambiguity of his ideological affiliations. Bacon grew up in Philadelphia, part of an old Quaker family. He studied architecture at Cornell in the early 1930s, and then did graduate work as a fellow under Eliel Saarinen at Cranbrook Academy. Before returning to Philadelphia, he worked in Michigan as the Supervisor of City Planning for the Flint Institute of Research and Planning. Bacon was fired from this Institute in 1939 and accused of being a communist for his advocacy of federal housing subsidies to aid the inconsistent incomes of General Motor's workers, who had staged a highly publicized sit-down strike in 1936–1937.[24]

The Philadelphia Bacon returned to in the early 1940s was in the early stages of a political transformation. Once described by the great muckraking journalist Lincoln Steffens as "Corrupt and Contented," Philadelphia and its physical decline – grimy streets, filthy drinking water, shrinking commercial venues – reflected the stronghold of an entrenched Republican political machine dominated by ward bosses and cronyism. Frustrated by the city government's resistance to the idea of active city planning, a grassroots movement of young, reform-minded individuals and civic groups formed the Action Committee on City Planning in 1939. This group later became a more permanent Citizen's Council on City Planning, with several members from its ranks appointed to important positions on the Planning Commission.[25] Bacon had been recruited back to the city by one of the civic reform groups associated

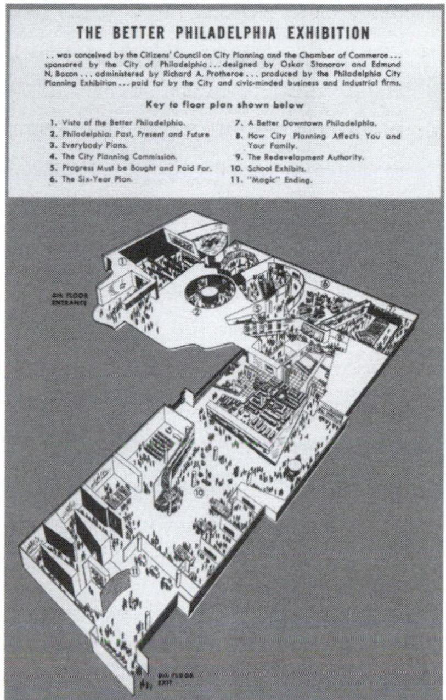

8.9
3-D plan and key, The Better Philadelphia Exhibition, Gimbels Department Store, Edmund Bacon and Oscar Stonorov, designers, 1947
Source: From pamphlet, *The Better Philadelphia Exhibition: What City Planning Means to You*, 1947

with the Citizen's Council to head the Philadelphia Housing Association. In 1947 the Citizen's Council on City Planning organized the "Better Philadelphia Exhibition." Bacon co-designed the exhibition with Oskar Stonorov (Figure 8.9).

Installed on the fifth floor of Gimbels Department Store in Center City, The Better Philadelphia Exhibition coordinated an ambitious, interactive display of the city and its planned projects with public programs meant to engage and inform a wide array of citizens. The exhibit was carefully choreographed using techniques drawn from both Worlds Fair pavilions and the kinds of modern retail displays found elsewhere in the department store. Heavily promoted through radio broadcasts, leaflets, newspaper and magazine articles, the Exhibition attracted over 385,000 visitors.[26]

The exhibition opened with the presentation of a 22- by 28-foot diorama, "Vista of a Better Philadelphia," a bird's-eye perspective depicting what the city and its surrounding environs would look like in 1982. Set within a converted auditorium, the diorama was supplemented by overhead images of past public works and an introductory text, "Philadelphia plans again." This narrative highlighted the ways in which changes to areas within the city's boundaries would transform them to be as compelling as the outlying suburbs, with their efficient highways and commodious industrial parks. A voice-over extolled the virtues of planning coordinated by local government, and the potential to achieve the city of civilized greenswards that William Penn had originally conceived. The city construed by the diorama, and other similar devices within the exhibition, served to orient visitors to the physical relationships between particular locales in which they lived and worked, and then, incrementally, to the larger district, city and region beyond. The exhibition featured displays explaining the specific benefits planning could offer in terms of the more everyday amenities that would improve the lives of people in the city's many neighborhoods, such as playgrounds, nursery schools, health centers and new housing.

To make the idea of a revitalized city palpable to the Exhibition's viewers, an extensive large-scale mock-up of a typical Philadelphia neighborhood composed of rowhouses was shown with new public amenities and tenant improvements to the individual houses and yards. A large section towards the end of the exhibition was devoted to the display of drawings and models made by the city's schoolchildren. Through schoolroom exercises, the students had been asked to survey their neighborhoods, make assessments of the overall quality of the environment, and develop, as individuals, an improvement plan for their part of the city. Students were then asked to work in groups to negotiate a shared plan, consulting with planning experts and city councilmen on what it would take to implement their plans. While this level of engagement in a participatory process would have been possible with a wider segment of the population, and welcomed by many reform-minded local activists in the city, it was limited to the schoolchildren's program.[27]

The Better Philadelphia diorama and the mock-up of a typical neighborhood were engaging, but the most promoted feature of the exhibition was a 30- by 14-foot model of the downtown. It contained a highly animated display of new developments projected over a 35 year period. Panels on the model would flipped over in sequence, synchronized with dialogue and spot lighting, to reveal one new initiative after another, including a series of new transportation, civic space, recreation, arts and business improvement projects. Displayed in parts, and not yet given a specific alignment, was a new expressway surrounding the entire downtown. Also included was the verdant, three-block long scheme for Independence Mall and a new boulevard between City Hall and the Main Commuter Train Terminal at 30th Street, replacing the elevated train tracks, known as the "Chinese Wall," that divided the northwestern portion of the city. A consolidated distribution facility replaced the city's waterfront food markets, and the spaces were replaced with piers and harbors for recreation and pleasure boating. The improved automobile access and open space amenities, while modeled as improvements to the city's efficiency, were also linked to new, fashionably modern housing and cultural facilities.

As Amy Menzer points out in her detailed study of the Better Philadelphia Exhibition, the spectacle of the downtown model differed in format and content from many of the other, more pedagogical displays in the exhibition, in the ease and Madison-Avenue way in which it showed the downtown transformed as if by a benevolent yet absent hand. This consumerist tone was furthered by another nearby display, consisting of a conveyor belt with a series of public projects on it, complete with price tags, under the banner "Progress Must Be Bought and Paid For."

Menzer has argued that the Exhibition contained the potential of a radical "environmental [urban] politics" in its attempt to spur citizen participation in a vision of the city that could provide a compelling alternative to suburbanization. She concedes that the exhibition, like much subsequent urban renewal, suffered from "ambivalences and missed opportunities" typical of the "post-war labor management consensus, racial and ethnic segregation and discrimination and anti-communism which undergirded a coalition of largely white male housing reformers, patrician civic leaders, socialist architects, and representatives of the chamber of commerce."[28] The Better Philadelphia Exhibition *was* radical in its attempt to take the need for visionary planning directly to the citizens, demonstrating its promise and the virtues of the initiatives it advocated. The Exhibition's subtle emphasis on the downtown and its muted take on the social inequities inherent in the city's allocation of physical resources also reflected the source of its funding; three-quarters of the $400,000 cost of the exhibition had been raised from local businesses by Edward Hopkinson Jr. Hopkinson was a financier, and, chairmen of the City Planning Commission, which covered the remaining balance.[29] The perhaps unspoken goal of the exhibit was to leverage the public interest it generated into increased support, stability and power for the recently revived Planning Commission, still fledgling under the Republican city government.

The Better Philadelphia Exhibition coincided with a period in Philadelphia when several discreet groups of civic and business leaders, fearful that the city's physical decline and reputation for corruption was beginning to stymie new business investment, joined together to form "The Greater Philadelphia Movement." Charged with the dual purpose of answering to the aroused civic interest in the city and "preserving the value of business interests," the group assembled a trust and combined assets in excess of ten billion dollars to be devoted to the transformation of the city.[30] Around the same time, the membership of Philadelphia's chapter of the Americans for Democratic Action – drawn from local labor unions and members of the community chest – was organizing independent voters in opposition to the republican regime. In 1952 they helped elect one of their members, Joseph Sill Clark Jr, as the city's first Democratic Mayor in 67 years.

A new reform-minded city government and a business community willing to cross traditional party lines empowered the Philadelphia's Planning

Commission as never before. Bacon was made Executive Director of the Commission in 1949. While his direct influence on political decisions concerning development and redevelopment is hard to assess – for example, he did not have a seat on the mayor's cabinet until the last years of his directorship in the late 1960s – his power seems to have lain in his capacity to stay ahead of the politicians. Ascribing his effectiveness to the "power of ideas," Bacon claims to have "dealt with the future beyond the view of the mayor's cabinet, and when they got there, they found me in possession: they found I had staked out the territory. By the time they became concerned with a problem, I had already developed a proposal."[31]

Almost all of proposals unveiled in the downtown model of the Better Philadelphia Exhibition were undertaken by the Planning Commission under Bacon and eventually achieved within the projected 35-year time frame. Beginning with a discreet set of projects, many of which he inherited, Bacon eventually developed a comprehensive vision of a revitalized center-city Philadelphia. The original borders of the city platted by William Penn were to be re-inscribed with a ring of expressways. New, large-scale building complexes and greenswards were to be woven into the existing streets, highlighting the monuments of the Old City (Figure 8.10).

As with Independence Mall, the accommodation of automobile circulation provided the initial impetus for planning the city. In 1952, Bacon laid out his understanding of the important relationship between traffic planning and rational redevelopment patterns in a lecture given to the College of Engineering at Rutgers University. Drawing on detailed planning commission studies which surveyed types and patterns of automobile usage and parking affecting

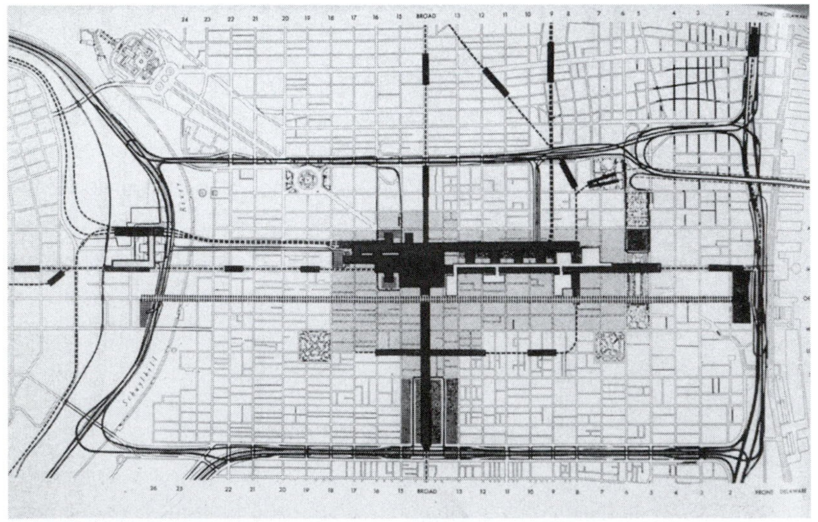

8.10
Comprehensive plan for downtown Philadelphia, 1961
Source: Philadelphia Planning Commission Report, 1961

TRAFFIC VOLUMES ON EXISTING MAJOR HIGHWAYS
AND CITY THOROUGHFARES

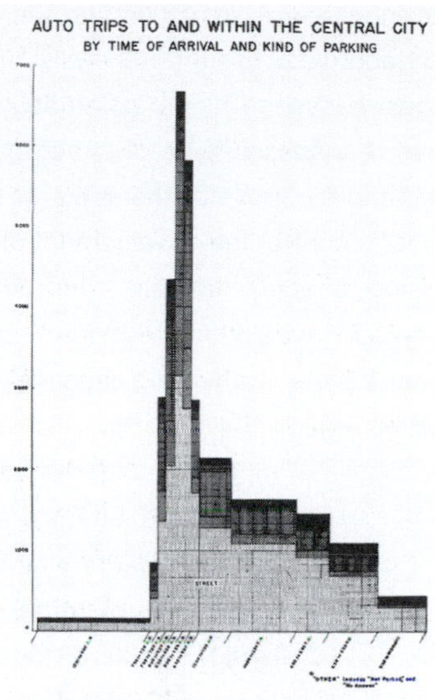

8.11
Origin and destination traffic surveys, 1947. Philadelphia Planning Commission's Technical Advisory Commission, 1947
Source: As published in Edmund Bacon, "Highway Development Related to Land Use in an Urban Area," *Spencer Miller Lecture Series: Landscape Design and its Relation to the Modern Highway* (New Brunswick, NJ; New Jersey Roadside Council/College of Engineering, Rutgers University, 1950–52)

the downtown, Bacon stressed two aspects of traffic; how to analyze its effects and patterns in the city, and how to plan for it more efficiently.[32]

The study Bacon drew on sought to document "desire lines" – where people were coming from and going to, and what they were doing when they got there (Figure 8.11). His analysis showed that already at mid-century, a relatively small percentage of overall auto trips into the city was devoted to shopping, and that those trips were short in duration. He also showed evidence that although a much greater percentage of trips into the city was undertaken by those working or doing business there, they also tended to stay in the city for a much shorter duration than might be expected – less than three hours.

If the who, what and when of automobile use came first in the approach taken by Bacon, then the ways to serve more efficiently, and perhaps even increase circulation into the city followed as a response. Bacon's empirical approach to traffic analysis later found expression in plans for the downtown based on highly differentiated forms of circulation, keying each kind of use to a specific type of street, parking or mass-transit system. In his Rutgers lecture, he spoke of the need for the city not only to control road planning, but also to control the development of property adjacent to roadways through exercising eminent domain over blighted areas of the city. This coordinated approach would ensure that future projects would perform in the best possible way from a "traffic and appearance point of view, but also from a tax point of view. . ."

> . . . Lombard Street runs along the southern edge of the business center parallel to Vine Street on the north, and it happens that there is a band of extremely bad housing between [the] two rivers right along the route of the proposed Lombard Street highway. We have determined that if the redevelopment authority condemned all of the land involved and put it all into one control, the amount of land now occupied by *useless little alleys and streets which criss-cross this area* would be roughly equivalent to the land required for the widening of Lombard street to a six-lane highway. . . . It would also be possible to prevent use of any of the Lombard Street frontage for access. All of the access could be from the North–South streets because the area would be developed as a unit.[33]

(My own italics.)

Bacon had inherited the highway plan encircling the city from the previous Planning Director. The cross-town expressway on Lombard Street was eventually shifted one block south to the original city border on South Street. Aside from the general goal of better servicing the city with highways, the specific alignments of the proposed highways to the north and south appear to follow no formal logic besides the re-inscription of the historical borders. While ward lines reinforced these historical borders, the zoning patterns tell a somewhat different story. On the South Street border there was a fairly swift transition from commercial to residential uses, but to the north there was primarily commercial and industrial use until Spring Garden Street. Had Penn's plan been completed on its northern side, with five blocks extending symmetrically in each direction from High (now Market) Street, Spring Garden Street would have been the city's northern border. Greber's plan had acknowledged this in 1917, by figuring Spring Garden Street to terminate directly into the head of the Benjamin Franklin Parkway at Fairmount (Figure 8.6). By implementing the construction of a six-lane expressway on Vine Street (completed in the early 1980s), Bacon effectively sealed off the northern border, misreading Penn's ambiguous plan and forestalling the historically established tendency of the downtown to drift north.

Having used new expressways to encase the city within the literal boundaries of Penn's plan, Bacon then went on functionally to code and optimize each element of the encased city at the scale of both the immediate project and of the downtown as a whole. Emblematic projects, separately addressing office, bureaucratic uses, shopping, and dwellings, were to be linked by overlapping but discreet networks of automobile, mass-transit and pedestrian circulation. It is almost as if each of the groups of different downtown "users" identified in the early traffic studies – shoppers, businessmen, workers, those seeking arts and leisure – might be given their own circulation network within the city.

Projects were undertaken to reinforce the hierarchical importance of the two main arteries within the downtown – Market and Broad Streets – with "super-block" projects. A roughly six-block parking lot/transit hub straddling Broad Street was projected as part of the South Street cross-town Expressway. Market Street projects included the construction of the Penn Center Office Complex to the west of Penn Square, and later the Market East Shopping Mall to the east. Each of these (now built) Market street developments incorporated complex, multi-level circulation concourses. When Penn Center was begun in the late 1950s, it was the largest mixed-use office complex undertaken in the US since the building of Rockefeller Center in the 1930s. Expressing his frustration with the difficulty of fully integrating several levels of circulation below and above the street grade at Penn Center, Bacon noted his satisfaction with the later design solution developed for the Shopping Mall at Market East (Figure 8.12):

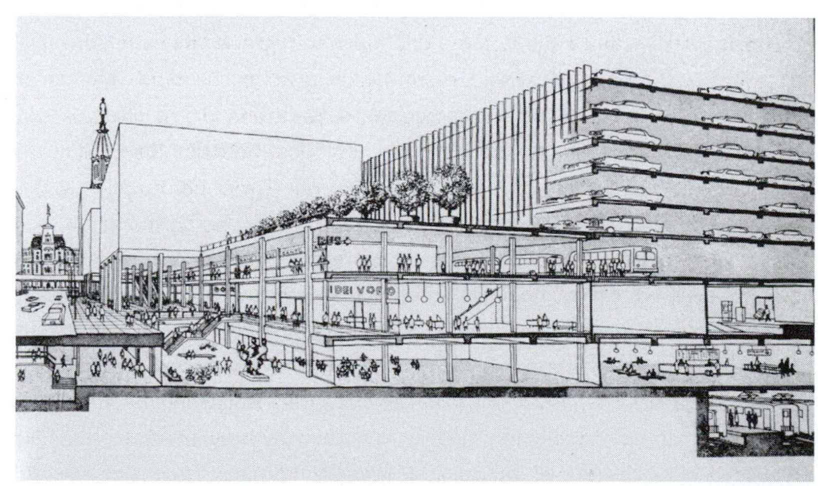

8.12
Sectional perspective, study for Market East Urban Mall, 1960. Drawn by Willo von Moltke, Philadelphia City Planning Commission, 1960
Source: As published in Edmund Bacon, *Design of Cities*

> The architecture of the buildings which penetrate this space rises clear from the pedestrian level [note: below grade] to the level above the street with *no expression at the street plane, so oppressively present in Penn Center*. . . The Vertebrae Structure of the bus terminal and parking garage, an architectural extension of regional movement systems, asserts itself across the composition in the background.[34]

(My own italics.)

Such an abundance and articulation of circulation could only be borne out by high levels of density, such as one might find in contemporary Asian cities. The projected 30-year population figures assumed in the traffic studies cited by Bacon in the early 1950s saw the city's population increasing until 1970 and declining slightly thereafter, with the region continuing to grow. Instead, the city's overall population stayed stagnant until 1970, and declined precipitously thereafter – dropping by almost 15 percent between 1970 and 1980 alone – and losing roughly a quarter of its mid-century population of two million people as of the Year 2000 census. It is doubtful that, even if the city had gained in population and managed to maintain a majority of those inhabitants, Bacon's duplicitous circulation schemes would have been much warranted.

Bacon's concern with functionally determining circulation was not limited to highways and mega-projects. Alongside the "super-sizing" of portions of Market Street to the east and west of Penn Square, and effectively evacuating whatever street-life previously existed in these areas, he proposed (and partially achieved) closing Chestnut Street, one block south of Market Street, to automobile traffic in order to restore its role as "the great walking street" from river to river (but proposed a new trolley there for the less hardy). If Market Street was to act as the modern, infrastructural east–west spine of the city, Chestnut Street was to serve as the main spine of an alternative, small-scale pedestrian network linked to the restored Old City, passing directly in front of Independence Hall, between the new Independence Mall and newly renovated areas of Society Hill.

Perhaps the development most responsible for changing the perception of Philadelphia within the city's general population was the gentrification of Society Hill. Drawing its name from the Free Society of Traders, an early and short-lived group given settlement privileges by William Penn, the area is comprised of roughly fifteen blocks southeast of Independence Square. Adjacent to the heart of the colonial town, Society Hill had been the site of the city's finest homes during the colonial and revolutionary periods. The Park Service, which cleared all but the noteworthy colonial structures east of

Independence Square, saw its strategy extended by the city, as it cleared out the old food markets on Dock Street and demolished much of the remaining "non-colonial" fabric. Having taken many properties through foreclosure and eminent domain, they were then transferred into the hands of the private Old Philadelphia Corporation, which sold roughly 600 individual houses back to private citizens at very low prices, with a stipulation that they be restored to their colonial glory. The city, along with the OPC and other private development interests, undertook the process of filling in the rest of the demolished areas with sensitively-scaled townhouse developments and residential parks, making Society Hill an attractive and affluent enclave by the 1970s.[35]

Bacon's landmark project in the area was the construction of Society Hill Towers, a luxury high-rise and townhouse project designed by I. M. Pei. Built around the site of the old Dock Street markets, atop a hill formed by a parking plinth, the composition of the Towers extended from the axis of the restored colonial market Head House. Among other claims made for this project, Bacon stated that the vertical proportions of the Tower's glass and concrete face recalled the six-over-six windows of the surrounding colonial buildings, despite the more than ten-fold difference in scale. Bacon's touting of this project as a unique and harmonious blend of the (now clichéd) "old and new" is reinforced by the picture used on the cover of Time and in many other promotions for the city: Bacon is set against a background made by the abstract grid of the towers with a colonial light-post in the foreground in-between. The viewer of this illustration was to infer that Bacon was the medium through which these two distinct historical periods were bridged (Figure 8.8).

The rapid pace of the transformation of Society Hill produced several palpable effects that other longer-term projects had yet to yield. Wealthy Philadelphians were now not only reinvesting in the city through their business efforts, but were also moving into the Old City. The 1500 or so new and renovated residences completed by the middle 1960s formed a relatively small number compared to the general rate at which middle-class people were leaving the city's neighborhoods at that time. Nevertheless, the quaint postcard atmosphere of Society Hill had a symbolic impact, dovetailing nicely with the interest generated by the restored shrines of Independence National Park and the emerging nightlife on South Street. The area quickly began to lure significant numbers of tourists and suburban visitors eager for an adventurous outing in the "city."

By the early 1960s, Bacon's initiatives were beginning to have unanticipated effects. Expressways on the city's north, east and western eastern edge had been approved, and the long process of demolition and construction had begun. Although not yet approved, the planned cross-town expressway on South Street had by the late 1950s begun to depress investment and real estate values along the expressway's projected path. The South Street corridor had historically been an active area that welcomed immigrants to the city. Dominated by Jewish settlers and merchants from the late nineteenth century onwards, and later home to a Black community on its western extent, the area began to draw bohemians in the late 1950s, who were no doubt attracted to its cheap rents, funky atmosphere and jazz clubs. By 1963, the street's reputation was summed up in a line from a popular "Philadelphia Sound" Doo-Wop record, "South Street" by the Orlons: "Where do all the hippies meet? South Street! South Street!"

The anti-urban renewal ethos that began to emerge in the 1960s in the wake of Jane Jacob's consciousness-raising *Death and Life of the Great America City* found its local expression in Philadelphia in a fight concerning the South Street Expressway. Under the banner "Houses not Highways," a campaign to block the expressway was organized by the Citizen's Committee to Preserve and Develop the Cross-town Community. The CCPDCC was a coalition of Black residents living along and south of the proposed highway, affluent white residents from Rittenhouse Square and the recently gentrified Society Hill to the north, "hippie" homesteaders, and South Street merchants.

The Black community in particular objected in principle to the racial discrimination implied by the expressway's creation of an "effective buffer zone" between the Central Business District and the (poor) residential areas to the south. Along with the accusation of not-so-subtle racism, they faulted the city for its failure to offer a credible plan to re-house the several thousand residents that would be displaced by the highway. The coalition elicited the interest of a new generation of planners and architects – most notably Denise Scott Brown, who, having just undertaken a landmark study of "strip" urbanism in Las Vegas, was asked to develop a plan to show the viability of a revitalized South Street corridor. Sensing the political winds in 1967, then-Mayor Tate withdrew his support for the project and decided to "let the people have their victory," despite continuing pressure to build the expressway both from the city's chamber of commerce and from Bacon himself.[36] It took several more years' worth of battles before the expressway project finally died. Tired-out by the vociferous opposition of the "young liberals," Bacon retired as Executive Director of the Planning Commission in 1969.[37]

The agency of planning and design in Philadelphia

In the critical period of economic and urban transformation that followed the Second World War, Philadelphia consistently reinvested more in its downtown than in the extended network of neighborhoods that make up the bulk of the city. It is difficult to discern the degree to which Edmund Bacon, or the Planning Commission he directed, would have been able – had they been inclined – to guide or influence these decisions in another direction. By mid-century, downtown business and real-estate interests had for years been paying taxes to the city on properties whose assessments had been maintained at artificially high levels. By bringing pressure to bear on the city's planning and redevelopment efforts, the financial establishment sought not only to reach their broader, long-term goal of stimulating new, outside investment in the city, but also to recoup their losses in property values and inflated tax payments.

The visions floated by the Better Philadelphia Exhibition may have stressed the importance of re-planning the whole city, but the substantial resources commanded by the backers of the Greater Philadelphia Movement appear to have been primarily expended on the downtown. Nevertheless, for Bacon and the group of design and policy professionals empowered by Philadelphia's reform-minded democratic city government, the emphasis on the core of the city surely must have been justified in more altruistic terms. In her assessment of the Better Philadelphia Exhibition's attempts at constructing a common ground of urban interests free of the ideological extremes of conservatism and liberalism, Amy Menzer refers to Arthur Schlesinger's roughly concurrent concept of the "Vital Center."[38] Built upon the supposed understanding of democratic notions of freedom and liberty shared by a plurality of Americans during the Cold War, Schlesinger's Vital Center was a political concept posing a "middle way" of militant liberalism against the threats of communism and totalitarianism. In 1947 Schlesinger was a founding member of Americans for Democratic Action an organization that counted among its members many of the reform-minded politicians, activists and intellectuals that took the mantle in Philadelphia at mid-century, including Edmund Bacon. It is perhaps not too far-fetched to imagine Bacon and his cohorts conceiving of the downtown's symbolic potential as a physical embodiment of the "vital center;" that is, as the common ground of an entire city's shared interests.[39] If the city's center could be revived and prosper, especially considering its historic role as the "cradle of liberty," then perhaps it could act as a catalyst for remaking the disparate communities and interests composing the rest of the city.

The "vital center" imagined by Schlesinger was more an idealistic concept than a documented, stable consensus of broadly-shared values held across a range of political constituencies. As the local struggle over the South Street cross-town expressway revealed, groups with diverging political, economic and racial interest may temporarily join forces over a shared cause, but such groups do not necessarily constitute a "vital center." Moreover, if by the late 1960s the concept of a "vital center" was giving way to more contentious models of political organization, a political figure could no longer justify his actions by claiming to represent what was never more than a fugitive political body.

The question of whether Philadelphia's downtown was revived at the cost of the rest of the city cannot be clearly ascertained here, as the factors that would have to be considered in making such a judgment go well beyond the purview of planning and design. Moreover, because very few formerly industrial American cities with profiles similar to Philadelphia's have been able to stave off population loss and physical decline, it is difficult to provide analogous examples of how better planning and design might have overcome the ravaging of much of Philadelphia outside its downtown. However, the consistent effects of urban policy in the US notwithstanding, agents of planning and design in Philadelphia, whether as visionary advocates or mere facilitators, did play a substantial role in construing the city's current form.

Bacon credits his success in transforming Philadelphia's downtown to the "power of ideas." Yet once he became Executive Director of the Planning Commission, Bacon seems to have focused little effort developing new ideas for the metropolis as a whole, and certainly no ideas with as much potential to capture the public imagination as those he advocated for the downtown. Early on in his directorship Bacon took a principled stand against the over-large, a-contextual format of federally-funded housing projects, opting instead to support programs to reinforce existing neighborhood patterns through the renovation of existing housing stock and the development of scatter-site housing. Although Bacon sought out high-caliber architects, including Louis Kahn, to do this work, and some laudable "model" projects were built, he never achieved his scatter-site scheme in any substantial way.

Today, faced with many sparsely populated neighborhoods and thousands of abandoned buildings that are literally falling down, Philadelphia's Planning Commission has undertaken an ambitious program selectively to clear many parts of the city deemed to be obsolete remnants of the city's industrial past. Harking back to the emphasis of the regionally-focused, social equity planners at mid-century, the commission is studying and implementing new, more suburban (or at least lower-density) block and settlement patterns. Unfortunately, the financial resources available at mid-century are now gone, along with the city's broader tax base. This financial circumstance has forced the planning commission to explore schemes that might have helped unify the city in the relatively more flush times at mid-century. In order to facilitate the reduction and redistribution of public amenities such as health centers, schools, libraries and public safety infrastructure, planners have begun to think beyond the boundaries of historically established neighborhoods and reconceive the city as a network of services shared across many communities.

Taking the towne for the city: the purview of urban design

Edmund Bacon's work followed a period of unprecedented urban expansion and modernization in the late nineteenth and early twentieth centuries, when the fundamental nature of cities, Philadelphia included, had changed. The concept of urban design emerged in the late 1940s as a way for the professional apparatus of architecture better to address these changes. As the director of Philadelphia's Planning Commission, and later as the author of *Design of Cities*, Bacon played a seminal role in establishing urban design as both a discipline and an actor in the shaping of cities in the mid-twentieth century.

Bacon conceived urban design as a means to recover the civilized form of the European city within the modern metropolis, bringing the new scale and complexity of modern architecture and development under the discipline of a more humanistic order. This attitude is well-illustrated in Bacon's *Design of Cities*, where a majority of the examples are drawn from a western tradition of city building, in which Renaissance Florence is taken as the great paradigm. In *Design of Cities* and many public statements about his work in Philadelphia, Bacon devotes much rhetoric to the importance of "public process," "feedback mechanisms" and "democracy in action." Yet he states that city making is "an act of will," and draws inspiration from the harmonious design of cities executed by mostly monarchic or papal authorities. Was the "will" Bacon referred to his own, or that of the "the people," transfixed by "power of ideas?"[40] Certainly, prior to the reform movement that brought him into power, no clear public authority existed in Philadelphia, where almost since its inception private, patrician interests and commercial enterprise had shaped the city.[41] That most of great public works and monuments in Philadelphia's downtown are named after figures from the seventeenth and eighteenth centuries – William Penn and Benjamin Franklin are the most numerous – speaks not only of the way in which the city's colonial past provides the sustaining mythology of the city's importance, but of the reticence on the part of Philadelphia's citizens to put their own mark on the city in the intervening years.

Bacon's recourse to William Penn is neither innocent nor inconsequential. Rather than contend with the physical 300-year history of Philadelphia – a speculatively driven, redbrick, mercantile city – Bacon instead chose to focus on a reification of Penn's original plan for a "green county towne." An early scheme related to the Penn Center development epitomizes both Bacon's attitude toward the built history of the city that preceded him and his use of Penn as a symbolic figure. Finding fault with the inefficient traffic patterns produced by the diagonal of Greber's Benjamin Franklin Parkway (Bacon planned to replace the Parkway's function as a gateway into the city with the Vine

8.13
Model, proposal for Penn Center and altered City Hall, Redevelopment Area Plan, Philadelphia Planning Commission, 1952
Source: Redevelopment Area Plan, Philadelphia Planning Commission, 1952

Street expressway), Bacon terminated the Parkway two blocks before Penn Square, "restoring" the surrounding rectilinear blocks. Linked to this reorganization of traffic patterns was a proposal to tear down the imposing City Hall on Penn Square, another "inefficient" nineteenth-century structure, leaving only the tower at its center (Figure 8.13).

Conceived in an allegorical mode by Alexander Milne Calder, along with other sculptures depicting the history of the city and state, a 37-foot-high bronze statue of William Penn, Philadelphia's great patriarch, sits atop the tower of the massive City Hall.[42] The statue of Penn faces northeast, towards Penn Treaty Park, the supposed site of a treaty signing between Penn and the Lenni Lenape Indians. The Charter of Pennsylvania is held in Penn's left hand. Following the erection of the statue in 1894, a "gentleman's agreement" emerged among planners and real-estate developers, prohibiting buildings in the center-city from surpassing the brim of Penn's hat in height.[43] When Bacon proposed to remove all of City Hall, except the tower and Penn's statue, he was not only reinforcing the importance of Penn's control over the height of buildings in the city and the symbolic function of his backward glance, but also revealing two other biases. First, it showed his distaste for everything the City Hall stood for; its decadent, Second Empire style would have been anathema to a mid-century modernist such as Bacon, and redolent of the corrupt city government that had built and occupied the building in its first 50 years of existence. Perhaps more critical was the desire to manifest Penn's most enduring physical legacy in the city – the green public squares – by returning an open space to Central (now Penn) Square, thereby linking the figure of Penn to the very open space he had envisioned.

By using Penn as the animating figure for the urban design of the city, writing the "old" into the "new," Bacon was also working in an allegorical mode. Invoking the moral authority of the colonial age inaugurated by Penn, and the rather puritanical character of its architecture, he attempted to erase as much as possible the detritus of 200 years of urban speculation. In so doing, he hoped to kindle a rebirth of the city with a puritanical urbanism characterized by discreet circulation, structural clarity, visual transparency and pastoral open space. Egbert's 1928 scheme for Independence Mall had contained the entire formula: eliminate, as much as possible, all but the colonial structures, whose established historical significance and small scale made them entirely accessible to a suburban population increasingly less inclined to dense, complex forms of urbanity; optimize access, first by automobile and then by mass-transit; and finally, leverage the restored "history," new transportation infrastructure and open space to promote new commercial development – the only truly bankable form of rebirth (Figure 8.14).

While the allegory of the old colonial city giving birth to a new modern city appealed to the city's chauvinism, it was destructive in the way that it ignored those aspects of the city that had emerged during the intervening

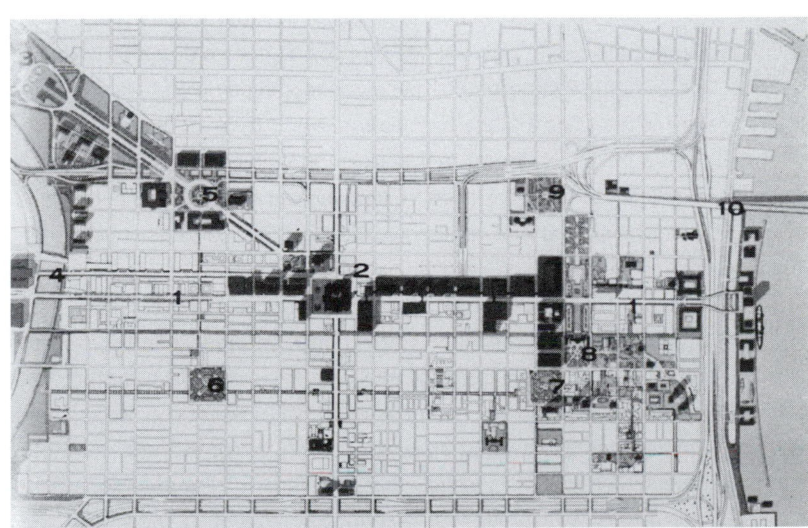

8.14
Illustrative plan for downtown Philadelphia, 1961
Source: Philadelphia Planning Commission Report, 1961

years, particularly the bulk of the city built in the nineteenth and early twentieth centuries. Thus the colonial allegory failed to provide a historical idea or sustaining myth that encompassed the whole city, as opposed to focusing selectively on its old center.

Louis Kahn, Bacon's contemporary and Philadelphia's most esteemed architect of the period, gave the theme of defending the old center above all else its most potent and explicit expression. During the period 1947–1962, Kahn developed a series of studies and proposals that addressed many of the same issues and assumptions as those undertaken by Bacon and the Planning Commission. Highly enigmatic and romantic in flavor, Kahn's ideas influenced many of the more seemingly sober schemes that were adopted. Most famous among Kahn's many studies for Philadelphia was one from 1953 addressing the reorganization of traffic in the center-city. Attempting to reunify the downtown through a new "order of movement," Kahn redefined streets in the existing grid by referring to the kinds of "activities" or traffic they would serve – bus, pedestrian, automobile, etc. The new order of movement was to be held in balance by encircling the original bounds of Penn and Holme's plan with large expressways. Monumentalizing the planning commission's traffic scheme, Kahn likened the expressways to the fortifying walls of the medieval city at Carcassonne, only now understood as "viaducts" channeling automobile traffic around the city. Kahn even replicated the architecture of fortifications with large, cylindrical parking towers lining the edge of the expressways. The parking towers were to act as great lithic gates to the city, keeping the hordes of automobiles from entering the city and disrupting its pedestrian life – a scheme not unlike those later adopted in pre-industrial European city centers ill-suited to automobile traffic. Anticipating Bacon, but perhaps drawing more inspiration from an Ur-city of ancient roman ruins than from Bacon's Ur-colonial city, Kahn shows the existing center-city reduced to historical monuments, circulation, and swaths of open green space (Independence Mall). Having taken the reification of the city's historic form to a greater extreme than Bacon, Kahn then reinhabited the city with space-frame-like buildings that projected a new, progressive image for the city. In one highly evocative bird's-eye perspective sketch of this scheme, the only existing building depicted is Independence Hall (Figure 8.15).

Bacon and Kahn, both highly influential figures within their respective professional communities, aimed their efforts in Philadelphia towards the retrieval of a more humanistic, pre-industrial city, as embodied in the potential of the physical layout of the old center. Kahn's rendering of the old city as a defensive fortress revealed what may have been a widely held sentiment among architects and urbanists; a fear that the old city, with its grand institutions and high culture, was going to be lost to decentralization and the growing

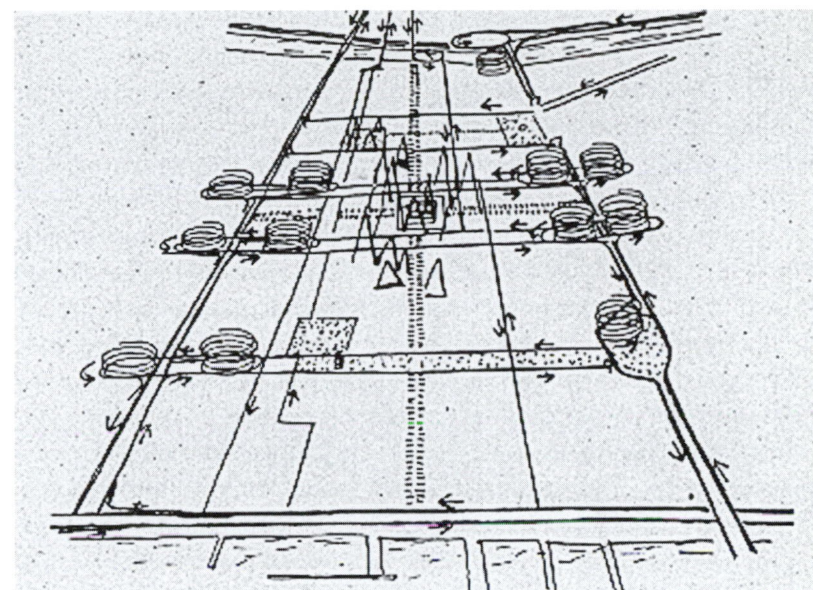

8.15
Sketch, Louis Khan study for Philadelphia, 1953
Source: Kahn Collection, Architectural Archives of the University of Pennsylvania, Gift of Richard Saul Wurman

popularity of suburban life. The fact that the new city walls created by the expressways corresponded to boundaries that defined well-established race and class distinctions within the city speaks two things: either these architects were naive in refusing to see that their plans materially solidified spatial, political and economic cleavages in the city, or they were acquiescing to the political and economic power of their sponsors – or both.[44] Certainly the question of who gained and who lost in the transformation of the city overseen by Bacon and imagined by Kahn is easy to answer. Downtown business interests, those wealthy enough to invest in real estate within the center-city, downtown arts and educational institutions and tourism, hospitality and restaurant industries all gained. With a few exceptions, everyone outside the downtown area lost in terms of investment in infrastructure, city services and declining land values.

The urban design of Philadelphia in the post-war period can be taken as constitutive of the historical viewpoint and methods that define urban design as a practice. The most frequent justification for concentrating on the city centers was that the centers offered a level of authenticity and dynamism that could provide an attractive counter to the lure of the suburbs. Yet the attribution of authenticity to "place" in a society characterized by mobility and change may be as fleeting as the attribution of "newness." Where the redesign of Philadelphia's center was concerned, it is certainly ironic that the monuments supposedly contributing to an authenticity of "place" were framed by an infrastructure of mobility.

The reactionary posture taken by many of the founders of urban design practice towards the new city is an aspect of their nostalgia for an historical form of city and a corresponding aversion to the "vital messy-ness" found in the "difficult whole" of the contemporary city.[45] Their nostalgia was inspired by the European cities they may have experienced as soldiers or as tourists, or perhaps by way of the European "masters" that they studied under, or conceivably was based on a longing for an apocryphal small-town America. Predisposed by their nostalgia against the seemingly endless, unbounded extents of the new metropolis, and lacking the analytical and representational tools to read the physical and programmatic patterns of these new spaces, they focused on the old centers. Urban design, as Bacon conceived it, still understood the city in static, historical terms as a center with discreet subsidiary districts. By the mid-1960s, research by figures such as Melvin Weber revealed that large cities like Philadelphia had already become something else; a complex, multinucleated network of commercial, industrial, domestic, recreational and cultural uses linked by rapidly evolving transportation and communication technologies.

William Penn had conceived of Philadelphia as a modern city, where an experiment with religious tolerance and town planning was to be financed by the selling of bonus plots to investors in Pennsylvania land. Cities were not in need of fortification by the seventeenth century, and Penn clearly foresaw an advantage in the open, ambiguous boundaries of the city. By cauterizing the city within its historical boundaries, and concentrating too much on the literal dimensions of Penn's plan, the schemes brought to fruition by Bacon overlooked the larger lessons that can be taken from Philadelphia's historical development as the outcome of Penn's broad vision. Taking Penn's scheme for Philadelphia literally, one would start by understanding the city as a center of cultural and economic exchange for a vast region. Given that the region has continued to grow exponentially since the colonial period, it follows that for the city to continue to function as not only a symbolic but also a substantive center, it too would have to expand exponentially in both scale and in the diversity of its programs and inhabitants.[46] Instead of envisioning this new metropolis, those entrusted with the urban design of Philadelphia consistently mistook the *towne* for the city.

Notes

1 Distinctions between a town and a metropolis would typically hinge on considerations such as population size, geographic extent and other factors, including physical density and the cultural diversity of inhabitants.

2 Reps, 1965, pp. 152–153.

3 Bronner, 1962, pp. 81–82.
4 Bronner, 1962, p. 85.
5 Bronner, 1962, p. 87.
6 Bronner, 1962, p. 87.
7 Meyers (ed.), 1959, c.1912, pp. 261–273.
8 Bronner, 1962, pp. 97–101.
9 Reps, 1965, p. 161.
10 Bronner, 1962, p. 102 .
11 By 1850, just prior to the incorporation of Philadelphia county, the population of the city's adjacent liberty lands, which came to be know as the Northern Liberties district, was, combined with the more westerly Spring Garden district, approximately 100,000 people, making this area alone the sixth largest city in the U.S.
12 Reps, 1965, p. 172.
13 Penn has considered building his own house on the site.
14 At this, the country's first public, popular museum, Peale combined his portraits of luminaries from the American Revolution with paleontological finds, including the mastodon from Newburg, New York, which Peale advertised as "the great incognitum." Constructing a pre-historic lineage for America, Peale's museum reflected late-eighteenth-century efforts to legitimize the American project in the light of natural history.
15 Green, 1993, p. 197.
16 Currently the site is overseen by the National Park Service, whose renovation projects on the site continue into the present. See National Park Service, 1994, pp. 11–20.
17 National Park Service, 1994, pp. 22–28.
18 Among approximately twelve proposals developed made between 1915 and the adaptation of a plan in the mid-1940s, Paul Cret's was perhaps the most sophisticated. Clearing a half block of buildings north of Chestnut Street to Ludlow Street (one of the built-up secondary alleys), Cret proposed two similar schemes, the first with a semicircular plaza and the second with a square plaza. Cret's schemes kept the plaza small and located a flight of steps below-grade, a gesture that would have limited long views toward the diminutive colonial statehouse, thereby increasing the perception of its scale. See National Park Service, 1994, pp. 27–28.
19 National Park Service, 1994, pp. 20–32.
20 National Park Service, 1994, p. 63.
21 For an account of opposition to the wholesale clearance of the mall site on the part of the Park Service's architect, Charles E. Peterson, see Greiff, 1987, pp. 49–58; Mumford, 1957.
22 Extending the logic of the easterly portion of the National Park, Edmund Bacon later developed a meandering route to the eastern riverfront through a series of leafy, inter-block pedestrian walks.
23 Bauman, 1983, pp. 174–176.
24 Barnett and Miller, 1983, pp. 5–7.
25 Constance Dallas, as quoted in the "The Philadelphia Story," American Planning and Civic Association, 1953 pp. 13–16.
26 See "Philadelphia Plans Again," *Architectural Forum*, 1947, pp. 65–68.
27 For a detailed account of the programs associated with the exhibition, see Menzer, 1999, pp. 112–136.
28 Menzer, 1999, p. 115.
29 Menzer, 1999, p. 118.
30 Constance Dallas, as quoted in the "The Philadelphia Story," p. 15.
31 Bacon, as quoted in Barnett and Miller, 1983, p. 7 .
32 Bacon, 1950–1952.

33 Bacon, 1952, p. 56.
34 Bacon, 1974, p. 126.
35 Neil Smith has made a detailed study of the collusive political and business relationships that allowed the gentrification of Society Hill. He has shown how wealthy individuals appointed to commissions overseeing initiatives in the environs of the Center City were, at the same time, directing local banking and financial institutions making loans and guarantees in the area. Some of these same individuals were then able to buy property as private citizens at greatly reduced prices, and reap great profits after renovating them. See Smith, 1996.
36 For an account of the fight over the expressway, see Clow, 1989.
37 Bacon, as quoted in Barnett and Miller, 1983, p. 4.
38 Schlesinger, 1949.
39 Amy Menzer has argued that the Better Philadelphia Exhibition was an attempt to empower a process through which a vital political and physical "center" for the whole city could be engendered. Yet subsequent to the exhibition, the downtown, by virtue of the planning and investment processes actually undertaken, became, as a site and an idea, the de facto center.
40 Bacon, as quoted in Barnett and Miller, 1983, p. 9.
41 See Bass Warner, 1987.
42 Philadelphia's City Hall is the largest single municipal building in the U.S.
43 The agreement to not build above Penn's Hat was not broken until 1986.
44 I use the word sponsor as opposed to the larger public body design professionals are typically assumed to represent.
45 These quoted terms refer to concepts of urbanity first advocated by Robert Venturi and Denise Scott Brown in the 1960s.
46 The reform of Philadelphia might have concentrated on expanding the boundaries of the center to at least include the areas north of Vine Street – areas that were once the center of the city's residential population, but are now devastated.

Chapter 9

San Francisco – San Francisco in an Age of Reaction

Mitchell Schwarzer

In San Francisco, the movement toward self-realization has reached such heights of indulgence that it is leveling the creation of inspiring urban design. Since the early 1980s, in a city that celebrates individualism, the collective discipline of architecture has taken a pounding. Here on the western shores of the North American continent, the American dream has taken a turn into activism bred on affluence and adversity. San Francisco's public planning process is lousy with naysayers. At the initial whiff of a new project, opponents spring up like oxalis, a prolific weed with yellow flowers that carpets the ground here after the first winter rains. These not-so-laidback Californians, who stymie architectural innovation in this once innovative city, defend a medley of values premised on history, esthetics, cultural politics and, most of all, an impossible-to-generalize set of self-interests. They fight to keep precious vistas and exclude new buildings – new building that add cars to the streets, new buildings that look different, any structure of monolithic stature, steely materials, odd angles. Strange that in a place distinguished by progressive politics and an artistic spirit, the reactionaries stand out when it comes to urban design.

If you're going to San Francisco, the best new architecture you see might be the International Terminal (2001) at the SFO airport, about eight miles south of city limits. Designed by Craig Hartman of Skidmore Owings and Merrill, its soaring flights of trusses and space, foregrounded by a minestrone of freeway and parking-lot structures, would likely have been grounded by the municipal planning process had the building been located in the city proper. Practically the only place within San Francisco where far-out architecture has been realized of late is the Yerba Buena Redevelopment Area, a new downtown district of convention centers, museums, hotels, and entertainment spots built atop what was once skid row. Yet Mario Botta's eyepopping San Francisco Museum of Modern Art (1995) or James Polshek's functionally expressive Center for the Arts Theater (1994) might never have risen outside redevelopment jurisdiction. Swarms of opponents would have massed like the birds in Alfred Hitchcock's film, lining up ominously at meetings and cackling that the museum's faceted brickwork and sliced cylindrical tower had no local precedents, or that the theater's collage of cubic volumes and vivid colors wasn't consistent with the historic materials and textures of the area.

Just about the only thing that flocks of people can agree on is that San Francisco is worth fighting for. The city dons a wardrobe of arresting visages. San Francisco, gridded, whitish, wooden and stucco, rolls up and down over 40 hills, the building-enhanced last dance of the California Coast Ranges as they shoot down to the sea. Many valuable struggles have been undertaken in the name of these beauties and intricacies – against billboards that mar the skyline, chain stores that put local stores out of business, and unfair tenant evictions that force poorer people out. Yet some San Franciscans are loving a traditionalist esthetic vision of the town to death.

Love is often blind. Because many of San Francisco's vocal citizenry came to this city from elsewhere, and because they came here not by accident but by intention, they hold particularly strong attachment to early impressions, memories of youthful romps from bay to breakers, and carefree days spent in small cream-colored flats that rented for pittance. Proposed changes threaten people's core identities. If San Francisco doesn't look the way it did, they too will have changed. The love of older architecture and hatred of the new expresses a fear of aging and the loss of one's lodestar. Someday the city might be looked at as a museum to the region's cult of perpetual youth, just as Venice, Italy, has become a museum of Renaissance *coloratura*. And as in Venice, in San Francisco tourism sways the urban design process. San Francisco holds greater claim (through frequent use) to the nickname "America's Favorite City" than any other place. In the media, million-dollar images treat the city as a cable-car ride to the stars or a spin under the Golden Gate Bridge. Not only do famous sites like the bridge, Transamerica Pyramid or Coit Tower hold court; ridges of Victorians and Edwardians also file out peaked, turreted, and reliably recognizable rhythms. Alas, postcard San Francisco makes it hard for the real city to grow. Through mass exposure in magazines, films, and television, San Francisco is immediately and spectacularly identifiable, branded,

9.1
A steely prototype for the narrow lot, 1022 Natoma Street, Stanley Saitowitz architect
Photo by Pad McLaughlin

9.2
The bane of the bay window, recent condominiums, 16th and Missouri Streets
Photo by Pad McLaughlin

marqueed, a reel of appetizing scenes. The success of tourism encases "Baghdad by the Bay" in imagistic scaffolding that blocks deeper visual grains.

While tourism has been a part of San Francisco's mix since the nineteenth century, the city's architectural vision turned from the future to the past during the 1970s – the decade during which tourism once and for all eclipsed shipping and manufacturing as the number one industry. Nowadays, factories, warehouses, dry docks, and bridges embody a little noticed industrial San Francisco. Despite their showcasing in movies, like Clint Eastwood's *Dirty Harry* series, such structures hardly figure in public debate about the city's architectural identity. The Eastern Waterfront is left to rot, a vast memory-tomb of the city's former working classes and mechanical innovations. Out of benign municipal neglect, some innovative architecture has been built in these coarser warehouse and factory barrens. In particular, Stanley Saitowitz's loft projects propose an inventive typology of continuous living space expressed through large clear-span windows and assertive industrial materials. However, implausible as it sounds, even amid the decaying hulks of manufacturing and shipping some other designers sweeten their facades with Victorian finery and lace. In a Potrero Hill complex completed in 1999 bay windows protrude out of a loft, despite the fact that the nearest residential building with bay windows is several blocks away and the immediate surroundings stare back corrugated metal, cracked cement, and clumps of anise weeds. If architecture that expresses contemporary lifestyle and historical industry can't be built here, then where?

Certainly not in the other new city district – besides Yerba Buena – of the past twenty years, South Beach, located along what had been a working waterfront of piers and warehouses south of downtown. Past the palm-lined Embarcadero, South Beach revels in patent-yuppie historicism. When the San Francisco Giants baseball team decided to build a new ballpark (completed in 2000) there, the architectural team, Hellmuth Obata and Kassebaum, looked for inspiration to nearby brick warehouses and not nearby concrete warehouses. In spite of the fact that brick bearing wall construction makes no sense in earthquake country and was abandoned after the 1906 earthquake, brick veneer covers most of the ballpark's forceful concrete and steel skeleton as well as other new buildings in the vicinity. Along with fake stone copings and a clock tower, Pacific Bell Park (while a wonderful place to watch a baseball game) looks from the outside like any other retro ballpark or a Rouse festival marketplace, a neo-Baltimore by the San Francisco bay.

Two major urban design controversies of recent years stand out. In 1999, needing to replace their seismically-damaged building, the M. H. de Young Museum proposed a new building for its site in Golden Gate Park. With great foresight, the museum's trustees chose the firm of Herzog & de Meuron. Known

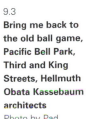

9.3
Bring me back to the old ball game, Pacific Bell Park, Third and King Streets, Hellmuth Obata Kassebaum architects
Photo by Pad McLaughlin

for their approach to building skin as an urban-scale screening room, the architects unveiled a façade of glass and dimpled/perforated copper that would generate intricate textures playing off light and nearby flora. Nonetheless, the feat of getting their proposal for a new de Young approved by the city has approached the magnitude of Hercules's fifth labor cleaning the Augean Stables. Through several seasons of public meetings, opponents argued that the design didn't harmonize with the natural context of the park, even though no building presumably could meet that demand, and despite the fact that the park's tall cypress, pine, and eucalyptus trees are themselves an artificial terrain, planted during the nineteenth century atop an unglamorous landscape of shrubs, grasses, and sand dunes. Some citizens loudly advocated resurrecting the Museum's former Spanish Revival design on the grounds that its historicism better matched the traditions of the city, and ignoring the fact that such period revivals bring back to life architectural symbols of colonialism offensive to some Latinos and Native Americans. Finally, their arguments faltering, diehards settled on battling the education tower proposed by Herzog & de Meuron. Incredibly, after several millennia of cultures around the world erecting towers so that they could be viewed from long distances and provide a focal point for a place, the diehards felt the only appropriate tower should be one that can't be seen from afar. Eventually, the museum was forced to cut the height of the tower from 160 feet to 144 feet.

In 2002, a second controversy came to a close. After a long planning process, the Lesbian Gay Bisexual Transgender Community Center opened on Market and Octavia Streets. Designed by Jane Cee and Peter Pfau, the building's polychrome glass curtain walls brilliantly express the different shades of the LGBT community as well as their travails and triumphs. Unfortunately, only part of the center as originally proposed was built. Because a Victorian occupies the corner lot, the city's preservation community rose up in arms at the first mention of its possible demolition. Though the three-story wooden building has no striking architectural or historical features, and hundreds like it grace the streets, preservationists argued that it forms a unique trapezoidal response to Market Street's diagonal clash with the grid. A photo that shows the building standing at the edge of devastation caused by the 1906 fire also stirred emotions. These appeals worked, and the building was given landmark status. The architects had to forsake the far grander possibilities of using the corner, and instead settle for the mid-block lot. Together the two buildings look separated by more than just a century. They embody the city's quibbling march to the future.

Given all that has been said so far – the power of tourism, tradition, and all the trimmings – it's no wonder that the preservation of modernist architecture has been a low priority. In 1996, the Red Cross Building by Gardner Dailey, one of the city's leading mid-century architects, was demolished with little opposition. In 2001, the same fate befell the Daphne Funeral Home,

9.4
Building a diverse community, Lesbian Gay Bisexual Transgender Center, Market and Octavia Streets, Jane Cee and Peter Pfau architects
Photo by Pad McLaughlin

designed by the noted Los Angeles firm of Jones and Emmons. Even though the Daphne – the only small-scale public example of an open plan in the city – was a far more important work of architecture than the LGBT's corner Victorian, the battle to save it went down to defeat. The reason has to do with the fact that for preservationists, modernism has long been the enemy. Despite the current rise of worldwide interest in a revamped architectural modernism, post-modernism still reigns in San Francisco.

How did this reactive state of affairs acquire such tidal force? To understand the anti-modernism of the past twenty years, one has to go back several decades. In the late 1950s, San Francisco was the first American city to begin dismantling plans to throw a spaghetti-jumble of freeways atop the small 46-square-mile city. During the early 1970s, the term "Manhattanization" came into vogue as part of an attack on highrise towers. Referendums were held, and allowable building height and bulk came down. No downtown skyscraper would ever again approach the heights of the Bank of America (779 feet) or Transamerica Pyramid (853 feet), completed respectively in 1969 and 1972. Nor would historic buildings, like the lost Montgomery Block (a longtime artistic haven) or City of Paris Department Store, be demolished any longer. Plans for slab, super-block urban renewal similarly shrank in scale, even though areas like the Western Addition had already been severely torn apart. As elsewhere, the

9.5
The great ornamental leap backward, apartment building, 21st Street and South Van Ness Avenue
Photo by Pad McLaughlin

autocratic ways of modernist urbanism brought about citizen reactions and urban design re-evaluations. More than elsewhere, the San Francisco counter-attack hardened into dogma.

The *Urban Design Element* of the city's Master Plan has been the bible of San Francisco's architectural philosophy since its completion by the City Planning Department in 1971. Boldly, it shifts the focus of architectural design from issues of art, structure, and function to those of historic and geographic context. Much of the plan makes sense. For instance, architects are encouraged to preserve the city's precipitous landforms by grouping towers on the tops of hills instead of on their sides, where they would flatten the topography. However, the costs outweigh the benefits. Architects are pushed to replicate the contextual features of adjacent buildings in any new design. Even though most new buildings are far larger than their Victorian or Edwardian predecessors, the plan encourages that their massing be broken up to match the small lot sizes in vogue a century ago. But should transitions between old and new buildings reduce the latter's design to dull reiteration? Are visually strong buildings that contrast severely with their surroundings such a bad thing? If these policies had been followed earlier in the city's history, they would have prevented any serious architecture. San Francisco would never have seen the likes of Willis Polk's Hallidie Building (1918) – one of the world's first glass curtain walls – or Timothy Pflueger's 450 Sutter Street building (1930) – a streamlined appliqué of glass and terracotta Mayan ornament onto a steel frame.

After more referendums, a subsequent planning document, the

Downtown Plan (1985), extended the use of design guidelines. A highpoint of the plan is its strict preservation of over 500 significant historical buildings, setting a national standard. The *Downtown Plan* also mandates several conservation (or preservation) districts, intended to prevent new buildings whose scale and composition would overwhelm older structures. The plan goes too far, however, by telling architects *how* to compose, forcing them to clad steel frames with tops and veneers that cause new tall buildings to look all too much like wedding cakes. In their zeal to bring back the good old days of skyscrapers, the planners overlooked the fact that their model era, 1906–1933, wasn't any longer than the age of modernism, 1945–1975. In reality, the city's urban design policies regulate not as much on the basis of context – for the modern context is routinely excluded – but on preferred temporal style.

This post-modern ideology leaves out the critical post-war period of San Franciscan cultural ascendancy. In almost every artistic arena, from poetry to architecture, San Francisco came into its own after the Second World War – not before it. No reasonable San Franciscan would disavow such local post-war painters as Clyfford Still, Elmer Bischoff, Jay DeFeo, and Joan Brown; photographers like Minor White and Ansel Adams; poets such as Kenneth Rexroth, William Everson, and Michael McClure; independent filmmakers including James Broughton, Bruce Baillie, Bruce Connor, and Sidney Patterson; and landscape architects like Thomas Church and Lawrence Halprin. Why, then, should the debate on the city's architectural identity omit the important contributions of William Wurster, Joseph Esherick, Moore Lyndon Turnbull and Whittaker, Anshen and Allen, and Skidmore Owings and Merrill, all of whom built important buildings in the city and vicinity between the war and the 1970s? Why, moreover, should forceful engineering structures not be considered part of our urban design heritage? Eliminating modernism from the municipal debate on urban design cuts San Francisco off from its own artistic legacy, the great international works of the past century, and the most vital contemporary architectural discourse.

Since the 1980s, forward-thinking architectural discourse has been noticeably absent in San Francisco planning. After a history of proposing Utopian schemes and then retrenching into downzoning and design guidelining, the city has practically given up on long-range planning. Instead of moving forward and adjusting the reactive strictures of the 1970s and 1980s, instead of realizing that the reaction to modernism was as extreme as modernism itself, city planning in San Francisco has shriveled to permit processing and a regulatory scholasticism. One local architect compares going to the Building or City Planning Departments for permit approval to Franz Kafka's description of K.'s dealings with the authorities of *The Castle*.

In large part, as mentioned above, the planners are merely

responding to vocal activists. Before the 1970s, San Franciscans were so preoccupied with their dream city, they didn't have time to wallow in details. Yet nobody in his or her right mind would say that the city of late hasn't cultivated a weighty self-image. San Francisco's gentrified neighborhoods are hotbeds of opposition to architectural innovation or densification, masters of the arcane detail – whether architectural, historical, or legal. Merely mentioning the Telegraph Hill Dwellers or Noe Valley Neighbors is enough to strike fear into the heart of any progressive architect. Paradoxically, in such neighborhoods (and there are lots of them in the city) the disconnect between exuberant interior lifestyle and stolid exterior expression couldn't be greater. Gobs of money are spent on kitchen and bathroom remodeling, but, thanks to planning policies and neighborhood activists, gut-rehabbing homeowners go to great lengths to keep facades familiar. Maybe living lavishly indoors induces people to pretend, at least from the outside, that all's as modest as it was 100 years ago. Or possibly those San Franciscans who have cut ties to tradition and family find it more comforting to live behind traditional facades, the same look of building that their faraway families inhabit.

Sometimes planning shortsightedness has no neighborhood activist to blame. In 1999, the Prada Company hired Rem Koolhaas to design a flagship building on the corner of Grant Avenue and Post Street, in one of the *Downtown Plan* conservation districts. At a meeting of the San Francisco Planning Commission to approve the project in 2001, the City Planning Department, citing its interpretation of the guidelines for the conservation district, recommended disapproval. The basis for their negative recommendation? The proposed building didn't copy the compositional strategies of its older neighbors, cornice line for cornice line. Even worse, they stated that the proposed building stood out in excess of its public importance – whatever that means. Effectively, the planners were saying that new architecture in a conservation district established because of its prior architectural inventiveness must not be inventive or conspicuous. They couldn't see that Koolhaas's design actually advances the creative energies of its context. For starters, the Prada building's height and shape, and its articulation into a frame, fit squarely in the mainstream of the district. But Koolhaas wouldn't settle for meek replication. His proposed stainless-steel façade is composed of transparent holes and opaque discs that would create fantastic light effects on the interior and variable clouds of luminosity on the exterior. What makes these urban design gestures successful is that they ramp up the tradition of innovative illumination on Grant Avenue. During the district's reconstruction after the 1906 earthquake and fire, tone-setting buildings had simple facades and large square windows that responded to needs for illumination and exhibition. In sync, Koolhaas's unusual fenestration plays off today's different needs for retail pomp through architectural spectacle.

9.6
Towards a new shopping, proposed Prada Store, Grant Avenue at Post Street, Rem Koolhaas architect

Amazingly, in a city drowning in process and regulation, decades of planning can be tossed aside when powerful interests intrude. Atop Potrero Hill, the view north toward downtown San Francisco is the stuff car commercials are made of. Steep streets cut straight sightlines toward gleaming skyscrapers. While tall buildings make the panorama exciting, if a local government official has his way no further monuments of architecture will spoil the prospect. In March of 2002, with little more than a few telephone calls, State Senator John Burton stopped construction of a planned seventeen-story dormitory for the new University of California at San Francisco's campus at Mission Bay. No matter that the 700-bed dormitory would have helped to ease a drastic affordable housing crunch. No matter that the proposed building's 160-foot height met the guidelines of the Mission Bay Plan, approved in 1998 after fifteen acrimonious years in the making.

How could the desires of one politician and a few hill residents for an unchanged view trump the greater need for affordable housing? Why should the planning process make it so difficult to build challenging architecture? Have earlier struggles against historic demolitions, freeways, urban renewal, and skyscrapers carried over to a permanent war against anything new and different? While few San Franciscans dispute the sentiment that the city possesses an incomparable landscape and that architecture and engineering have improved this physical setting in the past, its citizens seem incapable of agreeing on how to enhance it in the future.

Such indecisiveness proves costly. From 1996 until 2001, dot-coms, dot-commers, and their martini-and-loft lifestyle overtook large parts of the city. San Francisco, along with nearby Silicon Valley, was ground zero for the Internet revolution, and as the economy boomed, the city underwent one of its most traumatic periods of upheaval. Ironically, in a city that thought it had regulated large-scale change out of existence, an economic gale blew into town and brought about as much dislocation as the great urban renewal efforts of the 1960s.

As the dot-com boom has busted, San Francisco's pivotal urban design challenge is to overcome the climate of opposition. Over the past twenty years, in any given situation, the naysayers have never held great numbers. Thanks to the city's exhaustive neighbor notification program and permit appeals process, even a single opponent can generate considerable hurdles. The problem has always been that the few people with an axe to grind are far more dogged than those in support of a project. Yet in some of the recent urban design controversies, an encouraging development has begun to manifest itself. Increasing numbers of citizens are fed up with design mediocrity, and are becoming more vocal. The long wave of architectural conservatism may have crested. The Herzog and de Meuron museum is proceeding, in part because of the intervention of local artists and architects. Despite the planners, the more visionary ordinary citizens who sit on the planning commission approved Koolhaas's Prada Building. International architects like Thom Mayne, Renzo Piano, and Daniel Liebeskind are in the final stages of designing significant museums and public buildings. Downtown, several elegant glass-curtain-wall skyscrapers have risen in the past few years, including Gary Handel's sleek Four Seasons Hotel (2001). Hopefully, in a few years time, the new wealth of world-class architecture might cause more San Franciscans to see their city in a new light, as a place of the future as well as of the past.

After all, the city doesn't have a long history. Founded only a century and a half ago, San Francisco's reactive preoccupation with its visual image might be understood as a momentary (although two-decade long) crisis in self-confidence. The climate for urbanistic experimentation is better in newer cities, like Houston or Phoenix, that don't dwell too much on their past identity. It's also better in older cities like London or Paris, where any new building joins an architectural assemblage impossible to generalize, centuries of building

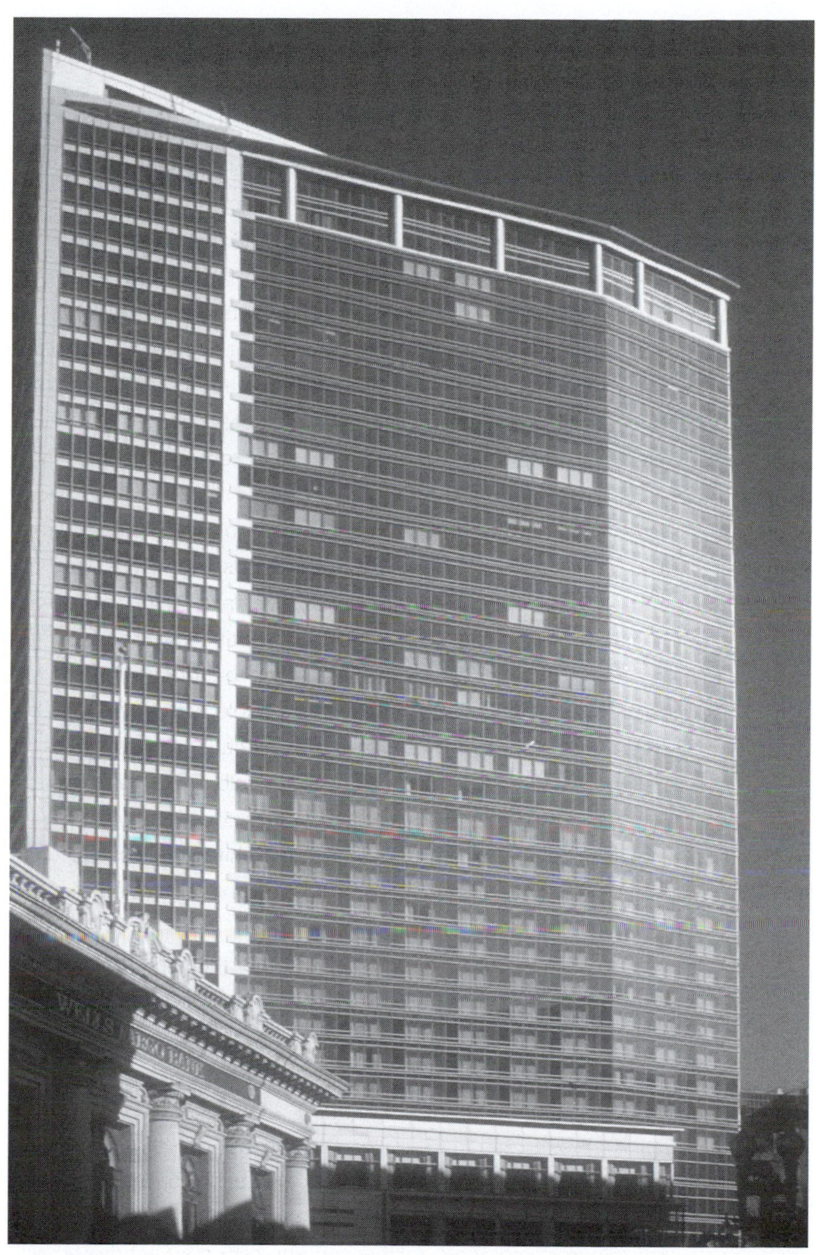

9.7
Curtain walls for our time, Four Seasons Hotel, Market Street at Grant Avenue, Gary Handel architect
Photo by Pad McLaughlin

activity that defeat any idea of a singular urban image. In both cases, youthful and mature, the urban climate accommodates new ideas and appearances. By contrast, San Francisco has seemed lately like an overly responsible 30-something, all too eager to cut off its wild years for a static ideal of ancestral foundations.

In retrospect, the age of reaction has been as severe as the preceding age of progress. From the late 1940s till the early 1970s, proponents of Utopian modernism cast their vision of the city in bi-polar terms like blight *vs* renewal, or outdated *vs* new. Then, from the mid-1970s onward, reactive post-modernists similarly used oppositional frameworks like small *vs* large, or harmonious *vs* contrasting. The past was seen by modernists as an impediment to the future, while post-modernists turned the tables to recast the future as an impediment to the past. Ultimately, aren't these visions opposite sides of a coin? The modernist highway to the future and the post-modernist detour to the past each offer limited and exclusionary understandings of the city.

Struggles against new architecture discussed in this article point out the dark side of urban design in conditions of affluence. For all that San Francisco's recent confrontational design politics (with its potent use of adjectives) suggests, what it yields really is the ethos of individualism. The neighborhood activist's view of the city is of a neo-city, nurtured not by a love of density, monumentality, and change, but by a power to control swathes of space, the signal quality of American suburbia – not social interest but defense of private interest, not people caught up in their desires to participate in a city but in their fears of the city intruding upon them. The activists see San Francisco as a patchwork of neighborly villages, yet in reality the city they envision is infected by a romantic sense of timelessness, a city without change, the same tomorrow as today, lovely, tidy, a closed canon. Do San Francisco's fringes, its non-traditional families, lifestyle experimenters, and counter-cultures add up to a reduction when it comes to urban design, the hot life chilled in reports, meetings, referendums, the protocols of mediocrity and resignation? Does the sum of individuals equal nothing more, nothing new?

In the first decade of the twenty-first century, one can do no better than expose this predicament of reactionary urban design. A city's context can never be a closed canon – indeed, the idea of canonical thinking is inimical to urban growth and vitality. If San Francisco's individuals truly want to build out from the city's context, they must acknowledge its complexity, volatility, and frequently severe contrasts. San Francisco's visual appeal has never rested on smooth transitions or steady repetition. Compare the stylistic and textural jumble of buildings on Russian Hill with the smooth monotonies on Sunset District streets. The glorious moments of the city abruptly contrast water with land, grid with topography, valleys with heights, nature with building, and buildings with each other.

The crux of architectural reaction in San Francisco can be traced to a narrow and superficial definition of urban design context. While the city's *Urban Design Element* takes into account pre-war architecture and topography, it ignores post-war design, infrastructure, technology, economics, and society.

The energies that can inform the design on any given parcel of land extend far beyond issues of façade and massing conformity. Urban contexts are like individuals before they congeal into the norms of identity, when they are still open to multiple affiliations, experiences, and energies. Urban contexts must be sought out in the moment like scents, the pungencies of San Francisco's natural environment, food culture, ethnic diversity, hi-tech economy, and complex history – Victorians and Moderns, tourist landmarks and neighborhood nooks, walking streets and driving streets. For example, the idea of the regional context has long been over-simplified. In the past, Bay Region architectural movements looked closely at local materials such as redwood and cedar trees. Yet the city of San Francisco never had such trees. Its native flora, nonetheless, offers other inspirations for design: looking at the chaparral alone – and its associations with fire, sand, wind, cool sea air, serpentine soil, and drought – inspires a wide range of colors, shapes, and patterns. San Francisco, as its internationally recognized food culture demonstrates, can realize original style out of the cornucopia of local substance. What's more, the city's population, to an unprecedented extent, represents all corners of the globe. What's local is most likely an import from somewhere else. But why aren't the visual symbols and design strategies of Asia, where over one-third of the city's residents trace their origin, or Latin America, where the largest group of Californians trace their

9.8
When structure mattered, Battleship Gun Crane, Hunters Point Naval Shipyard
Photo by Pad McLaughlin

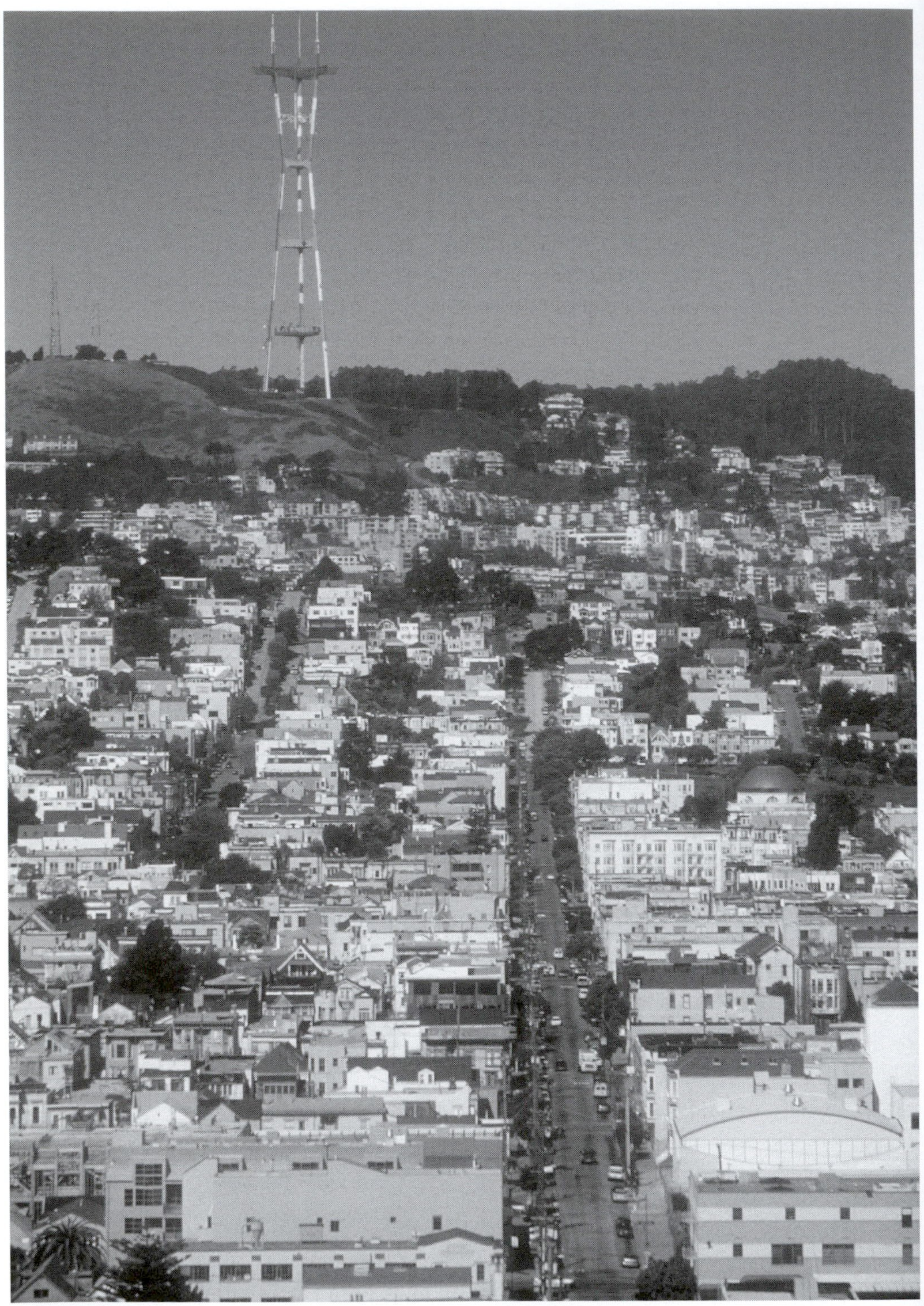

9.9
The unseen landmark, Sutro Tower
Photo by Pad McLaughlin

ancestry, a larger part of the debate on the city's architectural identity? How long must we recycle the same Victorian or Colonial details? San Francisco, as the Internet revolution in communication shows, needs to search for other images, forms, and dispositions of itself.

How refreshing it would be to re-imagine the city through its lesser-known industrial monuments. The most notable of these is certainly the unloved Sutro Tower (1968), a 977-foot television and radio tower. Perched atop a hill (and thus reaching 1,390 feet in the sky), the steel colossus dominates the city. Since it looks like the mast of a galleon, the Sutro Tower could symbolically guide San Francisco over the stormy seas of self-interest to new collective design destinations. Another striking and unrecognized landmark is the re-gunning mole crane (1947) at the Hunter's Point Naval Shipyard, at one time the world's mightiest hoisting machine. Visible from much of the southern part of the city and especially the bay front, the cantilever arms of the 200-foot steel-truss crane once lifted the turrets of guns onto the largest Second World War battleships. It's tempting to think of how the crane's power could be used metaphorically to raze bureaucratic gridlock and raise the city from its urban design doldrums.

Chapter 10

Asian Megacities

Richard Marshall

By 2008 more than half of the world's population is expected to be living in urban areas and by 2030, more than three fifths of the world's population will be living in cities.

United Nations – The Habitat Agenda

Size matters

Size is an important consideration in the debates that are central to the shape of contemporary urbanism. The acceptance of size as a determinant to the definition of "city" and "urban project" has undergone a conceptual change in the Asia Pacific Rim as a result of the explosive growth in the scale and nature of urban conditions there. The design of Asian cities has come to be defined by huge urban agglomerations as the basis for a new kind of city form. This has forced a rethinking and radicalization of fundamental concepts such as center and edge, inside and outside, urban and rural. The very nature of our understanding of what is "city" and what is "not city" has been called into question. The results of these transformative influences has not only affected the mechanisms of urban planning and the production of urban projects but also created a set of conditions in which large size has become something to embrace and to celebrate.

In contrast, urban design in the United States seems increasingly concerned with issues of smallness. Large size in the form of sprawl, unalloyed growth and urban development is rejected as anathema to smart urban design and livable urban forms. While we in the West focus our attention towards the

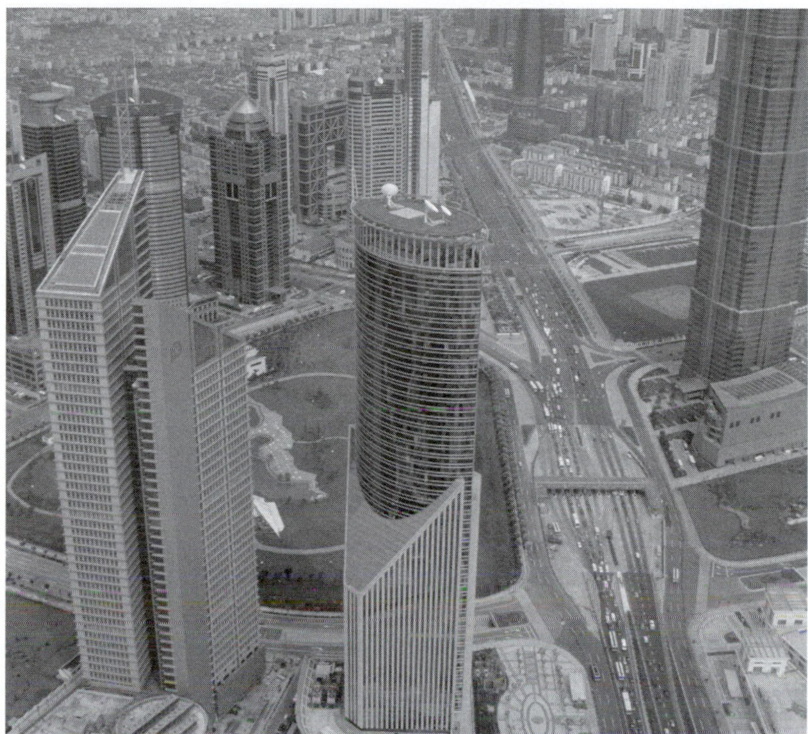

10.1
The emerging urban contexts of cities such as Shanghai will fundamentally alter the way that we think about and design in cities

making of small places and "community-oriented" developments, urbanization in Asia seems to be taking a different course – one that embraces much of what has been rejected in the West. In the urban situations in many parts of Asia urban agglomerations have expanded far beyond government's abilities to provide infrastructure; at the same time a series of megaprojects has been constructed accommodating millions of square feet of commercial space and housing millions of people, at scales that recall Le Corbusier's Ville Contemporaine. Large size, both in terms of the size of urban agglomerations and also the size of architectural projects, is clearly part of Asia's contemporary urbanization experience.

The basic foundations of planning and design as we understand it in the United States seem at odds with the realities of the emerging urban conditions in the Asia Pacific Rim. There appears to be a widening fissure between these realms to a point where the conventions of practice developed in the West have no relevance for these new conditions. The reasons for this are numerous, but increasingly it appears that the sheer size and the speed of change of these urban agglomerations forces a radical shift in the possibilities of planning and urban design. This warrants immediate attention for the simple reason that in the next 50 years the urban experience of the majority of the

world's population will be of living in conditions similar to those in the megacities of Asia.

10.2
View across the city of Tokyo. Despite its density, the majority of the city surprisingly comprises small-scale buildings. However, as is obvious in this image, Tokyo suffers from a lack of open space

New urban forms

Never in human history have we been faced with urban situations the likes of which we will see in the Asia Pacific Rim over the next 25 years. New urban forms are emerging in cities such as Bangkok, Beijing, Bombay, Calcutta, Dhaka, Jakarta, Karachi, Manila, Osaka, Seoul, Shanghai, Tianjin and Tokyo. Once thought of as distant and exotic locations, these dynamic urban centers provide us with a glimpse of the future of human habitation. Interestingly, these situations have for the most part been "off the radar" of European and American urban scholars. Writing about a different place, Koolhaas states that the Metropolis "annuls the previous history of architecture" and generates its own urbanism – "an architecture with its own theorems, laws, methods, breakthroughs and achievements that has remained largely outside the vision of official architecture and criticism."[1] Could the urban situations in the Asia Pacific Rim likewise annul the previous history of architecture? At stake is the very

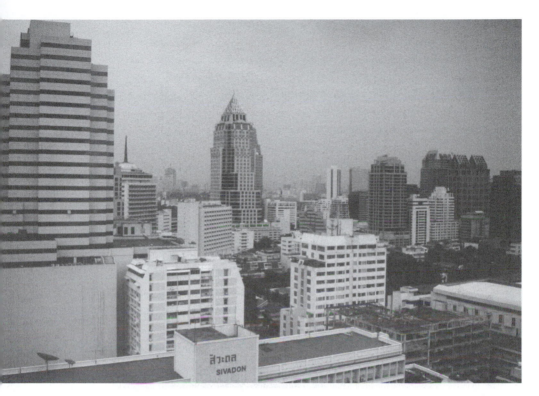

10.3
The influx of FDI into Thailand can be seen in the number of high-rise commercial developments that exist in Bangkok. This view is taken from Silom Road looking towards Sathurn Road

10.4
View of the high-rise residential towers at Muang Thong Thani, Bangkok

notion of the city – what it is, how it works, and the kind of urbanities it is capable of supporting.

Asia is fast becoming an urban continent, and its future will be a crowded one: by 2020, half its population will be living in cities. The tremendous growth in population, combined with an increasing awareness of the limited capacity of the environment, has led to new ways of thinking about, managing and designing in the Asian city. The rapid growth of Asian cities has been taking place at a time when the impacts of free trade associations, the globalization of decision-making on investment location, and the impacts of new information-based industries are having a profound effect on city development prospects. As the work of Dean Forbes notes, among the most striking consequences of the impact of the global economy on the production of urban situations within the Asian Pacific Rim has been the accelerated creation of new urban forms.[2]

Throughout the Asia Pacific Rim, the magnitude of these changes has radically transformed the historical dichotomy between rural and urban. Bangkok is a clear example. With a population of twelve million people it is one of the largest primate cities in South East Asia, with approximately 20 percent of all Thais living in the city. It is also a city with tremendous problems and continues to suffer with the worst possible traffic congestion, with urban poverty, poor air quality, limited sanitation facilities, inadequate garbage disposal, insufficient green space, and recurrent flooding. Bangkok's expansion was (and continues to be) uneven. While areas of housing and industry can be found as far as 40 kilometers from the center, there still exist vacant sites closer to the center. This is due to the patchwork nature of the road system, which means that some areas within the urban landscape are simply inaccessible. Indeed, the arterial road system to a great extent has defined the form of the city. This patchwork produces a "leap-frogging" of development activity as projects respond to the chaotic roadway organization. Better road access exists to the north and east of the city, and subsequently the city has expanded in this direction.

In addition, the impact of the global economy on cities in Asia has led to the creation of "world city" services which produce both the dispersal of productive functions and the concurrent centralization of nodes within cities.[3] At the same time that Bangkok expanded in a carpet of uneven development, for example, there are also instances of tremendous concentrations of urban development. The best example is Muang Thong Thani, a new city created almost instantly on the outskirts of Bangkok, designed to house a million people on 750 hectares. Built over a period of four years, the most striking aspect of the project is a line of 24 apartment towers standing 30 stories tall marching down one side of an artificial lake. Situated amongst a sea of red, green and brown tiled villa roofs, the towers rise like some enormous mountain range on the otherwise flat alluvial plain of Bangkok. These concrete towers are arrayed at intervals along a two-kilometer long street called Bond Street. The towers sit on top of a continuous six-story plinth of shopping and parking that runs the entire length of the street. Housed within this row of towers are 3,500 residential apartments, the majority of which today stand empty – a stark reminder of the impact of the Asian Economic Crisis.

Bangkok is not alone in courting megaprojects. In Kuala Lumpur also, large architectural projects provide a means for a city to claim a certain moment in the international spotlight. The development of projects such as the Multimedia Super Corridor, Putrajaya, Cyberjaya, the Petronas Twin Towers (the tallest buildings in the world), Kuala Lumpur City Center, KL International Airport (the largest in the region), Kuala Lumpur Linear City (the longest building in the world), the environmentally controversial Bakun Dam, the Kedah Reclamation, the Northern International Airport, the Bridge to Sumatra and the New Johor to Singapore Bridge all represent Malaysia's expression of itself in built form, and are the direct result of a conscious effort on the part of the Malaysian government to secure competitive advantage through the construction of large scale architectural projects. And while it may be too soon to evaluate the success of these large-scale projects, they pose both interesting and troubling possibilities for the role of urban planning and design in the contemporary city.[4]

In addition to issues of size, density will be one of the defining attributes of the new urban forms of the Asian city in the years ahead. Muang Thong Thani also includes high-density residential areas, which consist of low-cost housing in 27 blocks of 15 stories, totaling 27,000 apartments. The design of the apartments, some as small as 40 square meters, expresses a severe economic rationalism. Dejan Sudjik is pointed in his description of them, writing;

> [that] negotiating the double-loaded corridors . . . at night is going to feel like a journey through the lower decks of a crammed migrant ship crossing the Atlantic.[5]

Nowhere else in Thailand do people live in such densities. Although estimates of how many people live in Muang Thong Thani vary, some assess that about 75,000 people live there. If this number is indeed correct, then the resulting density within this district is in the order of 700 people per hectare. Even by Asian standards this is high. The result of this density is a remarkable active street life, facilitated by retail and services stores located on the ground floors of the condominiums. The street becomes a hive of activity and, similar to conditions in Hong Kong, where apartments are small, people actively seek street life as a way to escape the claustrophobic housing conditions.

The design of Muang Thong Thani raises a crucial question – the relationship between traditional urban patterns and the emerging realities of development in the Asia megacity. Nowhere in Asia are "traditional" forms of city-making defining the shape of the contemporary city. Across the urban landscapes of Asia new kinds of urban elements are creating new conditions which are, both in form and scale, radically different from traditional village structures. Of interest is the speed at which these urban environments have developed and the consequential adjustments that urban inhabitants have been forced to negotiate. In less than one generation villagers have moved into radically new accommodations, and with this a plethora of issues have surfaced. The majority of urban inhabitants now living in the megacities of Asia have been living there for less than twenty years, and one can only wonder what psychological and societal impacts this is having on these people.

High-density living environments are not unique to Muang Thong Thani. In a number of emerging urban conditions in the Asia Pacific Rim, people live at densities unimaginable in the West. Not only are these urban environments growing to tremendous geographic extents; they are growing in population terms as well. Hong Kong is the best-known example. Of the 1000 square kilometers that constitute Hong Kong and the New Territories, the urbanized portion is 200 square kilometers. With an estimated population of 7.1 million people (2000), this equates to a density of 355 people per hectare in the urbanized area. (Comparable figures for other cities include Tokyo, 24 people per ha; Shanghai, 126 people per ha; New York, 6 people per ha; and London, 10 people per ha).

Density has become one of the defining aspects of many Pacific Rim cities, and is responsible for a great deal of the particularity of urban culture in these locations. The implication of density for framing new ways of conceiving the city is a theme that reoccurs in Western urban theory. Henri Lefebvre[6] differentiates between the city dweller living in high-density urban situations and the suburban householder living in low-density peri-urban situations, he writes that the city dweller today has a different relation to everyday life than that suffered "unwillingly" by the suburban householder. The city dweller reaps the benefits of chance encounters and the various distractions forming part of his everyday experience.

Lefebvre argues that the drama of life is extended in urban areas, simply because there are lots of people to interact with in close proximity. One wonders what he would have thought of situations like Hong Kong, Shanghai or Tokyo. In these locations, where people "live so close together" (remembering Arendt), we begin to understand the implications of density for the creation of a particular culture within the city. This culture of density benefits from the heightened possibility of communicative action, of chance encounters, of seizing initiative and doing the unanticipated, from the contradiction between the appearance of security and the constant threat of the occasional eruption of violence. In these environments we witness an urban model of extreme inclusiveness and proximity. Although there are no conclusions that can be drawn about the future of these urban environments, it is clear that tremendous changes are occurring and that these are having a profound impact on the way we plan cities and on the design and production of urban projects in them. One thing is clear, cities are bigger now than they ever have been.

10.5
Sunday afternoon in Takeshita-dori, Harajuku, Tokyo. Japanese people seem to seek out the small and intimate spaces of older parts of the city and feel quite at home amongst masses of people

Urban bloat

The second half of the twentieth century saw the emergence of the urban environment as the predominant habitat of our species. Never before have we been able to say that the majority of the world lives in cities, but this time is fast approaching. Not only will urbanization increase, but also urban population will be more and more concentrated in what we now call the developing world. By some measures the relative ratios of urban population in the developed and developing world will be 20 percent and 80 percent respectively by the year 2030.[7] This bears tremendous consequence for the professions of planning and design, and forces us to accept, perhaps for the first time, that what we know as "city" is no longer going to be defined in the developed world but is right now being defined in Asia and Latin America. In these situations emerging urbanities are being developed which will not only influence the urban situations there, but also intrinsically impact the way we all think about cities.

Asia is urban due to recent economic prosperity and industrial growth. Today, the continent is home to nine of the world's seventeen megacities of more than ten million people, and experts at the Asian Development Bank predict even more monster cities on the horizon: by 2015 Asia may have seventeen of the world's 27 megacities.[8] Asia's nine megacities (Beijing, Bombay, Calcutta, Jakarta, Osaka, Seoul, Shanghai, Tianjin, and Tokyo) will soon be joined by four more, including Bangkok, Dhaka, Karachi, and Manila. The population of Asian cities has exploded over the last quarter-century. In 1965 the urban population of Asia was in the order of 430 million, with 1.5 billion people living in rural situations. Today the urban population is about 1.2 billion, and by 2025 the urban population is projected to soar to a staggering 2.5 billion people. At this time half of Asia's population will be living in cities. The demographic trends evidenced in Asia are also being experienced in other parts of the developing world, and the implications for urbanists are tremendous. In a few short decades urban life will be the primary experience for most of the world's population. At this time the experience of urbanity will become common to us all, a shared perspective. Does this represent the ultimate victory of the urban? Is the idea of city life validated beyond repute? Or are we witnessing one of the world's greatest environmental and social disasters?

The megacities of Asia are the setting where these questions will be answered. These enormous urban conurbations are in many cases responsible for a higher-than-average proportion of their nation's output of goods and services; are centers of innovation in science, the arts, and culture; and offer some of the best opportunities for people to find higher-paying employment, education, and social services. Despite this, many suffer from endemic water shortages, land-use conflicts, under-provision of basic urban services, environmental pollution, traffic congestion, and rampant proliferation of slums, crime, and other forms of social alienation. With the increasing globalization of business and industrialization of Asian economies, most of the region's megacities will continue to grow at unprecedented rates and to play vital roles in their country's development. Of concern, however, is the capacity of their respective governments to deal with these social and environmental problems. If this capacity issue is not addressed the Asian megacity may herald an urban nightmare the likes of which we have never seen.

New growth patterns

Megacity growth tends to sprawl along major expressways and railroad lines radiating out from older urban cores, leap-frogging in all directions, building new towns and industrial estates in areas hitherto agricultural and rural. In such areas, regions of dense population and mixed land uses are created, in which traditional agriculture is found side by side with modern factories, commercial activities, and suburban development.[9] The concept of extended metropolitan regions or *desakota* zones (*desakota* comes from Bahasa Indonesian for village-town zones) has been coined for this amoebic-like spatial form. These *desakota* zones seem diametrically opposed to the city-based urbanization to which we are accustomed, where downtown cores radiate rings of lower and lower density. These new urban phenomena cannot be analyzed with ideas developed for the reality of the ancient town or the old industrial metropolis.

One of the most visible urban forms that has emerged in these urban situations is the development of mega urban regions or extended metropolitan regions (EMRs). Terry McGee, among others, has documented this phenomenon in different parts of the Asia Pacific Rim.[10] EMR development is a kind of sub-urbanization that extends for 50 to 100 kilometers from the historic urban core. Often these regions involve contiguous territories that span over several countries.

An example of this is the Indonesia–Malaysia–Thailand Growth Triangle (IMT-GT), where economic cooperation pacts cut across borders and regions. The IMT-GT includes the development of common border towns, a road link between the Malaysian state of Perlis to Satun in southern Thailand, the construction of industrial estates in Northern Sumatra, and the development of the IMT-GT corridor between Songkhla/Haadyai in Thailand through Pulau Pinang in Malaysia to the Indonesian provinces of Belawan and Medan. The basis of this economic pact includes simplified border crossings using advanced information technology and industrial support infrastructures.

10.6
View of Silom Station. Bangkok's elevated rail system locates itself on top of the roadway, plunging the congested streets into darkness

The project aims at encouraging transborder production networks. Another perhaps better-known example is the Singapore–Johore–Riau growth triangle, which starts in Malaysia, includes Singapore, and ends in the Riau Islands of Indonesia.[11] As urban and regional development intensifies, the urban fabric coalesces to form urban regions of unprecedented size. Their stories inform the future of city thinking.

Differences in kind, or differences in degree?

Writing about the urban environment of Hong Kong, Peter Rowe notes that urban phenomena change as one or more parameters affecting their identity change. Moreover, the result is sometimes a difference in kind rather than simply a difference in the degree of its defining characteristics.[12] Appropriating Rowe's argument for the purpose of this chapter, is the megacity a different category of urban situation, or still a qualification, by degree, within the same continuum of urban situations? Is there a point at which the urban condition becomes so large that it mutates into something else entirely? If this is possible are the descriptors that we use to talk about urban situations still valid, or at some point do they require a radical redefinition to maintain their validity?

When we talk of "city," is it the same thing in Dhaka or Bangkok as it is in New York or Chicago?

It becomes apparent that various definitions need to be repositioned in light of the emergence of the Asian megacity. With the extent of urbanization that has occurred in the Asia Pacific Rim over the past two decades, the historical dichotomy between rural and urban has been repositioned. The nature of *desakota* urbanization has blurred the rural–urban distinction, and the very definitions of what is "urban" and what is "rural" have to be reconceptualized. The historical model of an expanding core encroaching outwards and consuming a rural hinterland has given way to a patchwork pattern of urban fragments mixed with rural fragments. This patchwork is uneven, driven mostly by imbalances in the provision of transportation infrastructure. The neat line of demarcation between city and country no longer exists, and instead one is left with a thick band of ambiguous fuzziness that denotes the transition from one to another – neither wholly urban nor wholly rural, but something new entirely. The point where the city stops and country begins cannot be clearly articulated. The result is that the landscape of the city becomes a new kind of urbanscape.

The absence of knowing where the city ends means that one is always left wondering about limits. As Paul Virilio wonders. . .[13] [w]here does the edge of the outer city begin when the classical notion of city and wall has ceased to exist? The difference between the space of civilization and the space of nature has become diluted. This produces a crisis of perception, the loss of an understood distinction and, predictably, confusion in terms of what we are actually describing. The problem is that the way we understand design and planning operations continues to hold on to the idea of distinction and of boundaries derived from historically developed and known models. The history of urban design is one based upon an understanding of the historical evolution of known morphologies – from village to town to city to metropolis.

The loss of understood distinctions leads to two concurrent ends. On the one hand it leads to an outpouring of negative appraisals of the new urban situation, and on the other it leads to a crisis of confidence in the design and planning professions – a crisis of professional insecurity. The new urban situation, characterized by amorphous form and diffuse boundaries, denies the possibility of difference between inside and outside, city and nature, civilization and barbarism. Instead the result is an undifferentiated hybrid, a patchwork quilt of various fragments taken from the classical city but cut up and organized in new ways, often without apparent order, and the traditional ways of "knowing" the city are inappropriate to understand this new thing. We have moved from the traditional city as object in a field to a new idea of the urban as a field that spreads out in all directions. This new landscape is certainly not uniform. It is not flat. At points it is stretched thin, at others it is folded and twisted and doubled over. It contains objects and spaces that are ordinary as well as objects and spaces that are extraordinary. It has the capacity to host both the ordinary and the extraordinary without prioritizing one over the other. The relationship between the ordinary spaces and objects and the extraordinary spaces and objects are not determined and instead occur in random combinations, not driven by the same logics as those with which we are conversant, which derive from classical ideas of the city. The urban field covers everything to the point where once there may have been difference, now there is only sameness. Within this urban field we fail to find orientation, fail to understand where we are in relation to anything else, fail to know if we are at the center or in the middle or close to the edge. Our urban compass, our way of understanding our position in the urban order seems to dance before us. The urban field of the megacity produces the ultimate generic urbanism, without order, hierarchy, definition or directionality.

The generic urbanism of the urban field does not care for rules of proportion or the golden mean. It refuses to acknowledge the possibility of "ordering," and instead is morphogenetic. Places and objects have no relation to each other within the urban field. Instead the new urban condition operates

10.7
View of the Central Business District of Kuala Lumpur

in a free, dynamic network of relations – seemingly arbitrary. Planning as a rational ordering practice finds no role here. Strategic interventions into the field will be the only other course of action, with an understanding that as one intervenes in the urban field the field itself changes, modifies itself, flattening in some parts and thickening in others. This is the future context for urban design operations within these new spatial forms.

Implications for thinking about urbanism

What these emerging urban fields mean for our conceptual understanding of the city is unclear. What is clear, however, is that such conditions necessitate a radical revision of the definitions upon which we base the disciplines of planning and urban design. Most critically, the emerging urban fields force us to negotiate new ways of understanding urbanism and its potential. What appears evident is that we have to rethink the strategic intervention of our actions and understand that to operate within this urban field we must be cognizant of a

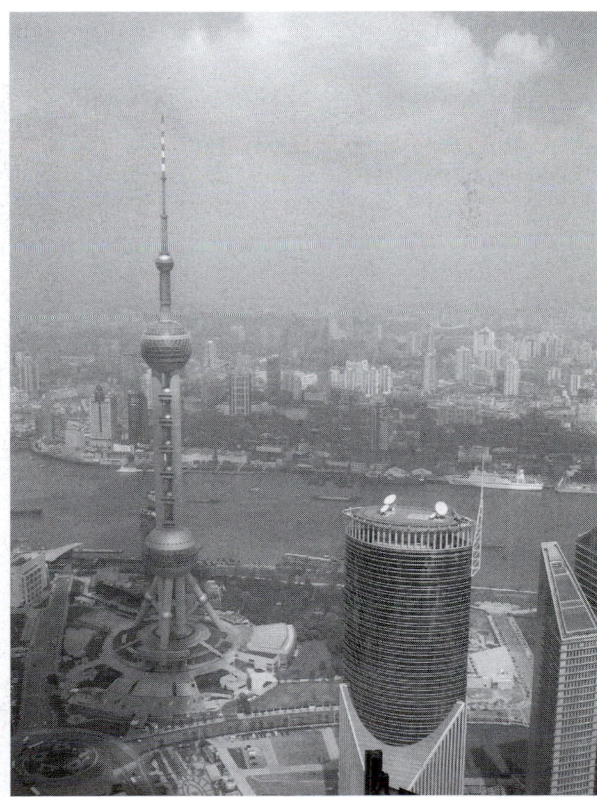

10.8
View from the Pearl Television Tower looking into the Central Park of Lujiazui

new reality that does not attempt to order and control, but rather aims at the potential of new urbanities. We must acknowledge the impossibility of ordering the urban field, and accept that our interventions will do nothing more than influence layers of the field while leaving the essential nature of it to forces beyond our control.

Writing about Los Angeles, Reyner Banham notes that planners and designers were mostly irrelevant to the formation of the city's development. Banham lauds Los Angeles as a triumph of contemporary urbanism and questions whether the city would have developed in the manner that it did if planners and designers had exercised more of their authority over it. And while we may argue with Banham's description of Los Angeles, his point is that new urban forms are evolving outside of the scope of professional jurisdictions, and to suggest that this is *a priori* a negative thing is to adopt a naïve and elitist attitude. Koolhaas too argues that there may be much about these "non traditional' urban situations that may open new possibilities for the professions, writing:

> The generic city presents the final death of planning. Why? Not because it is unplanned . . . [but that] planning makes no difference whatsoever.[14]

Both Banham and Koolhaas speak of an understanding that the complex array of forces that shape a city's development are not only beyond professional authority but are beyond predictability, and are therefore deeply troubling for the planning and design professions. In stark contrast to some who advocate the "power of good design to overcome the ills created by bad design, or, more accurately, by design's conspicuous absence,"[15] the Asia megacity, prelude to our urban future, defies control. If we as professionals are to have any hope of engaging in an urban future, we must give up our professional biases and bigotries. We must work against the obstinate and unreasoned attachment of our own professional beliefs and opinions. We cannot control the city, and we should cease fooling ourselves that we can. If we truly embrace the idea of urban culture – urbanity – we must recognize that it is not a predictable thing and at times can be ugly. Neighborhoods can be either good or bad, depending for example, on who you are. Cities and urban culture can be inclusive or exclusive, they can be open or prejudiced. This is one aspect of cities that has always been present. The history of planning has been about the elimination of the bad and the promotion of the good. The megacities of Asia shows the futility of this pursuit. In his conclusion to *Cities and Civilization*, Peter Hall writes that the greatest cities have never been "earthly utopias," but rather;

> . . . places of stress and conflict and sometimes actual misery . . . places where the adrenalin pumps through the bodies of the people and through the streets on which they walk; messy places, sordid places sometimes, but places nevertheless superbly worth living in . . .[16]

This above all else should be our motivation – to make places superbly worth living in. This will require new ways to understand and work in the new urban forms of the future city. On the fringe of the megacity, fragments sprout without intrinsic relationships to existing organization, responding only to the geometry of freeways, railways and airports. Here the fragments of the modern city deploy themselves continually outward, jumping over areas with inadequate access. The blurry hybrid of the edge of the megacity, where city and natural landscape overlap, calls for strategic visions to orchestrate thickenings and thinnings in the web of the urban field. In this zone, somewhere between landscape and city, there is hope for a new synthesis of urban life and urban form. This is the context of the emerging urban situations in the Asia Pacific Rim and the future of urbanism.

Appendix: populations for the largest 50 cities on Earth: 2000 estimates

(Asian cities in bold.)

Metropolitan area	*Nation*	*Population*
1 Tokyo-Yokohama	**Japan**	**33,190,000**
2 New York	United States	20,270,000
3 Seoul-Inchon	**South Korea**	**19,920,000**
4 Mexico City	Mexico	19,620,000
5 Sao Paulo	Brazil	17,720,000
6 Mumbai (Bombay)	**India**	**17,580,000**
7 Osaka-Kobe-Kyoto	**Japan**	**16,930,000**
8 Los Angeles	United States	16,200,000
9 Manila	**Philippines**	**14,140,000**
10 Cairo	Egypt	14,000,000
11 Calcutta	**India**	**13,940,000**
12 Delhi	**India**	**13,720,000**
13 Shanghai	**China**	**13,580,000**
14 Buenos Aires	Argentina	13,390,000
15 Jakarta	**Indonesia**	**13,330,000**
16 Beijing	**China**	**13,160,000**
17 Moscow	Russia	13,100,000
18 London	United Kingdom	12,130,000

19	**Karachi**	**Pakistan**	**11,020,000**
20	Rio de Janeiro	Brazil	10,810,000
21	**Teheran**	**Iran**	**10,740,000**
22	Paris	France	10,600,000
23	Istanbul	Turkey	10,430,000
24	Lagos	Nigeria	10,030,000
25	**Tianjin**	**China**	**9,920,000**
26	**Hong Kong-Shenzhen**	**China**	**9,180,000**
27	Chicago	United States	8,960,000
28	**Dhaka**	**Bangladesh**	**8,610,000**
29	Washington-Baltimore	United States	7,430,000
30	Lima	Peru	7,420,000
31	**Taipei**	**Taiwan**	**7,260,000**
32	**Bangkok**	**Thailand**	**7,250,000***
33	Bogata	Colombia	6,990,000
34	San Francisco	United States	6,940,000
35	**Chennai (Madras)**	**India**	**6,700,000**
36	**Hyderabad**	**India**	**6,390,000**
37	Philadelphia	United States	6,010,000
38	**Lahore**	**Pakistan**	**5,920,000**
39	Detroit-Windsor	United States-Canada	5,810,000
40	Essen (Rhein-Ruhr)	Germany	5,790,000
41	Kinshasa	Congo	5,750,000
42	Boston	United States	5,690,000
43	Santiago	Chile	5,610,000
44	Johannesburg	South Africa	5,530,000
45	Toronto-Hamilton	Canada	5,470,000
46	**Bangalore**	**India**	**5,430,000**
47	St Petersburg	Russia	5,410,000
48	**Nagoya**	**Japan**	**5,130,000**
49	Dallas-Fort Worth	United States	5,010,000
50	Madrid	Spain	4,950,000

*Bangkok figures quoted equate to the area of the BMA not the BMR.

Source: Prepared by Demographia based upon multiple sources, the most important being national census administrations in Canada, Japan and the United States, Rand McNally, Thomas Brinkhoff: Principal Agglomerations and Cities of the World (http://www.citypopulation.de/) and local sources. © 2000 www.demographia.com – Wendell Cox Consultancy – with permission. http://www.demographia.com/db-world-metro2000.htm

Notes

1 Koolhaas, 1978, p. 123.
2 See Forbes and Thrift, 1987, pp. 67–87; Lin, 1994, pp. 1–24; Forbes, 1999, p. 241.
3 Freidmann, 1986, p. 72; Lo and Yeung, 1996.
4 See Marshall, 2002.
5 Sudjik, 1993, p. 19.
6 Lefebvre, 1996.
7 United Nations, 1998.
8 Asia Development Bank, 1997.
9 McGee and Robinson, 1995, p. ix.
10 Ginsburg *et al.*, 1991; McGee and Robinson, 1995.
11 See Macleod and McGee, 1996, pp. 417–464; Perry, 1998, pp. 87–112.
12 Rowe, 2001, pp. 14–39.
13 Virilio, 1986, pp. 540–541.
14 Koolhaas, 1978.
15 Duany *et al.*, 2000, p. xiii.
16 Hall, 1998, p. 989.

Chapter 11

New Urbanism

Edward Robbins

Some critical ideas that have shaped our cities are the product of our experience of actual physical forms and designs rather than self-conscious design principles: Las Vegas and Los Angeles come to mind. Others often are the result of a judicious mix of actual design and the writings that accompany them: Hausmann's Paris and Cerda's Barcelona are examples. Still others are better known for their writings and organizational activities rather than actual projects and the effects these have had on the larger discourse about urbanism. The New Urbanism, which claims so many different designs, from tall buildings to small town Americana, is such a movement. As we shall see, the New Urbanism is mostly a commitment to: "The poetics of small town life, the virtues of sustainable communities, and the appeal of environments that emphasize the pedestrian over the automobile"[1] and a set of ideas of how this commitment might be achieved. Few, though, of the many and different projects New Urbanists claim as theirs have been actually realized and none have met the goals set out in their various charters and written texts.[2]

Nonetheless, any discussion about urban design and the city in the late twentieth century would be incomplete if it did not include the "New Urbanism." It has taken center stage as the most discussed architectural response to the plight of our cities in the last decade or so of the twentieth century. The architecture critic of the *New York Times* has called the New Urbanism "the most important phenomenon to emerge in American architecture in the post-Cold War."[3] At the same time it has been argued, "this emperor may have no clothes."[4] Thus it is important to not only understand what the New Urbanism claims, and its relation to earlier thinking about urban design. It also demands a critical analysis of why the New Urbanism has received so much attention and whether it has or can deliver on its promises.

Conceptual roots

There is some that is new in the New Urbanism, but for the most part it is deeply rooted in approaches to urban design that have preceded it. The New Urbanists, most crucially, are directly bound to their forebears by their faith in their own all-encompassing vision for the design of a better world. It is, in their view, the only answer to the critical problems that our contemporary cities face. If Le Corbusier argued that it was either "architecture or revolution," (that is to say, his architecture), Leon Krier, one of the heroes of the New Urbanism, has argued similarly that:

> If the United States is to solve its social and environmental problems in the future, it must revise the whole national philosophy of settlement, the very notion of civil society . . . Only when this possibility is secured . . . can states and governments take up their original constitutional aim as guardian and patron of the *res publica* of the civic realm and its welfare.[5]

Of course, unlike Le Corbusier, the philosophy of settlement he is talking about is that to which Krier is allied: the New Urbanism.

The design of housing and the residential landscape has been associated throughout the twentieth century, especially in the United States and United Kingdom, with the development of better citizens and a better society as much as it has been concerned with the design of commodious and esthetically pleasing residential developments. Like so many urban designers before them, the New Urbanists "speak of community and neighborhood as physical rather than social activities, as if community resulted from the built form rather than from people who inhabit it.[6] As Gwendolyn Wright writes: "For centuries Americans have seen domestic architecture as a way of encouraging certain kinds of . . . social life."[7] In England, too, from at least the middle of the nineteenth century, commentators like Frederich Engels[8] and Samuel Kingsley linked housing with the moral state of its inhabitants. As Kingsley argued as early as 1857, the social state of the city depends on its moral state and that, in turn, depends on the "lodging of its [the city's] inhabitants."[9] In the twentieth century, too, architects as different as Ebenezer Howard and Le Corbusier, Tony Garnier and the designers of failed developments like Thamesmead in England and Pruitt-Igoe in St. Louis, have offered their design visions as the singular answer to the social and cultural problems of urban life.

The work of Patrick Geddes (1915), Ebenezer Howard (1898), Raymond Unwin (1909),[10] and German town planners of the 1920s provided a legacy from which the New Urbanists have borrowed heavily. What binds these designers is a "belief in the scale and spatial organization of the traditional town as the basic building block for human settlement."[11] The New Urbanist emphasis on density and compactness also echoes the 1940's trend, among English planners for a fondness for dense old villages and small towns. It was felt that these kinds of dense and enclosed spaces fostered community and more energetic urbanity: the desire for active streets with mixed use, greater density and neighborhood coherence was the order of the day long before the New Urbanists came on the scene.

In their search, the New Urbanists have been strongly influenced by the work of Werner Hegeman and Elbert Peet (1992) and their taxonomy of different types of urban places, plazas, intersections, and gateways, and road arrangements that provide a sense of the civic scale and civic art. So too did the New Urbanists borrow the notion of the relatively self-contained neighborhood as a critical scale of design from the work of Clarence Stein, at Radburn among other places, and Clarence Perry. They, like the New Urbanists who followed, placed great importance and gave new life to the idea of the neighborhood, the priority of the pedestrian over the car in order to make a social and hospitable community. As Perry argued as early as 1929: "By some sociologists the automobile has been regarded as a destroyer of neighborhood life . . . Thus the automobile menace has set up an imperative demand for a definition and standardization of the neighborhood district."[13]

The New Urbanist's strong emphasis on the streetscape and street use is part and parcel, as well, of a long and continuous concern with street life[14] that re-emerged again in the 1960s. In the work of Jane Jacobs (1961), the Smithsons,[25] Gordon Cullen (1968) and, more recently, Robert Venturi and Denise Scott Brown (1977), there is a strong stated desire to return to an emphasis on life in the street in contrast to the thinking of modernists like Le Corbusier. There is a sense that the street is critical to urbanity and community even if the streets to which each architect saw us returning varied from the building corridors of the Smithson's, to the strip of Venturi and Scott Brown and the nostalgic main street of Cullen.

In many ways, though, the most influential urban design movement, ironically, is the one that the New Urbanists most vilify: modernism.

Modernism and the New Urbanism

The New Urbanists acknowledge their legacy, even their connection to the modernists, at least in part. They readily admit that: "In important ways the Congress for New Urbanism is modeled on CIAM [The Congress of Modern Architecture] . . . Our methodology is the same . . ." But they also emphasize that they offer a critical antidote to the errors of modernist thinking about city making. As one of the founding fathers of the New Urbanism has succinctly put it: "Our ideology is different."[16]

New Urbanism has borrowed the structure of CIAM, and adapted it to contemporary circumstances. Mirroring CIAM practices, there are annual congresses where members discuss and debate old and new approaches to the task of urban design and renew their allegiance to the general principles of the New Urbanism. There are working groups to discuss and report on particular issues. Most notably, proponents of the New Urbanism have produced a founding Charter of the CNU (2000), which has much in common with the Charter of Athens (1933), so central to the work of CIAM. The Charters of both groups address similar issues, such as reforming the chaos of existing cities, linking physical with economic and social issues, and providing clear guidelines on how to proceed in practice. Both set out to create community and social good through their designs. In practice, members of CNU, similar to CIAM, work assiduously to influence government agencies and other important groups central to the development of urban projects. Also like CIAM, they have produced more publicity, more publications, and more interviews and programmatic statements than projects that have been realized.[16]

Unlike CIAM, which limited its membership to architects and designers, and remained relatively small, the CNU is open to anyone who wants to join, and receive their publications and participate in their work. At CNU gatherings one will find students, developers, community organizers, politicians and city administrators along with architects, urban designers, and planners participating actively in both the official and informal discussions and activities. There is an active effort to capture the press and broadcast media by inviting them to CNU events and programs. The CNU accepts much of the organizing principles of CIAM but rejects its elitism.

Even though New Urbanists insist that their thinking and approaches critically contrast with those of modernism, they share many substantive ideas with it as well. Indeed, as John Dutton points out so succinctly: "The irony is that the New Urbanism is in many ways a resurrection of modernism but cloaked in the dress of the pre-modern era."[17]

The CNU, like CIAM, focuses not only on design but also on reforming the building industry to get it to understand the advantages and superiority of their design approach in comparison to more conventional design. Similar to CIAM there is also a strong belief in the efficacy of standards, codes, and written conventions. Like the modernists, the New Urbanists are also not adverse to working with big developers in realizing their goals but at a scale of design that is less monumental than that of the modernists. New Urbanists also share with CIAM an interest in the making of community through the design of town centers and, like many members of the MARS group, an offshoot of CIAM, they believe that urban design has to address the design of the street. And, it bears repeating, like CIAM, the CNU has a fundamental and almost evangelical belief in the role of design not only in forming a better city but also in shaping a better society.

Still, it is clear that in many ways the New Urbanism is a rejection of modernist approaches to urban design. Unlike CIAM and other modernists, the CNU seeks to work with people who are not professional architects but who are willing to join in the effort to realize the New Urbanist project. New Urbanists also repudiate the notion, central to modernist ideology, that one single architectural genius is and should be responsible for the design of the totality of any project: be it at the scale of house or of a whole city like Le Corbusier's Plan for Algiers.

Most crucial to the popularity of New Urbanists, among many of its followers and the media, is that they eschew the modernist aversion to popular taste and traditional building types. They reject the reliance on a single master-plan that works from universal ideas about the city, often ignores, even at times obliterates, the traditional urban fabric, and makes no reference to the surrounding street grid and adjacent buildings. In contrast, the New Urbanists have looked to the particular and local because:

> Each community shared a local vision and language of how to build their world . . . They shared common customs and culture that led them to create places that were a part of a larger, coherent, ordered and intrinsically beautiful whole.[18]

How do they do it?

Contemporary urbanism for New Urbanists is characterized by urban sprawl, placelessness, the domination of the automobile and mediocre urban design[19] that create suburbs that are noteworthy not only as esthetic failures but also "as civic environments [that] . . . do not work."[20] New Urbanists promise to remedy this condition through their own good design principles and practices, and to reintegrate dwelling, working, and schooling, worshiping and recreating, and to put an end to the domination of the automobile. In the place of the classic suburb – less a community in their eyes than an alienating agglomeration of houses – the New Urbanists assure us that their design principles will create a sense of place, which will re-engage the spirit of the traditional American small town and reinvigorate urban community.[21]

Vision will be made reality if one follows a set of design approaches central to New Urbanist thinking and practice. At its core is a series of scales that New Urbanists believe essential to the generation of good urban environments, the region, the neighborhood and the street, and a set of town-making principles and an architectural lexicon that provide a methodology for practice.

The region, neighborhood, and street

New Urbanists contend that it is essential that designers and planners engage the regional scale if they are to address the problems of air quality, water, issues of economic equity, urban decay, sprawl, social segregation, and the growing importance of the metropolitan culture in general. Without a regional plan, for example, neighborhood and village scaled developments can create the very sprawl and social segregation that should be prevented. Nonetheless, designers have as yet "no framework for this new reality, no handle to guide it."[22]

Although it is continually alluded to, the region is not rigorously defined by New Urbanists. It may be bounded by topography, watersheds, coastlines, river basins, and other natural features of the landscape, or may be described as comprised of cities, towns, and villages: regions may also be defined by reference to economic, political, and cultural attributes. There are, however, a number of principles that derive from addressing the region.

For the New Urbanists, designers should respect the edges of the metropolis so that sprawl and development do not replace agricultural and natural landscapes. With this in mind, they place great stock on infill development within existing areas rather than development of marginal or peripheral areas to the core city.

Where possible all development should be contiguous with existing urban boundaries. Non-contiguous development should be designed as towns and villages with their own employment, civic, and cultural base rather than as bedroom communities to avoid sprawl. Development should respect the local historical patterns of urbanism and the physical organization of the region should be supported by a transportation structure that provides for mass transit, pedestrian movement, bicycles and any other means of transportation that lessens the use of the automobile.

The neighborhood for New Urbanists is the essential element of development and redevelopment in the metropolis. It is critical that neighborhoods be compact, pedestrian friendly and provide for mixed use. Neighborhoods are to be designed and seen as coherent wholes. Districts, though within a neighborhood, should emphasize a single use as a civic or commercial center, for example. As many activities as possible, shopping, schooling, using parks, and local governmental facilities should be accessible by walking, especially by the young and the old. Other desirable features of a neighborhood are easy access to mass transit, codes that provide guidelines for building, and the dispersion of parks, ballfields, gardens, and such throughout the neighborhood rather than being concentrated in one single-use area.

It is also important that, within neighborhoods, a broad range of housing types, from single family to multi-family, from more to less expensive, be made available so that people of diverse backgrounds and incomes can find a place to live within the development. But to make a neighborhood work, it is crucial that the streets that make up a neighborhood be designed to allow for the elements that need to be accommodated and in an aesthetically pleasing way.

For the New Urbanists, whether correctly or not, the "fault line between Modernism and traditional urbanism"[23] is in the respect traditional design and the New Urbanism shows for the street. Any designer who thinks that "urban squares are obsolete, or that traditional, figural spaces clearly shaped and defined by buildings are somehow irrelevant"[24] should think again. A primary task of architecture, urban and landscape design, according to New Urbanists, is to assure that streets are designed as places of shared and mixed use. These streets should be designed seamlessly with their surrounding streets, and not as isolated pods so common to contemporary design. Local context and precedent should always be taken into account and the design of any street should be undertaken in relation to the overall plan.

Streets should be designed to be safe and secure without the use of overt signs of policing. Rather, such things as human presence through such elements as front porches and windows facing the street and street dimensions and scales that encourage congeniality are better ways to create a sense of security. Visibility, good lighting, well maintained publics spaces, the legibility with which one street or neighborhood site connects with another are other ways to make people comfortable with using what they will sense to be secure and inviting streets.

Clearly, New Urbanists are aware that cities have to accommodate the automobile. But in neighborhoods, the use of the automobile must be made to respect the pedestrian. This implies the use of such elements as on-street parking to protect the pedestrian from auto noise, traffic calming devices that slows the auto in densely used pedestrian areas, narrowing street width, and providing fewer traffic lanes, among other things.

Town-making principles, codes and lexicon

There is, at the heart of New Urbanism, a professed set of town-making principles as a guide to town design. These, they claim, are based on observations of patterns revealed by looking at traditional American communities. The principles describe the fundamental physical elements that embody community, although the principles are flexible in relation to local landscapes and programs.

At the core of any urban design is a master plan; a composite drawing that includes all the critical information needed to develop a town plan. It attempts to exemplify the patterns of what the New Urbanists claim to be the typical American town: a geometrically located town center surrounded by an interconnected street network. The town is made up of, in the parlance of the New Urbanists, a series of "neighborhoods and villages"; in effect, smaller quarters that connect to create a whole. In larger towns, the plan will also account for the ascending scales of urban development: the neighborhood, the village, the town, and the region.

Commercial activity and work places are concentrated in the town center. Civic spaces and buildings, like schools, parks, and community centers are distributed throughout the neighborhoods. Each neighborhood, mirroring the earlier work of designers like Clarence Perry, is planned so that, from edge to center is a quarter-mile or a five-minute walk.

Street size, depth, and length are developed so that building lots front the street and traveling distances are reasonable. All the streets, at least all that are possible, should connect and the street layout should allow for connections to new streets so as to create a regional network of streets. Along with streets, there should be pedestrian paths that connect civic spaces as well as, where possible, alleyways that also provides alternative pedestrian routes through the neighborhood. The street section provides carefully detail building heights, parking lanes, and street landscape to assure that the scale of the elements that surround the street make it attractive to pedestrian use.

It is also crucial that dwellings, shops, civic uses, and workplaces be in close proximity to each other and that squares and parks be distributed throughout the neighborhoods. Civic building should be prominently sited to serve as nodes or landmarks and as terminating places. The goal of all these design principles is to encourage active social use of the streets and other spaces of the neighborhood.

What the New Urbanists hope by the instantiation of their town-making principle is that issues of growth, traffic, and affordability are addressed through physical design. Traffic by the design of streets; affordability by preventing large-scale, single-income tract housing and encouraging homes over stores, garage apartments and other forms of mixed use usually prohibited by the design of most new suburban tracts.

The town-making principles are embedded within a series of Codes, which regulate and ensure that the principles embodied in New Urbanist town-making are implemented.

Much of suburbia is the product of codes and conventions. The NU rewrites these codes and conventions to restructure the nature of urban and suburban development. New Urbanist codes are a series of ordinances that regulate everything from the masterplan to the streetscape, the building types and distribution to the architectural design of all building types.

There are five basic documents that lay out the Codes. The Regulating Plan sets out the terms of the master plan in detail, and outlines where residences, civic spaces and commercial activities are to be located. What are called "Urban Regulations" delineate such things as how much of a building must be on a common frontage line, where parking is allowed, encourages such elements as porches and stoops, and provides for rentable outbuildings. It tends to be prescriptive rather than proscriptive. Architectural Regulations set out such things as materials, methods of construction, acceptable architectural elements to ensure that there is a harmony among the building types. They vary from strictly deterministic, to more open-ended, depending on the development. Street Types and Landscape Regulations set out the rules that govern everything from street widths and alignments to encouraged street plantings.

The Codes do not set out the design in exact detail; they are guidelines and limits to design within which architects can work. They are used to control the shape and the social reality of neighborhoods by providing not only boundaries for what is allowable but providing strong suggestions about what is considered admirable and complementary to the neighborhood as a whole.

In 1999 to provide a more exhaustive guide for the analysis of urban space and to create standards for a common urban language, Andres Duany and Elizabeth Plater-Zybeck, central figures in the New Urbanist movement, developed what they called a *Lexicon of the New Urbanism*.[26] It sets out a taxonomy of urbanism, provides a terminology with which to describe the form of the city, and its structure from the regional scale to the building type. The Lexicon also provides a strategy for implementation and ideas about how to best represent urban plans.[27]

From whence the popularity/why the criticism?

Whether the combination of scales, town-making principles, codes and lexicon works in practice, and what kind of world it is creating are the issues that are most often debated about the New Urbanism. It is noteworthy that these are usually debated in the abstract, with pieces of parts of various projects, often unbuilt, used as examples of this or that point in favor or against the New Urbanism.

The problem with the New Urbanist projects is, as John Kaliski points out,[28] New Urbanism claims so many different approaches to the city in its name – everything from Brownfield development to Clearfield development – that what constitutes a New Urbanist project is at best elusive. It might include everything from the key projects of DPZ such as Kentlands, Seaside, Windsor, Wellington, to the work of Peter Calthorpe at Laguna West that is full of builder-standard cul-de-sacs. It also includes work by people like Daniel

Solomon and his infill projects of medium density in places like San Francisco and San Jose, for example, Communications Hill. One also gets such places of urban infill and building-by-building restoration and redesign and projects like SOM/Calthorpe's Atlantic Center in Brooklyn that are indistinguishable in scale, scope or corporate gigantism from projects done throughout the country but not claimed (and even criticized) by NU.

It is thus difficult in a sense to come to any general understanding about the success or failure of the New Urbanism on the basis of any one or other particular project. The most written about projects associated with the New Urbanism are, at best, problematic as archetypes for critical review. Seaside celebrated, or denigrated, depending on your point of view, in the movie *The Truman Show* is a vacation development, and not an everyday community. Celebration, built by Disney, is not strictly speaking a New Urbanist community in the way it was created and designed, even though it has become one of the icons of the movement in the popular press. Other "iconic" projects, as we shall see, also raise serious issues about just what New Urbanism is and why one or another development is New Urbanist. Nonetheless, the New Urbanism is not without its strong support and equally strong criticism.

The support

There are many reasons for the apparent celebration of the New Urbanism among designers, developers, and the larger public. For some proponents, the New Urbanism, as the former Mayor of Milwaukee, John O. Norquist points out, is a significant part of the resistance to continued urban sprawl and fragmentation.[29] New Urbanism provides a voice for those unhappy with inner-city decline, the social alienation produced by conventional suburbs, and a world that seems to be increasingly dominated by the automobile. The call for towns and neighborhoods that build community, bring a sense of regional order and are less dependent on the car and more amenable to pedestrian traffic suggests that there is an important anodyne to the prevailing planning and development practices responsible for our current plight.

Moreover, for many people, the apparent concern New Urbanists have with the community voices and attitudes are a salutary alternative to the often dictatorial and unresponsive design strategies of many urban designers and planners of the modernist and also bureaucratic mode. In an attempt to include local visions and languages, New Urbanists often try to work with the local community in design charrettes to develop a contextual solution, grounded in local circumstances and attitudes. Whether this is a marketing strategy or a genuine attempt to include locals in developing the design (or a bit of both) is open to question. That it is an attractive element of New Urbanist practice and ideology is not.

For those developers that support the New Urbanism, it is not only an answer to sprawl and reliance on the automobile, it allows for, indeed encourages, development of sites that, previous to the New Urbanism, would have had fewer units in the same size tract. Real estate developers embrace the New Urbanism in the name of community development but, as Norman Blankman, writing in *Real Estate Finance Journal*, makes clear:

> The single most important thing that should be done to bring affordable housing within reach for millions of people is to change zoning laws to permit more compact development. The first steps have been taken by a nationwide movement [The New Urbanism] to reform US urbanism.[30]

Also, as one CEO of an important development firm once told me, the New Urbanism, by providing more restrictive building codes, in effect alleviate many of the problems of customer choice associated with new suburban development and the complications and increased costs this creates. It simplifies the developer's design process. Issues of access, house type, lot, and street configurations, front door location and other such decisions are limited and, as a result, so are the ensuing problems that this often causes between potential neighbors, as well as between customers and the developers of new suburban and urban tracts.

There may be a more profound explanation for the New Urbanism's popularity and the support that it appears to engender. Throughout the nineteenth and twentieth centuries, architects and urban designers, whether modern or postmodern, radical or conservative, have tried to realize an enlightenment dream to forge a satisfactory city through the cauldron of design and thereby produce good citizens.[31] One continually reappearing vision in that quest is that of a tidy, small, and gentile urban place, which in the words of Prince Charles would "nurture human life and imbue people with a sense of . . . community."[32] As David Harvey so aptly puts it:

> Faced with the innumerable problems and threats that urban life poses, some analysts . . . have reached for one simple solution – to try and turn large and teeming cities so seemingly out of control, into urban villages where, it is believed, everyone can relate in a civil fashion to everyone else in an urban and gentle environment.[33]

The New Urbanism in a sense makes a kind of Freudian trade-off.[34] Freud in his *Civilization and Discontents* argues that civilization provides freedom from fear and guarantees what he calls, in German, *Sicherheit*, in exchange for accepting certain constraints on the self and individual liberty. *Sicherheit* as Zygmunt

Bauman suggests is more than just "security." It also refers to "certainty and safety." Security guarantees us that what we have gained or possess will retain its value and that the world we have learned how to act in will remain reliable. Certainty provides us with the knowledge that the distinctions, between let us say useful and useless, proper and improper, will allow us to act in ways we will not regret; will tell us what is a good life. Safety is the awareness that if we behave correctly we will experience no danger, threats to our bodies or our property, home and neighborhood.

In a critical way that is precisely what the New Urbanist vision provides many people. It offers security by establishing a set of limits that helps to establish and guarantee the value of the home that has been purchased. The restrictions that are set by the Codes also appear to guarantee that the community will not change its physical form and appearance. New Urbanism also sells a vision of community, rooted in our nostalgic memory of small town life, that sets out a notion of the good life and provides assurances that this life will be maintained. It also sets out to make us feel safe through the notion of the eyes on the street, the familiarity with our neighbors, and the bounded, if not gated, form of the neighborhood letting us know who belongs and who doesn't. The emphasis on traditional house types and urban esthetics that signifies memories of a certain and controllable past suggests that this world can be resurrected. The assurances that tradition seems to convey also appears to provide a place for safe investment in a neatly bounded universe in a world that is increasingly diverse and threatening.

In exchange for *Sicherheit*, the New Urbanists ask that, as a member of their development, one accepts strict codes and conventions. These strictly limit individual freedom to use and design a house and property in any way an owner might see fit, to accept a number of standards that prescribe what your neighborhood can look like and a strong sense of neighborhood control – albeit mostly informal – over public practices. In some New Urbanist developments, when and how one could place political signs and how often one could have garage sales are among the regulations set for the community. In other New Urbanist projects, the color of houses, the type and height of fences, the range of ornament for homes, even the types of curtains one could have are regulated by codes. As the architect Robert Stern put it:

> In a free-wheeling Capitalist society you need controls – you can't have community without them. It's right there in de Tocqueville; in the absence on community of an aristocratic hierarchy you need firm rules to maintain decorum. I'm convinced these controls are actually liberating to people. It makes them feel their investment is safe. Regimentation can release you.[36]

This is a statement with which so many of the residents of New Urbanist developments could agree or if not agree in principle, in which they could at least find some comfort in practice. For critics though, such sentiments raise serious questions about whether the New Urbanism is worthy of the praise it has received.

The critiques

The questions about the New Urbanism revolve around a number of issues, both technical and ideological, and in many ways go to the heart of so much discussion about contemporary urbanism as a physical and social reality. If for no other reason, it is why the New Urbanism has been so central to architectural debates.

Most often voiced within the architectural community is a critique of the traditionalist architectural bias of the New Urbanism. For many architectural critics the nub of the matter is what they see as a tacky populist reliance on traditional American house types and a spurning of more modern and adventurous housing and architectural forms. New Urbanism's greatest sin in this view is that it is boring, commonplace and without any formal or aesthetic merit. The criticism is characterized by the New Urbanists as the ramblings of an elitist minority without concern for the larger issues that face people in their everyday lives in the city. But there are criticisms that are not as lightly dismissed.

There are a number of critics who do not challenge the architectural and esthetic qualities of the New Urbanism but argue that what the New Urbanists propose cannot alleviate the very problems they claim to solve. So far, these critics contend, the New Urbanism offers more in rhetoric than reality. And their rhetoric holds a number of assumptions that stand in want of serious questioning.[37]

Few, if any projects built by the New Urbanists provide all that they promise. In one of the most publicized, Kentlands (which has gone belly-up a number of times), the village relies on a conventional mall, which is based on regional automotive traffic for its economic survival, and to which the residents of the Kentlands go to shop for necessities like food. Laguna West neither has its promised commercial center nor its rapid transit link to Sacramento, residents still drive to work and shop. Indeed studies appear to show that residents of New Urbanist developments do not drive less than those in more conventional developments. Seaside finally has its commercial center in place but it is dependent on tourism based on the automobile. On the way to Seaside, the highway is littered with poor copies of Seaside that increase, not decrease, sprawl. Certainly, the New Urbanists cannot be held responsible for weak imitations. Seaside, Kentlands, and Laguna West, among others, remind us, however, that the New Urbanists have as yet been unable to deliver the kind of regional plans they promise. They have yet to integrate the proliferation of small, pedestrian-based places in a way that does not also produce sprawl, fragmentation, and the domination of the automobile.

The failure of Kentlands, and of Laguna West, to "concentrate commercial activities, including shopping and working, in town centers"[21] and the regional traffic problems that Seaside poses are not accidents. Nor is the failure of the New Urbanists to take a critical look at these problems. Such commercial centers are not viable. Communities of 5,000–10,000 people cannot support economically feasible town centers that will adequately serve the shopping needs of its populace. At best, they might provide centers for the sale of convenience goods and personal services. The densities and population needed for a serious shopping street or center are simply not possible if one designs a community based on single family dwellings in today's commercial market, as studies by the Urban Land Institute make clear.[38] Such pedestrian-based commerce is more likely in a city with higher densities, large multi-family buildings, and larger populations.

Developing places where people would walk to work is just as problematic. Even in neighborhoods and cities with the densities to support a jobs/housing balance, it is unlikely that people would work where they live. Robert Cervero[39] has illustrated that, even where counties develop a job/housing balance, two-thirds of those who work in such counties live elsewhere, and two-thirds of those people who live in those counties work elsewhere. In my own city of Boston, one of three cities with more jobs than people, 31 percent of its citizens work outside its municipal boundaries. Clearly, many people cannot or would not choose to live and work in the same place. Even if people could be persuaded to work within walking distance from where they live, unless one divided a metropolitan region into company based towns, the possibility of designing such relationships is questionable at best.

For argument's sake, let us say that such pedestrian-based communities could be built. There are still questions begging answers: how do the New Urbanists plan to guarantee work for a community's residents near where they live? Do people have to move if they change employers that are not within walking distance of their homes? What are families with two working adults to do if the firms for which they work are far apart? How do the New Urbanists plan to guarantee homes to new employees if a company grows and people who have changed employers or retired do not move? Design principles are clearly not enough. What would be needed is a frightening scenario of an almost "1984-ish" control of residential choices and management of economic practices.

Just as the New Urbanists cannot make thriving commercial centers or guarantee that there will be enough jobs within walking distance for residents, even if they wanted to walk to work, they cannot provide sufficient civic, religious, and recreational facilities within easy walking distance for residents.

But, let us assume for the moment that the New Urbanists had succeeded in building the suburban metropolitan region following their principles. A region of a million people would have 200 neighborhoods of 5,000 or so people. A region of five million would have 1,000 such communities. If each community housed only five denominational churches, that would be 1,000 churches in the first metropolitan region and 5,000 churches in the second. (The Boston/Cambridge area of over 600,000 residents and a nearby region of another 2.4 million residents has 532 churches representing over 50 denominations.) These hypothetical cities would have 200–1,000 swimming pools, health clubs, movie theaters, libraries, and sports fields among other things. Even this would not prevent auto traffic, unless one assumed that use patterns and social interactions were limited to the community in which one resided. Picture such a regional plan, and then think of the sprawl as 200 to 1,000 separate communities each with its own town center spans across the metropolitan landscape.

Even if the New Urbanists do meet all their goals, they might still succeed as Vincent Scully argues "in creating an image of community."[40] Such an image, he goes on to suggest, will overcome the social dissolution which, he and other New Urbanists claim, is plaguing our society.

The New Urbanist belief that it is through neotraditonal design of their developments can resurrect a lost sense of community has come under significant criticism. At the core of New Urbanist thinking and design practice is:

> The presumption . . . that neighborhoods are in some sense "intrinsic," and that the proper form of cities is some "structure of neighborhoods," that neighborhood is equivalent to "community," and "community" is what most Americans want and need.[41]

It is a presumption that is open to serious question. Many Americans love living in the anonymous suburbs as well as in urban towers. Effective community can be and has been created by people who live in different neighborhoods, and even different cities through mutually shared interests. It is especially noteworthy that the members of the CNU, a community of like-minded designers from all parts of the country, have through their shared efforts created a major force in the American, indeed, international discussion about urbanism.

Moreover, as Thomas Bender points out, trying to recapture community by imputing it to locality-based social activity, regardless of the quality of human relationships, is misleading. And, "if community is defined as a colonial New England town"[42] or as some other nostalgic vision of small town America, as the New Urbanists do, "then the prospect for community today is indeed dim."[42] It trivializes the complex and sensitive mix of social and cultural practices and attitudes that go into making a community and it assumes that community should be or must be place-based. What few studies of New Urbanist developments there are suggest that community is no more likely to develop there than in other types of developments and urban and suburban places.[43]

Even where community is created, it may not always be the cure for urban problems. It might be useful in a time of increasing fragmentation, conflict, and a fast growing dual economy, to ask whether creating small, well-designed places built around their own commercial and social center, whether in the urban core or periphery, is the best way to deal with our urban condition. This is especially important as evermore community groups are beginning to reach out for more citywide strategic planning rather than mere community based development. The need for ties between communities is growing in a world in which bigness at the corporate and political level is growing.

New Urbanist design militates against the notion of broad-based community alliances. Even the way they visualize their developments suggests a fully bounded and singular community that is not represented as part of the wider world. This is unlike the representations, for example, of neighborhood design by such as Clarence Perry, where the neighborhood is represented as part of an almost infinite urban region. Moreover, so many New Urbanist designs, if they are not gated, have monumental entrances, clearly demarcating their separation from the urban context that surrounds them. If boundaries set out who and what we include in our world and who are appearing to reach out to and encourage being with us, then New Urbanist designs and representations appear to suggest exclusivity.

Further, creating "urban villages," even if it were possible to do so, may create more problems in our cities than it would solve. There are questions about how best to ensure cultural and social diversity. Commentators and citizens alike argue about whether it is better to mix peoples of different ethnic and racial backgrounds or to work within social enclaves to maintain tradition. While most of us would criticize creating islands of class privilege and underclass misery, it is not obvious that by intermixing people of upper-middle-class backgrounds in the same place as the poor will either create community or overcome privilege. More crucially, creating such mix does not simply come as a result of good design principles. The minimum price for a house in Kentlands, outside Baltimore, is over $150,000 more than ten-times the median income of people in Baltimore.[44] In Seaside the prices are significantly higher. This does not augur well for the notion of economic diversity.

In Kentlands as well, the number of minority residents is significantly lower than for the region at large.[45]. Although Andreas Duany suggests that it is the aim of the New Urbanism to create diverse communities, there is little evidence that they have done so. He also has said that he is not interested in designing communities that will not be built. Thus diversity, would not only appear to threaten their market as Gerald Frug has argued,[46] it ironically runs counter to the American small town they yearn for, with its clear social divisions and class and racial segregation. It is of note that even as the New Urbanists call for class and economically mixed communities, they also brag that house prices in their developments are invariably higher than in surrounding developments *not* based on New Urbanist design.

Finally, the most telling criticism has been that the new Urbanist, like so many architectural practitioners and theorists before them, and especially the modernist who they scorn, are guilty of a kind of designer hubris. The New Urbanism, like modernism, can be accused of a kind of essentialism, in which all aspects of the complex and diverse urban world is reduced to a set of singular and authoritative principles summarized in a set of simple statements and strategic visual and verbal discourses. Even more arrogant in the view of critics is the belief that these principles and discourses are crucial, indeed determinative of better social and cultural practices: a questionable assumption at best. Finally, at its core is an authoritarianism similar to that of modernism. The New Urbanist belief that their design solutions are the one and only answer to the problems that beset us is not only a conceit but it is a dangerous conceit. In their unquestioned belief in their own good works, New Urbanists try to close off discussion of alternative visions of urbanism and urban design. They try to limit the range and diversity of the discourse about a subject that can only be strengthened by more, rather than fewer, potential approaches to what has become an increasingly intractable problem: what to do about our cities and suburbs.

Conclusion

The New Urbanists have raised many critical issues facing our cities, both publicly and successfully. They have, unlike so many of their postmodern brethren in design, not walked away and refused to face substantive problems to which design may be able to make a solution. They have not hid behind an apolitical relativism and elitist poetics but, rather, have been willing to join some of the most political and quotidian realities facing people today. Like the modernists, they are relevant and important, they are engaged and energetic. In many ways they have made discussions of urban design a crucial part of the larger discussion of whither the city, and urbanism. Their contribution to the debates about the city should not be underestimated or go unappreciated.

But the opportunity opened by the New Urbanists should not force all those concerned with the future of urbanism to get on their bandwagon. It should generate a critical debate about new solutions for what have been and still are seemingly intractable and complex problems. Designers should learn from their past that there are no singular solutions to our urban problems and that no single, one-dimensional approach to urban design can or should shoulder such a monumental and intractable task. Rather, the hubris of the New Urbanist, like the hubris of the modernists, should teach designers to approach the problems of our cities open to a range of ideas and approaches to urban problems, which will provide the basis for flexible, creative, and appropriate responses to the urban condition.

Notes

1 Kaliski, 1999, p. 69.
2 That is why this chapter presents no project illustrations.
3 Quoted in Andersen, 2001, p. 102.
4 Robbins, 1997, p. 61.
5 Krieger, 1991, p. 119.
6 Southworth, 1997, p. 43.
7 Wright, 1981, p. xv.
8 See F. Engels, 1958,
9 Kingsley, 1880, p. 187.
10 For an insightful overview of their work see Peter Hall, 1988.
11 Krieger, 1991, p. 12
12 See Miles Glendinning and Stefan Muthesius, 1994.
13 Perry, 1929, pp. 31–32.
14 For an elucidating discussion of the street in design thinking and practice, see Vidler.
15 See Glendinning, 1994, for a discussion of the Smithson's notion of streets.
16 Duany, 1997, p. 48.
17 Dutton, 2000, p. 31.
18 Bothwell, 2000, p. 51.
19 See James Kunstler, 1993, for an energetic, and at times even vitriolic, polemic against the American city and suburb and its design.
20 Duany and Plater-Zybeck, 1992, p. 28.
21 See Duany and Plater-Zybeck, 1992.
22 Calthorpe, 2000, p. 15.
23 *Charter of New Urbanism*, 2000, p. 122.
24 Solomon, 2000, p. 123.
25 Lennertz, 1991, p. 21.
26 It is discussed and reproduced in Dutton, 2000.
27 Recently, Andres Duany has introduced a new set of coding procedures for the whole urban region, although not in time for analysis for this chapter. See Duany and Talen, 2002.
28 Kaliski, 1999, p. 70.

29 Norquist, 1998.
30 MacCannell, 1999, p. 109.
31 For a discussion of this effort, see Vidler, 1978.
32 Donald, 1997, p. 182.
33 Harvey, 1996, p. 424.
34 The discussion that follows borrows heavily from a brilliant discussion of public space by Zygmunt Bauman, 1999.
35 Bauman, 1999, p. 17.
36 Quoted in MacCannell, 1999, p. 112.
37 For example, see Robbins, 1998, from which much of what follows is taken.
38 Urban Land Institute, 1985.
39 Cervero, 1996.
40 Scully, 1994.
41 Harvey, 2000, p. 171.
42 Bender, 1982, p. 4.
43 For discussions of the extent to which New Urbanism leads to community, see B. Andersen, D. Frantz and C. Collins, A. Ross, among others. For a more detailed analysis of community and design see Robbins, 2000.
44 Harvey, 2000.
45 Andersen, 2001.
46 Frug, 1997.

Chapter 12

The Imaginary Real World of CyberCities

M. Christine Boyer

In the mental geography of architectural theorists, an affinity is often expressed between science-fiction narratives and contemporary cities.[1] This attraction involves speculating on how the possible worlds of artificial intelligence and cyberspace might affect the material reality of design, conceptual models of space, and architectural or urban intuitions. Since the new informational network, the computer matrix called cyberspace, is commonly defined as if it were a huge megalopolis without a center, both a city of sprawl and an urban jungle, we have to ask, what do these analogies do?[2] What does it mean for Los Angeles to be simultaneously offered as the visualization of cyberspace and promoted as the prototypical posturban metropolis (or perhaps *meta-polis*, a loose configuration of 66 nodes tied together by an elaborate freeway system where the foot on the gas pedal replaces the pedestrian's step on the path)? From the moment in 1984 that William Gibson first announced in *Neuromancer* that cyberspace looks like Los Angeles seen at night from 5000 feet in the air, what has this predilection for drawing parallels between the virtual space of computer networks and the posturban places of disorder and decay really expressed?[3] This unwieldy mixture of cyberspace and urban dystopia – which I call CyberCities – turns the reality of time and place into an imaginary matrix of computer nets linking together electronically distant places around the globe and communicating multilinearly and nonsequentially with vast assemblages of information stored as electronic codes. What does it signify that this electronic imagery generates a unique mental ordering that seems to parallel rather than represent reality? What significant effects result from the fact that the textual universes of postmodern accounts conjure up immaterial and fictional worlds that disavow any link with material reality, any connectivity with a shared community? It is to attempt an answer to these questions of the imaginary real world of information, to search for the meaning of CyberCities affected by the logics of computers and cyberspace, that I offer this account.

Most science-fiction descriptions of CyberCities assume or explicitly state that a profound mutation last taken place entailing a transformation from the Machine City of modernism to the Informational City of postmodernism. So it is said, this transformation displaces the Western space of geometry, of work of the road, the building, the machine, with new forms of diagramming, bar graphs, spreadsheets, matrices, and networks expressive of "a new etherealization of geography" in which the principles of ordinary space and time are being tampered with beyond recognition.[4] This matrix appears to be a metaspace, or hyperspace, superimposed above the level of reality. It is a space in which reality is deferred from the screen to the memory bank, to the video disk, to imaginary networks. Or perhaps a better analogy for the computer matrix of disrupted space and time is the audio-visual jumps and leaps – the blank spaces, arbitrary sound bites, and fragmented images – achieved by the viewer of cable television who, remote control in hand, flips through an array of television programs that never coalesces into a single knowable order.

If a transformation from the machine to the computer has taken place, even if it affects only the imaginary, we need to question what has been transformed and what these changes affect with respect to architecture in the city, for the imaginary and the artistic are closely aligned. As one cyberspace advocate, Michael Heim, reminds us, artistic and technological fascination are linked: "With an electronic infrastructure, the dream of perfect FORMS becomes the dream of inFORMation. Filtered through the computer matrix, all reality becomes patterns of information. . . . Further, the erotic–generative source of formal idealism becomes subject to the laws of information management."[5] Consequently, the absorption of architectural theory and architectural fascination into the language of computers – and I am not referring here to CAD systems but to the theory of information science and all the science-fiction imaginaries it seems to invoke – may make a categorical mistake: for one side of the equation in CyberCity is immaterial, while the other remains material; one side of the analogy is about the construction of information networks, the other about the construction of space. Indeed, this confusion of categories may undermine many of our postmodern architectural theories as they are applied to architecture in the city.

The machine city

Like the computer of CyberCity and the postmodern, the machine of the Machine City is ingrained in the way we represent and imagine (or have represented and imagined) the modern city. Metaphors of the Machine City linked to representations of and reflecting attitudes toward modernity and the metropolis at the turn of the twentieth century come easily to mind. Calvin Coolidge seemed to encapsulate the idolization of the machine age when he proclaimed, "The man who builds a factory builds a temple. The man who works there worships there."[6] The metropolis was believed to be an inorganic and fabricated environment, the product of mathematics and the creation of the engineer. Thus we find, for example, Ludwig Meidner in "Directions for Painting Images of the Metropolis" advising the artist of 1914 to pay attention to "tumultuous streets, the elegance of iron suspension bridges, the gasometers, . . . the howling colors of the autobuses and express locomotives, the rolling telephone wires, the harlequinade of the advertisement pillars."[7] And before long the dynamics of motion in the big city, as well as the visual juxtaposition of disparate elements (graphics, musical rhythms, typography, and photography) used to create picture poems, were captured by one of the machines of the twentieth century: the movie camera. Laszlo Moholy-Nagy explained in his fourteen-page film script for *Dynamics of the Metropolis* of 1921–22 that there were to be shots of construction sites from below, from above, from diagonal views, from revolving cranes, shots of the flashing letters of electric advertisements, and shots filmed from racing automobiles and moving trains, to set up the dynamic tempo of the city. Although Moholy-Nagy's script was never produced as a film, it seems to have reached fruition in William Ruttmann's *Berlin: A Symphony of the City* of 1929.

Now the Machine City of modernism, far from being only liberating and celebratory, also embodied a darker side: the mechanisms of discipline and the architectural spaces of enclosure that Michel Foucault has so brilliantly described – the asylum, the prison, the factory, the school, and the home. If subjects were once controlled through dramaturgical displays of might and ceremonies of exaggerated torture, from which could be deduced the sovereign's authority to appropriate wealth, taxes, goods, services, and life itself, then, beginning in the late eighteenth century, this power was transformed into a power to ensure, maintain, and develop the life of a social body, which, to this end, used space and architecture as its instruments of normalization.[8] Discipline, or the self-construction of the individual, became the most efficacious instrument of power deployed by these spaces of enclosure. Here the acts of comparing, contrasting, and categorizing were organizational relations that supported new disciplinary procedures; for the individual was forced constantly to stand in relation to the established norm, and this self-comparison determined the range of deviations and diversions to be brought under control. Thus the machine-like norm established authority over an individual without any external references to a sovereign's might.[9]

Certainly, we can extend this analogy to the Machine City, for disciplinary control proceeds by distributing bodies/uses in space, allocating each individual/function to a cellular partition, and creating an efficient machine out of its analytical spatial arrangement. In becoming a target of disciplinary control, the city offered up new forms of knowledge: its disciplinary methodologies came to describe an anatomy of detail. An ideal architectural model was conceived as well to house this disciplinary system, an architecture that would allow for the continuous operation of surveillance. A network of urban observatories bent the space of the city to a set of norms that both established the line of horizontal and comparative and surveyed the movement of each individual and every cellular space. So arose at the end of the nineteenth century the process of city planning.[10]

CyberCities

Gilles Deleuze has suggested recently that Foucault's spaces of enclosure are increasingly placed in crisis.[11] Thus the home, the factory, the school, the deindustrialized city, and certainly the process of city planning, are in various stages of dissolution, reflective of the disciplinary breakdown that CyberCities entail. So, Deleuze maintains, disciplinary societies that have molded behavior are giving way to numerical societies of modulating control facilitated by computer technology. From machines of production that require a disciplined labor force and an efficiently planned and organized city, we have evolved into a space of flows defined by worldwide networks of computers. This free-floating membrane of connectivity and control encircles the globe in ultrarapid fashion, enabling a new economic order of multinational corporations to arise. In these societies, control acts like a sieve whose mesh transmutes from point to point, undulating and constantly at work. The code, not the norm, becomes the important device; the password rather than the watchword now provides or inhibits access.

In addition, the coded figure of multinational corporations pulls an agoristic market mentality of competition, rivalry, and contests in its wake, conquering through colonization, specialization, and the deformable and transformable decisions that computer tracking allows. A market mentality of short-term advantages and high turnover rates overtakes any long-range and continuous planning endeavors. In computer-led societies, jamming, viruses, piracy, and corruption replace the machine-age dangers of entropy and sabotage. We are, if we accept Deleuze's description, at the beginning of the sociotechnological revolutions and dispersed systems of domination that societies of control comprise.

Now clearly the computer matrix is just a metaphor for patterns of information, a tool for examining our contemporary reality in which electronic machinery dominates our imagination. Or is it? For it seems increasingly difficult to erase imaginary forms from our feelings about reality. As Heim claims in "The Erotic Ontology of Cyberspace," the matrix holds out a promise of connectivity that reality denies: the technologies of networking through on-line communication, electronic mail, or news groups offer each unit at his or her terminal a way to counter urban isolation and alienation. Even though "new communities" are formed, Heim does acknowledge the dark side to networking: it operates through stand-ins of ourselves, representations in which we can lose our humanity, or hide our identity, and thus it may inspire an amoral indifference to human relations. "As on-line culture grows geometrically," Heim allows, "the sense of community diminishes."[12] Of course, human unity and community are totalizations that lie among the major conceptual fault lines that CyberCities display.

But let us return to the city; that is, if we can turn off the console and walk into the physical richness and energies of reality's world, if we can leave behind our metaphors of simulated connectivity and the synthetic world of the computer matrix that has supposedly supplanted physical space. It is curious that just as CyberCities narrate the dematerialization of physical space and chronological time, within postmodern criticism, "space" has become a dominant issue. Edward Soja in *Postmodern Geographies*, relates how the nineteenth century's affair with progress, which valued time over space, allowed space to be used as a veil drawn over the surface, hiding things from us. And David Harvey in *The Condition of Postmodernity* speaks of how space–time compressions, each revolution in communication technology causing an annihilation of space by time, produced crises of representation. While Fredric Jameson notes in *Postmodernism, or, The Cultural Logic of Late Capitalism* that the cultural conditions of postmodernity have created the need for cognitive maps to link our ideological positions with our imaginations and hence enable social transformations to take place.[13] In all three accounts, the postmodern body is surrounded by and bombarded with incoherent fragments of space and time. For we seem in CyberCity to be perpetually reflected from glass curtain walls and continuously in motion, whether driving the freeways, shopping at the mall, or pushing carts through supermarket aisles. And it has been argued that electronic telecommunications have so reformulated our perception of space and time that we experience a loss of spatial boundaries, of spatial distinctions. All spaces begin to look alike and implode into an undifferentiated continuum, while time is reduced to obsessive–compulsive repetitions. As a result, we are unable to map our contemporary terrain, to envision space and representational forms, and thus to weave things together, to conclude, to act.

Increasingly, in postmodernist criticism, as spaces of modernist enclosure are placed in crisis, there has occurred instead a massive restructuring of our perception of space and time to the point where we have assumed the nonlinear vision of a computer matrix full of ruptures, breaks, and discontinuities. Might our postmodern fixation on shifting positions in space and time and our common pronouncements of the disappearing or invisible city mask deeper anxieties and ambivalent negations within the metropolitan core? At the same moment that computational connectivity holds out the promise of nonhierarchical, multicentered, open-ended forms defining a "new community," voices from other times and different spaces are beginning to emerge and disturb the supposed unity. Is the gesture of electronic connectivity anything other than an attempt to contain contested terrains and to absorb excluded parts, thereby allowing the whole to reorganize without challenging its fundamental assumptions?

Lag-time places

In the late twentieth century unknown and threatening territories lie within the center, inside the boundaries of the metropolis where there are many lag-times, temporal breaks in the imaginary matrix, and areas of forced delay put on hold in the process of postmodernization.[14] These partitions, cuts, and interruptions in the urban imaginary allow us to deny our complicity in the making of distinctions between the well-designed nodes of the matrix and the blank in-between places of nobody's concern. Disavowed, overlooked, marginalized, left out of our accounts, these in-between spaces, the inexpressible, the incomplete, the unattended, the "etc." and the ". . ." are the center's truly invisible places.[15]

To attend to a few of these lag-times and spatial gaps within our metropolitan narrations, to note the margins and paradoxes of our postmodernity, we have only to turn to the *New York Times*.

> 5 November 1991: To visit Mott Haven [a neighborhood of some fifty thousand people around East 138th Street] – and there are Mott Havens in most large American cities these days – is to discover a world apart. Here, poverty cuts deeper than the lack of

> money, the lack of health care, the abundance of drugs. This gray place is largely bereft of many of the threads that knit other very poor neighborhoods together: strong tenant organization, powerful community groups, charismatic leadership, even a safe playground. The strongest neighborhood bind is its struggle with hardship. 'We're like the forgotten city.'[16]
>
> 26 April 1992: José Delgado lingered at the doorstep of a decaying South Bronx apartment building last week watching Mayor David N. Dinkins promise millions of dollars in development projects. After a while the politicians dispersed. The television cameras were packed up. The onlookers dribbled away. But Mr. Delgado remains, as he always does. 'Every time they want to be elected they come here,' said the forty-one-year-old building superintendent. 'They say they are going to do things to fix the neighborhood, but it's been like this since 1972.'[17]

These lag-time narrations, and there are numerous others, reveal how the imaginary matrix performs spatial and temporal disjunctions that enable us to think of city centers as if they were naturally bipolar places of uneven development rather than effects of a willful dismemberment that sites certain lives and places outside of, and only sometimes beside, the main events of contemporary cities.[18] It is this splitting that the binary logic of the computer matrix allows us to achieve with relative ease. Such an arrangement, for example, provides Paul Virilio with his images of the disappearing city – where chronological topographies replace constructed geographical space, where immaterial electronic broadcast emissions decompose and eradicate a sense of place. Virilio's city has lost its form except as a connector point or airport, as a membrane or computer terminal; this is a two-dimensional Flatland in which the city can vanish. Obviously, Virilio's position is overdetermined by the binary coding and switching logic of computer technology: the logical +/–, 0/1, on/off of electronic pulses and, hence, the appearance/disappearance of the city. But the point here is that this architectural theory ignores our involvement in the shaping of space, in the production of lag-time places and temporal disjunctions.

Agoric systems

The logic of computers engenders more than binary modes of thought. There is also within connectionist systems an interest in the capacity of machines to learn. Computer learning consists of the shifting of internal linkages (that is, the production of new representations) among units distributed throughout the network as they interact with the world/context and adapt to patterns that it presents.[19] In the attempt to develop expert systems, moreover, "the goal is to develop computer-implemented rule systems that can replicate aspects of the reasoning of humans who perform the function in an expert fashion." Such rules, usually obtained through interviews, are then encoded in a computer program.[20]

Returning to the agoristics of Deleuze's societies of control, Manuel De Landa explains in *War in the Age of Intelligent Machines* that the decentralization of intelligent computer networks around the globe introduces a problematic paradox, since they spawn "independent software objects," known as "demons," which may lie beyond the network's control. Demons operating within the membrane of global networks, De Landa proclaims, already display a tendency to form societies that resemble insect communities or economic markets:

> Independent software objects will soon begin to constitute even more complex computational societies in which demons trade with one another, bid and compete for resources, seed and spawn processes spontaneously and so on. The biosphere . . . is pregnant with singularities that spontaneously give rise to processes of self-organization. Similarly, the portion of the 'mechanosphere' constituted by computer networks, once it has crossed a certain critical point of connectivity, begins to be inhabited by symmetry-breaking singularities, which give rise to emergent properties in the system. These systems "can encourage the development of intelligent [software] objects, but there is a sense in which these systems themselves will be intelligent."[21]

In this scenario, the agoric, or marketlike, computer system takes on a life of its own. We seem entrapped within a giant machine from which we can never escape, a fear exploited by the best and worst of science fiction. Or, expressive of yet another postmodern narrative, we find ourselves in the nihilistic and deterministic terrain of Jean Baudrillard, where the computer "code is the unseen, 'ob-scene' vehicle by which that power [the power of corporations] moves toward global control, toward the profitable creation and regimation of ever more sign-oriented, media-bound, simulated and simulationist cultures."[22] But even a cursory look at computer literature reminds me that way back in 1959 Oliver Selfridge, searching for a means of pattern recognition for handwritten letters of the alphabet, came up with a theoretical model he called Pandemonium. "Cognitive demons" acting in parallel without attention to one another would each eventually "shout out" its judgment of what letter had been presented to it. A "decision demon" would then identify the letter based on which demon shouted the loudest. For each cognitive demon was, in its turn, responding to lower-order "feature demons," and the greater the number of features represented by the letter, the louder the demon could shout. In other words, the computer field is alive with attempts to develop network models of parallel processors trying to simulate cognitive processes.[23] Now what does this development of "smart computers" – able to learn from their environment, to plan problem-solving strategies at increasingly varied levels of complexity, and even to eliminate irrelevant details from consideration as they become endowed with a relentless common sense – I repeat, what does this have to do with the city and architecture?

Mini–max strategies

To begin with, we need to acknowledge that the history of computers has, from its inception, been deeply affected by military objectives, and this has tainted its logic and modes of operations. The paradigmatic decisionistic model is the Prisoner's Dilemma, a game articulated by John von Neumann that guided our military policy throughout the Cold War and still guides our corporate decision processes.[24] Every graduate business school offers a course in the theory of games – not intended for leisure-time sports. The purpose is rather to teach competitors how to minimize their maximum losses. Consequently, a proconflict/anticooperation bias is worked into the model. Need we be reminded that in the Cold War neither the Soviet Union nor the United States ever made a gesture of unilateral disarmament? – Instead, losses were supposedly minimized by supporting nuclear build-up. We can apply this Cold War rhetoric of chance and risk to the city: for, indeed, corporate adversarial politics, the agoristics of the market, affects the space of the city.

Look at New York City today and you will see von Neumann's "mini–max" logic at work. To maximize one's unilateral private gains at the expense of the collective good appears to be the rational move. I need only mention the twenty or so "business improvement districts" (BIDs) that in the last decade have pockmarked the city with privatized protected zones. These are commercial and business areas where property owners have agreed to assess themselves at a rate higher than the city's in order to generate funds to improve their local environment in the face of the disintegration of the whole. BIDs usually disperse their collective money to private security forces, private sanitation collection companies, or street and sign beautification programs.[25] However lucrative their assessments may be, it is hard to conceive how the problems of drugs, homelessness, and security can be treated as issues of boundary maintenance, for they permeate the city; minimizing the maximum risks of doing business in one area simply pushes the problems elsewhere. Or another example of these struggles can be found in the recent complaints from some builders that New York City has a faulty economic-development policy. Since 1976 the city has tried to form incentive packages through tax breaks and credits that would lure developers to the outer boroughs or above Ninety-sixth Street in Manhattan. As a consequence, downtown Brooklyn has experienced a surge of new development. Now, however, during economic recession, this policy is being called misguided because it was pursued to the detriment of Manhattan – the borough that must remain the epicenter of commerce if maximum losses are to be minimized.[26]

The city of artifice

Another aspect of the logic of computer mathematics applied to the city is the art of spatial and temporal ordering, what we might call the creation of the City of Artifice. As Margorie Perloff points out in *Radical Artifice*, our word processors and electronic devices have taught us to snip, to sort, to cut, to edit, to rearrange our data, our word-processed text, our VCR tapes, until they have become constructed artifices. In Perloff's domain of poetry, she finds that language has given way to a medium that, to quote Charles Bernstein, is "constructed, rule-governed, everywhere circumscribed by grammar and syntax, chosen vocabulary: designed, manipulated, picked, programed, organized, and so an artifice, artifact – monadic, solipsistic, homemade, manufactured, mechanized, formulaic, willful."[27] Perloff recounts how artifices have leaped off the page and moved into the public realm; in the poetics of greeting cards, in ingenious advertisements, in the sign inflection of billboards.[28] Such powerful images challenge the artist to move beyond mere duplication. Since images are now sold by corporations, Perloff argues, the poetic image has become problematic – as has the architectural image as well. "Given the sophisticated print media, computer graphics, signpost and advertising formats of our culture, all writing – and certainly all poetic writing – is inevitably 'seen' as well as 'seen through' or heard."[29] To understand the latter not as phonemic but as ink on the page is to contest the status of language as a bearer of uncontaminated meaning.[30]

And so we might say of the spaces of the city. In spite of all we may have learned from the semiotics of Las Vegas, pop architecture of the late sixties and seventies merely duplicated the commercial artifice, raising it to the level of high art. If we turn to our cities of the seventies and eighties, is it surprising to find their public spaces structured as if a labyrinthine network were thrown over their surface? These urban matrices become an aggregate of atomistic detail; for, indeed, the urban artifice valorizes the local, the regional, the particular – it becomes an array of historical and stylistic details and Wordsworthian "spots of time."

Returning to New York City, I would recommend a walk through South Street Seaport, Battery Park City, Times Square, the large historic districts of the Upper East Side, the Upper West Side, Greenwich Village, and Ladies Mile to examine the artifice at work. Here the nodes of the urban matrix have become cutouts of local details, controlled by design codes, historic-district regulations, and contextual zoning ordinances. In-between, of course, plenty of spaces are overlooked, left unimproved, dropped out of the transforming grid – those numerous lag-time spaces explored above. For detail owes its privileged status, as Freud proclaimed, to the primary process of displacement.[31]

Warring against totalities

The matrix of urban space, clearly an artifice with all of its contrived and manipulated details, positions itself in war against the reality of the city; it imposes itself as a gesture against totalities, as a recognition that harmony of life can never be achieved. Its commitment is to the struggle, to the resistance, to us versus them, and in this sense it is radically antiurban and highly postmodern. Modernism, by contrast, held artifice to be its enemy, searching for what Ezra Pound called "good art . . . that bears true witness, . . . the art that is most precise," in opposition to "bad art" that "is inaccurate art, . . . art that makes false reports."[32] Modernists intended images, both visual and verbal, to be precise and clear analogies of reality; postmodernists, on the other hand, discredit the use of imagery because contemporary culture is saturated with manipulated, commercialized signs designed and fabricated by product advertisers.[33] Confronted with these powerful and complex images, poetic discourse is challenged, in Perloff's words, "to deconstruct rather than to duplicate them. They prompt what has become an ongoing, indeed a necessary dialectic between the simulacrum and its other, a dialectic no longer between the image and the real, as early modernists construed it, but between the word and the image."[34]

So we find that on the edge of the twenty-first century our technological fascination with computers merges with our artistic conceptualizations of multivalent assemblages in which the individual, the collectivity, and the data set play separate parts. Yet how does the outside, the material world, penetrate and infuse the images and representations of this imaginary assemblage? How, in particular, is the community, the polis, the center allowed to inform our position? And why, precisely, is our contemporary time so afraid of centering devices, why do we speak so often of invisible cities, the disappearing, deindustrialized, disfigured, and decentered city? What is this fearful center but a point of concentration or gravity that holds together a verbal sequence and gives meaning to utterances? Centering is both recursive and precursive, helping to give order to what proceeded and to what will follow.[35] It is the sign we read as we enter the outskirts of every European metropolis, unerringly pointing the way "to the center." In the Western world, centering events or images are understood symbolically. Because they often mask the very powers that center a discourse and are feared for their potential enslavements, they demand interpretation and decipherment.

Postmodern critics, in particular, think that the notion of unity, totality, or "center" is an artifice – an arbitrarily constructed narrative whose implicit relationships can no longer be accepted as true or retain a stable significance. Lyotard tells us that "we have paid a high enough price for the nostalgia of the whole and one, for the reconciliation of the concept and the sensible, of transparent and communicable experience. . . . Let us [instead] wage war on totality, let us be witness of the unpresentable, let us activate the difference."[36] Eventually, however, we must come full circle to this decentering game of postmodernism and ask, in our war against all totalities and our contemporary discontent, just what is it that we affirm? We have, in turn, deconstructed the promise of the Enlightenment, the logocentrisms of Western discourse, the purposive, rational action systems of science and technology, the process of city planning, Marxism, and so on. Of course, architecture and the city are among postmodernism's major structures of ambivalence. The polis – the Greek city – was the center of Western communal life based on the now-faulty assumption of a common purpose and common consensus and an unmediated harmony and unity of all human life. In our postmodern deconstruction of totalizations, we think we have reinstated freedom of choice and enabled the voice of alterity to rise, but clearly at the cost of community.[37]

When Karl Scheffler, a member of the Deutscher Werkbund, confronted the reality of the metropolis in the early 1900s, he saw that the city was no longer a closed organism held together by small-scaled patriarchal groups in which "every man could recognize the whole, and [thus] . . . each took part in the prosperity of a whole on which one's own prosperity depended." The metropolis was devoid of a "spirit of community," was a mere accidental place of residence.[38] The move to the city was, then, a voyage away from home and toward the unknown. And once embarked on this voyage, there was no promise of a safe return, for the urge to travel was simultaneously a gesture that abandoned the security of home.[39] Consider how Kafka in 1912 used this motif of travel in his first novel, *Der Verschollen* (the missing ones, as in passengers missing at sea), written about New York although he had never been to the city.

"Traffic" is Kafka's metaphor for the transitory nature of things experienced in the metropolis – not just the comings and goings of subway trains and automobiles and the ebb and flow of crowds as they follow their daily rhythms, but also changes in fashions and architectural styles, and the fragmentary, illusory quality of perception itself. Each chapter is organized around a different mode of travel that propels the hero into a never-ending succession of new circumstances. Complex traffic patterns of New York City streets give way to pedestrians and automobiles along the highway, which are supplanted by vertical movements of elevators and sexual traffic, which finally lead into the subway and toward the endless expanse of the American continent. New York and America are landscapes without beginning or end, labyrinths of accident, disorder, and uncertainty in which the images of the city are continually destabilized, dematerialized, and erased, landscapes from which the protagonist is constantly expelled and forced to move on.[40]

Again we can draw parallels between the stabilities of home, the familiar enclosure, and the open-ended and rootless metropolis that defies connectivity and belonging. For Kafka's narrative opens as the hero is banished from his family for having fathered an illegitimate child; he is exiled to a world without a past and without a center, "a world of changing appearances, unstable impressions, accident, and death: a world of 'traffic' " that will not stand still and is oblivious to his presence.[41] Modernism set itself the task of describing these fragmented experiences of the metropolis, trying to close the gap between the individual and his environment, to recenter and reconstruct the city until it formed an organic whole. The city was a place of immigration and estrangement, yet simultaneously a register through which passed a dynamic array of local styles, cultures, and languages. Modernist artistic expression arose out of and through this metropolitan experience.[42]

To take up a postmodern narrative of travel, we need only turn to Italo Calvino's *Invisible Cities*. "Traveling," Calvino's Marco Polo reveals, "you realize that differences are lost: each city takes to resembling all cities, places exchange their form, order, distances, a shapeless dust could invade the continents."[43] The type of city is uniform, the detailed variations endless. Hence every city must be read in quotation marks, its representation excessive and privileged: we have to learn what is not present in "the city" and what this absence might mean. *Invisible Cities* is structured as a systematic artifice, a numerical set: there are fifty-five cities in all, five cities allocated to each of eleven different categories. The idea of city is fractured by this serial artifice, being influenced retroactively by the definition of each element in the set. As Marco Polo claims, "I will put together, piece by piece, the perfect city, made of fragments mixed with the rest, of instants separated by intervals discontinuous in space and time, now scattered, now more condensed, you must not believe the search for it can stop."[44]

Calvino's *Invisible Cities* bears a similarity to travel in the informational matrix of CyberCity, where borders are crossed with the help of a hypermedia navigator who guides the traveler in riding, traversing, browsing, playing the links between different texts, images, words, and graphs, moving across the grid of the electronic screen, establishing new relationships in unpredictable ways. Marcos Novak describes traveling through this hypertext:

> Every paragraph an idea, every idea an image, every image an index, indices strung together along dimensions of my choosing, and I travel through them, sometimes with them, sometimes across them. I produce new sense, nonsense, and nuisance by combination and variation, and I follow the scent of a quality through sand dunes of information. Hints of an attribute attach themselves to my sensors and guide me past the irrelevant, into the company of the important; or I choose to browse the unfamiliar and tumble through volumes and volumes of knowledge still in the making.[45]

Can this thrill of constantly traveling on into the unknown network of information without a centered focus or bounded domain make us critically aware of how abstract the matrix of CyberCity is and how far from reality it lies? The relays of references, the inversion of orders of precedence, the endless lists and enumeration of texts all present the chaotic effects of randomness and indeterminacy generating neither options nor choices. Being constantly on the move in order to escape the repressive machines of disciplinary societies or to exploit fully the uncertain voyages of complexities in societies of control offers us no foundation on which to stand, to criticize, to remember the past and plan the future.

The rhetoric of indeterminacy

So let us now analyze a text that prompted this entire discussion, Brian Boigon and Sanford Kwinter's "Manual for 5 Appliances in the Alphabetical City: A Pedagogical Text" published in *Assemblage* 15. Let us ask, What can these appliances do? Apparently, the Alphabetical City was a studio room in an architectural school open around the clock, an ideal space in which, to quote the authors, "every action and intervention . . . must be recorded in a logbook that will be present at all times." This studio was a "form of publishing, social life, billboard, historical inscription, archive"; it was a happening, a situation, a drift and *dérive*, both a collective memory and a "diagram of every fleeting moment."[46] The manual, of course, is the familiar tool kit, the ABC instructional book, for constructing the Alphabetical City. But far from being radically disruptive, this manual actually replicates disciplinary control: a set of orders and commands prescribed in military tones – "you are required," "we will be ruthless in our pedagogical approach" – reveals how embedded in decision controls the images of CyberCity can be. The mere reference to "pedagogy" as opposed to "performance" is sufficient to implicate these authors in replicating the deferential position of student to teacher, even though they disavow the power of authority.[47]

Borrowing from Le Corbusier, Boigon and Kwinter transform his five points of architecture into the five appliances of time, screen, sleep, information, and site/domain. Quite clearly, these appliances reflect a shift from the Machine City of modernism to the CyberCity of postmodernism, where theoretical architecture, the authors note, become "diagrammatical acts": radical machines or appliances internalizing an abstract mechanism (a computer code or program) for producing (in unspecified ways) political and social change. Memories of Le Corbusier's claim of "architecture or revolution" simply bounce off of their text, although in highly indeterminate ways. Of these radical appliances, however, it is probably "sleep" that will turn on itself – allowing the blank spaces of the contemporary city, the unknown lag-time sites outside of the computer mesh, the dream spaces of nightmares and repressed fantasies, to make their appearance as slips of meaning and translation.

Boigon and Kwinter claim that even "if the contemporary city has undergone a partial dismantling of its (traditional) spatial unity as well as a radical deployment of what used to be called 'time,' this does not necessarily imply that it 'expresses' any less coherently the regime silently working within it. . . . The Alphabetical City corresponds less to a formed and distinct object than to a specific *regime* (of power, of effects) that currently, or increasingly, inhabits the social field."[45] Now if we understand the mutations that coincide with the shift to CyberCity, these statements about regimes of disciplinary control appear to be misplaced, or exceedingly nihilistic, when their social fields are left indeterminate, never discussed or presented with any specificity. The open-ended networks of the Alphabetical City allow nomadic thought to skid across the computer matrix, reversing hierarchical order and closed representations wherever it may range. But Boigon and Kwinter never question who might control the programming, with what values, or to what ends, and how the monad can be manipulated at his or her isolated computer terminal. Nor do they ask what is being represented in the imaginary space of the network removed from the public sphere. For their narcotics are indeterminacy and iterability eliding criticism and commitment.

Manifestly, this manual desires to place itself among the *avant-garde* of architecture, for what does this Alphabetical City do but mimic the role of *avant-garde* texts by generating more discourse around it? Look at the epitaph of the demolished Alphabetical City: it lasted 1008 hours, its analysis filled 61 pages of logbook and a 92-page document, it generated a case of arson, several acts of vandalism, an article in *Assemblage*, and, following this publicity campaign, I would add perhaps more studio jobs for the two writers, this paper, some gossip. In other words, like a good *avant-garde* work of art it generated discourse to be distributed, bought, and consumed. The point being that architecture in the last two decades has become an important discursive event with weekly, if not daily, coverage in the print media, documentary films on television, and background advertisements for life-style consumer items. The value of an architectural work seems to lie in its ability to generate a discourse around itself: it is the claim that we need only care for our project until it has been photographed because at that moment it has been inserted into the endless circulation of cultural signs. Confusion over whether a theoretical discourse is productive or constraining, liberating or controlling, is one of the ways it sustains itself. Paul Mann has written in *The Theory – Death of the Avant-Garde* that

> . . . discourse thrives on negations, revisions, resyntheses and resublimitations: more texts can be produced, more claims and counterclaims, more theses and antitheses; vast researches and polemics sponsored by just such confusions as these. But not forever: this indeterminate movement of alignments and misalignments, the uncertainty of both Left and Right about the proper and plausible role of art, is acted out in the avant-garde until it is only theater, only a representation, and hence absorbed by the problematics of representation as such.[49]

The *avant-garde*'s position is an antiposition, a theoretical discourse constrained to relate to a dominant discourse that it rejects but cannot transcend. Its role is to articulate polarities: between innovation/tradition, destruction/creation, movement/stability.[50] Futurist manifestos were the prototypical antigesture, being both for and against the metropolis, breaking the frame and being enframed. Returning to the text of "The Alphabetical City," we note in Boigon and Kwinter's manifesto the following: "Hypothesis: architecture is the name of a universal system of oppression (of what Foucault called the 'human multiplicity,' the undifferentiated mass of human flesh, thought, and desire). In this sense, its domain is the social and psychological control of the environment, including images, odors, weather, sexual practices, fantasies, documents, collective representations (but this also suggests a guerrilla architecture of subversion and resistance)."[51]

We do not have to go very far to know that we are in the worst of science fictions: battling against the closed world of architectural studios, the purisms of high art, the regimes of domination within the disciplinary spaces of the architectural school. As the authors tell us, we must abandon the architectural jury that is the "squadlike spectacle of the review," with its "fascist-style adjudication techniques."[52] In another antigesture of radical inversion, "drawing becomes an editing, selecting, or sampling process, a wreaking havoc with the pre-existing, overcoded, collective, social drawing."[53] And, of course, robotic and cynical design students accept that there is no returning home, no private internal space of retreat, for they are impelled into the world to engage with forces that are always drawing up a social diagram or messing with ours.[54] They have become "itinerant warriors continually on the move," "punk guerrillas" replete with computer viruses and jamming mechanisms admitted "through back channels" to subvert and eliminate.[55]

Architecture, we are told, "must be seen as a collector, servomechanism, or sensitive screen, monitoring the results of endless and still-unnamed experiments."[56] "A piece of architecture . . . may be defined not by how it appears but by *practices*: those that it partakes of and those that take place within it."[57] Let me deal with the effects of these indeterminacies that plague Boigon and Kwinter's text, for it is the intent of their studio to open architecture to adjacencies, to pollutants and impure practices, to affect transformation within the institutions of architecture and the city.

Far from being radically new, however, these are the encounters and coadaptations of forms, the maps and diagrams suggested by Foucault, or the machine phylum of Deleuze, where disconnected elements upon reaching a critical threshold are expected to cooperate to produce order out of chaos. They are reminiscent of El Lissitzky's Proun Room, which he believed would have a profound effect on architecture. Lissitzky defined the Proun as "the station where one changes from painting to architecture."[58] In his view, the Prounen were experiments in architectural design: documents, indices of the world to come, and theoretical models for the revolutionary reality that needed to be built.[59] Closer to our time, these assemblages are perhaps reminiscent of the exhibitions proposed by members of the Independent Group in England – "Parallel of Life and Art," organized by Peter Smithson, Alison Smithson, Eduardo Paolozzi, and Nigel Henderson in 1953, and "Man, Machine and Motion," organized by Richard Hamilton in 1955 – a nonhierarchical approach to imagery, mostly photographs, that attempted to wring a new way of seeing things out of unusual juxtapositions. As Moholy-Nagy noted in *Vision in Motion*, a photomontage of the 1920s wanted to set up a "concentrated gymnastic of the eye and brain to speed up the visual digestion and increase the range of associative relationships."[60]

These loose arrangements of associative materials, based on notions that contiguities breed connections, are also prevalent in computer networks that model cognitive processes.[61] Since computers have been the most important instrument to enable a new cartography to arise in weather forecasting, in the study of DNA, in the mapping of atomic surfaces and subatomic particles, and, especially, in the visual exploration of chaos theory, then why not hope this juxtaposition of masses of visual information and high-tech appliances will produce a new map for the city and architecture, a map that will describe nonrandom order suddenly appearing in the midst of seeming disorder? But the analogies wear thin – for arrays of information are not the same as knowledge. Information is merely data, devoid of an abstract processing framework that can make comparisons, draw connections, recognize exemplars, and know how to accomplish, to perform, certain things. The science-fiction world of smart computers taking over executive control has yet to arrive at the architectural school.

And this is why, in the end, I question the meaning of the Alphabetical City: its open-ended rhetoric masks what it literally means. Does it refer to Jean-Luc Godard's 1965 movie *Alphaville*, in which a megalomaniacal computer, Alpha 60, embodied the triumph of instrumental reasoning and dehumanized control systems? But this is hardly reality today, when the guerrilla tactics of PC hackers can easily subvert such mainframe controls. Might it refer instead to "Alphabyte Cities," imagistic video elements that are recombined and rearticulated electronically as if they were letters in the alphabet? Or does it refer to the finite and fixed alphabetical ordering that eliminates hierarchy and significance in the arrangement of words in a dictionary or entries in an encyclopedia? Clearly, the use of "Alphabetical City" presents a paradox, for has not Derrida argued that "alphabetic writing . . . is a restrictive definition that ties the broad range of marks, spatial articulations, gestures, and other inscriptions at work in human cultures too closely to the representation of speech, the oral/aural word"?[62] Therefore, have not Boigon and Kwinter, far from liberating us to achieve new levels of perception and new orders for the city, slotted us back into the imposed discourse and analysis implied by alphabetical writing?

To return to the analogies that computer matrices imply, I am reminded of Stephen Tyler's remark that "the matrix makes the shape that has shaped Western thought since the beginning of writing."[63] Be it in the mark of the cultivator or the grid of the city or the matrix that alphabetical language implies, it is the Western face imposed on the land. Here we might also note, albeit briefly, another paradox that Boigon and Kwinter's text interjects: they have transformed the primary generative device of modernist urbanism – the plan imposed on the land – into the generative body, "a manifold endlessly generating structure (that is, desire) on the run."[64] Indeed, postmodernism has seen an entire restructuring of the body/machine relationship, refiguring the subject with the advent of the hybrid – part animal, part machine – cyborg citizen who dwells in a postgendered "technological polis."[65]

We need to read Boigon and Kwinter's inscription and the entire postmodern discourse and cultivation of the "clean body" against the grain of Foucault's *History of Sexuality*, where he cleverly warned us that "the emphasis on the body should undoubtedly be linked to the process of growth and establishment of bourgeois hegemony: not, however, because of the market value assumed by labor capacity, but because of what the 'cultivation' of its own body could represent politically, economically, and historically for the present and the future of the bourgeoisie. . . . One understands why it [the bourgeoisie] took such a long time and was so unwilling to acknowledge that other classes had a body and a sex – precisely those classes it was exploiting."[66] Perhaps therein lies our real fascination with the computer, the binary logic of computer codes, the cyber-networks that hold out the hallucinatory promise of virtual connectivity, for the computer seems to be our age's clean, innocent machine, promising a synthetic world born pure from mathematics and not yet tainted by the dark disciplinary devices of our all-too-human making.[67] And, once again, we might observe that just when bodies of race and gender begin to emerge in the lag-time spaces of the city, we can transcend our anxieties, and thereby refuse their corporeal demands, in the hypermaterialistic synthetic connections of computer networks where the body, technology, and community are reduced to the hallucinatory metaphors of cyberspace.

So, finally, we have to note an odd juxtaposition between text and image: the appearance of an image of Louis Aragon's poem "Suicide" – which reads "A b c d e f/ g h i j k l/ m n o p q r/ s t u v w/ x y z" – inserted into the text of "The Alphabetical City" underscores the ultimate rhetorical paradox of our postmodern position. As we war against totalities, afraid of their prescriptions and overdeterminations, believing this liberates us from tyranny and oppression, we are driven on and on by negativity, by standing against, by not being for, until we reach a state of abjection. Abjection, as Julia Kristeva describes, is a narcissistic crisis – a revulsion that hurls us away from that which limits our being – a crisis caused by the breakdown of our objects, or appliances, of desire.[68] A narrative of failure, the Abject Machine equals the Alphabetical City, an architectural enclosure of non-sense signifying nothing at all. Let the cortège pass by!

Notes

1 Willis, 1989, pp. 47–70; Boigon and Kwinter, 1991, pp. 30–42: Benedikt, 1992.
2 Heim, 1992, p. 77.
3 Gibson, 1984, p. 51.
4 Benedikt, 1992, p. 22.
5 Heim, 1992, p. 65.
6 Lucic, 1991, p. 16.
7 Quoted in Haxthausen, 1990, p. 63.
8 Foucault, 1973, p. 136.
9 Ewald, 1992, pp. 169–175.
10 Boyer, 1983, p. 71
11 Deleuze, 1992, pp. 3–7.
12 Heim, 1992, p. 76.
13 Harvey, 1989; Soja, 1989; Jameson, 1991.
14 The ideas of lag-times and temporal breaks are taken from Bhaba, 1991, pp. 193–219.
15 Liu, 1990, pp. 75–113.
16 Dugger, 1991.
17 Mitchell, 1992, p. 32.
18 For an account of splitting cuts, or temporal breaks, embedded "in" modernity, see Bhaba, 1991. Bhaba suggests that the nonplace is the template for colonial space.
19 Bechtel and Abrahamsen, 1991, pp. 70, 127–129.
20 Bechtel and Abrahamsen, 1991, p. 155.
21 "Two extreme forms of organization are the command economy and the market economy. . . . The command model has frequently been considered more 'rational,' since it involves the visible application of reason to the economic problem as a whole. . . . In actuality, decentralized planning [of the market] is potentially more rational, since it involves more minds taking into account more total information. . . . One might try to assign machine resources to tasks through an operating system using fixed, general rules, but in large systems with heterogeneous hardware, this seems doomed to gross inefficiency. Knowledge of tradeoffs and priorities will be distributed among thousands of programers, and this knowledge will best be embodied in their programs. Computers are becoming too complex for central planning. . . . It seems that we need to apply 'methods of utilizing more knowledge and resources than any one mind is aware of.' . . . Markets are a form of 'evolutionary eco-system' and such systems can be powerful generators of spontaneous order" (Miller and Drexler, quoted in De Landa, 1991, pp. 121–122.
22 Goshorn, 1992, p. 218.
23 Bechtel and Abrahamsen, 1991, p. 3.
24 This game is based on the behavioral expectations of two prisoners who have been jailed for an assumed crime and who are both offered, in isolation from one another, the following deal: if you tell on your partner in crime, even though he remains silent, you will be released from jail but your partner will receive a long sentence; if you squeal on each other, you will both get moderate sentences; if neither of you talk, your sentences will be short. Obviously, the best solution is to trust in one another's silence. But here the problem begins, for you must trust that your partner won't squeal and won't want you to receive the longest sentence. Therefore, the most "rational" individual decision is to betray your partner.
25 Oser, 1991, sections 10–5, 15.
26 Lucek, 1991, sections 10.1, 6.
27 Perloff, 1991, p. 47.
28 Walter Benjamin commented on this problem years ago when he saw that "the letter and

the word which have rested for centuries in the flatbed of the book's horizontal pages have been wrenched from this position and have been erected on vertical scaffolds in the streets as advertisement" (Benjamin, in Perloff, 1991, p. 93).

29 Perloff, 1991, p. 120.
30 Perloff, 1991, p. 129.
31 Schor, 1987, pp. 63–78.
32 Perloff, 1991, p. 55.
33 Perloff, 1991, p. 87.
34 Perloff, 1991, p. 92.
35 Crapanzo, 1992, pp. 30–32.
36 Lyotard, 1984, pp. 81–82.
37 Terdiman, 1991, p. 117.
38 Dal Co, 1990, p. 55.
39 Huyssen and Bathrick, 1989, p. 14.
40 Quoted in Anderson, p. 142.
41 Quoted in Anderson, p. 152.
42 Williams, 1989, pp. 37–48.
43 Quoted in Stratton, 1990, pp. 313–314.
44 Calvino, 1972, p. 164.
45 Novak in Benedikt, 1992, p. 230.
46 Boigen and Kwinter, 1991, p. 39.
47 For a deeper analysis of the tensions between "pedogogy" and "performance," see Bhaba, 1990, pp. 291–321.
48 Boigon and Kwinter, 1991, p. 40.
49 Mann, 1991, p. 55. Although Boigon and Kwinter proclaim that "pornography is the radical cultural form of our age" (p. 35 n. 8), it can quickly turn into theater and lose its critical edge. Judging from a performance piece by Arthur and Marilouise Kvoker (editors of *Body Invaders: Panic Sex in America.* St Martins Press, 1997), there is obviously a threshold at which saying dirty words in public takes on its own high, when the virtual-pornographic performance eradicates its oppositional claims, when, in other words, any critical stance is destroyed as it tends towards theater.
50 Mann, 1996.
51 Boigon and Kwinter, 1991, p. 40.
52 Boigon and Kwinter, 1991, p. 38 n. 16.
53 Boigon and Kwinter, 1991, p. 37.
54 Boigon and Kwinter, 1991, p. 35.
55 Boigon and Kwinter, 1991, p. 31, 32, 35.
56 Boigon and Kwinter, 1991, p. 32.
57 Boigon and Kwinter, 1991, p. 40.
58 *El Lissitsky*, exhibition catalogue, Eindhoven: Municipal Van Abbemuseum, 1990. pp. 73–74.
59 *El Lissitsky*, exhibition catalogue, Eindhoven: Municipal Van Abbemuseum, 1990. pp. 33.
60 Robbins, 1990, p. 57.
61 Bechtel and Abrahamsen, 1991, pp. 101–103.
62 Clifford, 1986, p. 117
63 Tyler, 1987, p. 37.
64 Boigon and Kwinter, 1991, p. 35.
65 Haraway, 1991, pp. 149–181.
66 Foucault, 1978, pp. 125–126.
67 Cubitt, 1991, p. 178.
68 Cubitt, 1991, pp. 178–179.

Bibliography

Chapter 3 Barcelona – rethinking urbanistic projects

Ajuntament de Barcelona, 1983. *Barcelona: espais i escultures.* Publicacions Ajuntament.
Ajuntament de Barcelona, 1983. *Barcelona. La segona renovació.* Publicacions Ajuntament.
Ajuntament de Barcelona, 1983. *Plans i Projectes 1981–82.* Publicacions Ajuntament.
Ajuntament de Barcelona, 1987. *Barcelona. Plans cap al 92.* Publicacions Ajuntament.
François Ascher, 1999. *Metrópolis, ou l'avenir des villes.* Odile Jacob.
Eve Blau and Monika Platzer, 2000. *L'idée de la grand Ville.* Prestel.
J. Borja, 1989. *El espacio público: ciudad y ciudadanía.* Diputación.
Fernand Braudel, 1972. *The Mediterranean and the Mediterranean World in the age of Philipp II.* University California Press.
Joan Busquets and J. Parcerisa, 1983. Instruments de projectació de la Barcelona suburbana. *Annales ETSAB.*
Joan Busquets and J. L. Gómez Ordóñez, 1983. *Estudi de l'Eixample.* Publicacions Ajuntament.
Joan Busquets, 1992. *Barcelona: Evolución urbanística de una ciudad compacta.* Mapfre.
Joan Busquets *et al.*, 2003 *The Old Town of Barcelona. A Past with a Future.* Publicacions Ajuntament.
Gianfranco Canniga, 1979. *Composizione architettonica e tipologia edilizia.* Cluva.
Ildefonso Cerdà, 1992. *Cerdà y Madrid, Cerdà y Barcelona.* Facsímil. Ajuntament de Barcelona + MOPT.
Ildefonso Cerdà, 1995. *Trabajos sobre Cerdà.* MOPT.
Fabián Estapé, 1971. *Teoría General de la Urbanización.* Instituto Estudios Fiscales.
Fabián Estapé, 1977. *Cerdà 1876–1976: Construcción de la Ciudad.*
Jole Garreau, 1991. *Edge City: Life on the New Frontier.* Doubleday.
David Harvey, 2000. *Spaces of Hope.* University of California Press.
Patsy Healey *et al.*, 1995 *Negotiating Development.* Spon.
Laboratori d'urbanisme, 1978. *Ensanches I y II.* Publicacions UPC.
Laboratori d'urbanisme, 1992. *Trabajos sobre Cerdà y Barcelona.* Ajuntament de Barcelona + MOPT.
Aldo Rossi, 1982. *Architecture of the City.* MIT.

Chapter 4 Scale and monumentality in Brasilia

Robert Alexander, 1991. *Juscelino Kubitschek and the Development of Brazil.* Ohio University Center for International Studies.
Raul de Sá Barbosa. 1960. Brasília. evolução histórica de uma idéia. *Módulo,* 18.
Lucio Costa, 1957. Memória descritiva do Plano Piloto.
Lucio Costa, 1987. *Brasilia Revisitada, 1985/1987.* Photocopy.

Lucio Costa, 1995. Ingredientes da concepção urbanística de Brasília. *Registro de uma vivência.* Empresa das Artes.
Warren Dean, 1987. *Brazil and the Struggle for Rubber.* Cambridge University Press.
Edital do concurso do plano piloto da nova capital do Brasil, 1957. *Brasília*, 3, 20.
William Holford, 1957. Parecer *Arquitetura e Engenharia*, 44.
Oscar Niemeyer, 1960. Minha experiência de Brasilia. *Módulo*, 18.
Osvaldo Peralva, 1988. *Brasília, Patrimônio da Humanidade.* Ministerio da Cultura, Brasilia.
Angelo Pereira, 1946. *Os filhos de el-rei D. João VI.* Empresa Nacional de Publicidade.
Ernesto Silva, 1970. *História de Brasília.* Editora de Brasilia.
Yara Vicentini, 1996. História e cidade na amazônia brasileira: a utopia urbana de Henry Ford, 1930. In: *Cidade, povo e nação: gênese do urbanismo moderno* (Luiz Cesar de Queiroz Ribeiro and Robert Pechman, eds). Civilização Brasileira.

Letters and interviews

Lucio Costa, 1957. Letter to Jayme Maurício. *Correio da Manhã*, 27 March.
Lucio Costa, 1961. Interview by Cláudio Ceccon. *Jornal do Brasil*, 8 November.
Lucio Costa, 1990. Letter to Ítalo Campofiorito, 1 January.
Oscar Niemeyer, 1989. Letter to José Aparecido, 4 October.
Marcelo Roberto, 1957. Interview by Jayme Maurício, *Correio da Manhã*, 24 March.

Chapter 5 Chicago – superblockism: Chicago's elastic grid

James Silk Buckingham, 1842. *The Eastern and Western States of America.* Cited in John Reps, 1965. *The Making of Urban America.* Princeton University Press.
Bureau of Land Management, 1947. *The Manual of Surveying Instructions of 1947* (Washington, D.C.).
Chicago Plan Commission, 1945. *Chicago Looks Ahead: Design for Public Improvements.* Chicago Plan Commission.
Alan Colquhoun. 1971. The Superblock. Republished in Colquhoun, *Essays in Architectural Criticism: Modern Architecture and Historical Change.* The MIT Press.
Carl Condit, 1973. *Chicago: 1910–29.* University of Chicago Press.
Sigfried Giedion, 1944. Need for a New Monumentality. In: Paul Zucker, *New Architecture and City Planning.* Philosophical Library.
Bertrand Goldberg, 1985. Marina City. In: *Goldberg On The City* (Michel Ragon, ed.). Paris Art Center.
Bertrand Goldberg, 1985. The critical mass of urbanism. In: *Goldberg On The City* (Michel Ragon, ed.). Paris Art Center.
Homer Hoyt, 1933. *One Hundred Years of Land Values in Chicago: The Relationship of the Growth of Chicago to the Rise of its Land Values, 1830–1933.* University of Chicago Press.
Jane Jacobs, 1961. *The Death and Life of Great American Cities.* Vintage.
Hildegard Binder Johnson, 1976. *Order Upon the Land: The U.S. Rectangular Land Survey and the Upper Mississippi Country.* Oxford University Press.
Rem Koolhaas, 1984. *Delirious New York.* Monacelli Press.
Katherine Kuh, 1971. *The Open Eye: In Pursuit of Art.* Harper and Rowe.
Phyllis Lambert (ed.), 2001. Bas-Relief Urbanism: Chicago's Figured Field. *Mies in America.* CCA and The Whitney Museum of American Art.
Kevin Pierce, 1998. IIT at a crossroads. *Competitions*, 8(2).
Albert Pope, 1996. *Ladders.* Princeton Architectural Press and Rice School of Architecture.
John W. Reps, 1965. *The Making of Urban America: A History of City Planning in the United States.* Princeton University Press.

Ron Shiffman, 2002. As quoted in A Wellspring of Grief and Hope, Lyne Duke, *Washington Post*, September 9.

Frank Lloyd Wright, 1901. Home in a prairie town. *Ladies Home Journal*, February, 18.

Alfred B. Yeomans, 1916. *City Residential Land Development: Studies in Planning*. University of Chicago Press.

Chapter 6 Detroit – Motor City

Michel De Certeau, 1984. *The Practice of Everyday Life*. University of California Press.

Ze'ev Chafets, 1990. *Devil's Night: And Other True Tales of Detroit*. Random House.

Chicago Tribune, 2000. Census should show if Detroit is successful in its comeback. June 5, pp. A1, 10.

Detroit Vacant Land Survey, 1990. City of Detroit City Planning Commission, August 24.

The Economist, 1993. Day of the Bulldozer. May 8

Michael Hays, 1995. *Modernism and the Posthumanist Subject*. MIT Press.

Jerry Herron, 1993. *AfterCulture: Detroit and the Humiliation of History*. Wayne State University Press.

Ludwig Hilberseimer, 1945. Cities and Defense, 1945. Reprinted in: *In the Shadow of Mies: Ludwig Hilberseimer, Architect, Educator, and Urban Planner*. Richard Plommer, David Spaeth, and Kevin Harrington (eds.). Rizzoli/Art Institute of Chicago.

Ludwig Hilberseimer, 1949. *The New Regional Pattern*. Paul Theobald & Co.

Dan Hoffman, 2001a. Erasing Detroit. In: *Stalking Detroit*, pp. 100–103. ACTAR.

Dan Hoffman, 2001b. The best the world has to offer. In: *Stalking Detroit*, pp. 48–56. ACTAR.

Sanford Kwinter, 1994. Mies and movement: military logistics and molecular regimes. In: *The Presence of Mies* (Detlef Mertins, ed.). Princeton Architectural Press.

Sanford Kwinter and Daniela Fabricius, 2000. Contract with America. In: *Mutations*, p. 600. ACTAR.

Metropolis, 1998. Dismantling the Motor City. June.

Richard Pommer, David Spaeth and Kevin Harrington (eds), 1988. *In the Shadow of Mies: Ludwig Hilberseimer, Architect, Educator, and Urban Planner*. Rizzoli/Art Institute of Chicago.

Witold Rybczynski, 1995. The zero density neighborhood. *Detroit Free Press Sunday Magazine*, October 29

Joseph Rykwert, 1988. *The Idea of a Town: An Anthropology of Urban Form in Rome, Italy and the Ancient World*. MIT Press.

Patrick Schumacher and Christian Rogner, 2001. After Ford. In: *Stalking Detroit*, pp. 48–56. ACTAR.

Thomas Sugrue, 1996. *The Origins of the Urban Crisis*. Princeton University Press.

Andrey Tarkovsky, 1986. *Sculpting in Time: Reflections on the Cinema*. The Bodley Head.

Paul Virilio, 1986. Overexposed city. *Zone*, 1–2.

Charles Waldheim, Jason Young and Georgia Daskalakis, 2001. *Stalking Detroit*. ACTAR.

Chapter 7 Los Angeles – between cognitive mapping and dirty realism

Theodor W. Adorno and Max Horkheimer, 1994. *Dialectic of Enlightenment*. Continuum.

Stephanie Barron and Sabine Eckmann, 1998. *Exiles + Emigrés: The Flight of European Artists from Hitler* Los Angeles County Museum of Art.

Jean Baudrillard, 1984, Precession of the Simulacra. In: *Art After Modernism: Rethinking Representation* (Brian Wallis, ed.), New Museum of Contemporary Art.

Jean Baudrillard, 1987. Forget Baudrillard: an interview with Sylvère Lotringer. *Forget Foucault.* Semiotext(e).

Marco Cenzatti, 1993. *Los Angeles and the L.A. School: Postmodernism and Urban Studies.* Los Angeles Forum for Architecture and Urban Studies.

Dana Cuff, 2000. *The Provisional City: Los Angeles Stories of Architecture and Urbanism.* MIT Press.

Mike Davis, 1990. *City of Quartz: Excavating the Future in Los Angeles.* Vintage Books.

Mike Davis, 1998. *Ecology of Fear: Los Angeles and the Imagination of Disaster,* Metropolitan Books.

Michael J. Dear, H. Eric Schockman and Greg Hise, 1996. Preface. *Rethinking Los Angeles.* Sage Publications.

Stephen Dobney, 1997. *The Master of Architect Series III: Johnson Fain Partners: Selected and Current Works* The Images Publishing Group.

Umberto Eco, 1987. *Travels in Hyperreality.* Picador.

Nan Ellin, 1999. *Postmodern Urbanism* Princeton Architectural Press.

Robert M. Fogelson, 1967. *The Fragmented Metropolis: Los Angeles, 1850–1930.* University of California Press.

Hal Foster, 1996. *The Return of the Red: the Avant-garde at the End of the Century.* MIT Press.

Michel Foucault, 1993. Of Other Spaces: Utopias and heterotopias. In: *Architecture Culture 1943–1968: A Documentary Anthology* (Joan Ockman and Edward Eigen, eds). Rizzoli Press.

William Fulton, 2001. *The Reluctant Metropolis: The Politics of Urban Growth in Los Angeles.* Johns Hopkins University Press.

Mario Gandelsonas, 1996. X-*Urbanism: Architecture and the American City.* Princeton Architectural Press.

Sir Peter Hall, 1998. *Cities in Civilization.* Pantheon.

Dolores Hayden, 1995. *The Power of Place: Urban Landscapes as Public History.* MIT Press.

Anthony Heilbut, 1998. *Exiled in Paradise: German Refuge Artists and Intellectuals in America from the 1930s to the Present.* Viking.

Greg Hise and William Deverell, 2000. Preface to the Master Plan. *Eden by Design: The 1930 Olmsted–Bartholomew Plan for the Los Angeles Region.* University of California Press.

Catherine Ingraham, 1998. *Architecture and The Burdens of Linearity.* Yale University Press.

Frederic Jameson, 1988. Cognitive Mapping. In: *Marxism and the Interpretation of Culture* (Cary Nelson and Lawrence Grossberg, eds). University of Illinois Press.

Frederic Jameson, 1991. Postmodernism or, The Cultural Logic of Late Capitalism. In: *Postmodernism or, The Cultural Logic of Late Capitalism.* Duke University Press.

Frederic Jameson, 1994. *The Seeds of Time.* Columbia University Press.

Charles Jencks, 1993. *Heteropolis: Los Angeles, the Riots, and the Strange Beauty of Hetero-Architecture.* Academy Editions.

Norman Klein, 1997. *The History of Forgetting: Los Angeles and the Erasure of Memory.* Verso.

Richard Lehan, 1998. *The City in Literature: An Intellectual and Cultural History* University of California Press.

Jean-François Lyotard, 1984. Foreword. In: *The Postmodern Condition: A Report on Knowledge* (trans. Geoff Bennington and Brian Masumi). University of Minnesota Press.

John McPhee, 1989. Los Angeles against the mountains. *The Control of Nature.* Farrar, Strauss, and Giroux.

Carry McWilliams, 1946. *Southern California: An Island on the Land.* Gibbs Smith.

Elizabeth Moule and Stefanos Polyzoides, 1994. Five Los Angeleses. In: *World Cities: Los Angeles* (Maggie Toy, ed.) Academy Editions.

Office for Metropolitan Architecture, Rem Koolhaas and Bruce Mau, 1995. *Small, Medium, Large, Extra Large* (Jennifer Sigler, ed.). Monacelli Press.

Leonard and Dale Pitt, 1997. *Los Angeles: A to Z: An Encyclopedia of the City and County.* University of California Press.

Thomas Pynchon, 1965. *The Crying of Lot 49.* Lippincott.

Dagmar Richter, 1991. Reading Los Angeles: a primitive rebel's account. *Assemblage* 14, MIT Press.

Colin Rowe and Fred Koetter, 1975. *Collage City.* MIT Press.

Charles G. Salas and Michael S. Roth, 2001. *Looking for Los Angeles: Architecture, Film, Photography, and the Urban Landscape.* The Getty Research institute.

Allen J. Scott and Edward W. Soja, 1996. Introduction to Los Angeles. In: *The City: Los Angeles and Urban Theory at the End of the Twentieth Century.* University of California Press.

Edward Soja, 1989. *Postmodern Geographies: The Reassertion of Space in Critical Social Theory.* Verso.

Edward Soja, 1996. *Thirdspace: Journeys to Los Angeles and Other Real-and-Imagined Places.* Blackwell.

Michael Sorkin, 1992. *Variations on a Theme Park: the New American City and the End of Public Space.* Hill and Wang.

Douglas R. Suisman, 1989. *Los Angeles Boulevard: Eight X-rays of the Body Public.* Los Angeles Forum for Architecture and Urban Design.

Douglas R. Suisman, 1992. *Wilshire Boulevard, L.A.* Casabella.

Roemer van Toom, 1999. Architecture Against Architecture: Radical Criticism Within the Society of the Spectacle. *Ctheory* (Arthur and Marilouise Kroker, eds). www.ctheory.net/text.file?pick=94.

Kazys Varnelis, 2003. Los Angeles, Cluster City. In: *Future: City* (Jürgen Rosemann, Stephen Read and Job van Eldijk, eds). Routledge.

Chapter 8 Philadelphia – the urban design of Philadelphia: taking the towne for the city

American Planning and Civic Association, 1953. *American Planning and Civic Annual.* American Planning and Civic Association.

Edmund Bacon, 1950. Highway development related to land use in an urban area. *Spencer Miller Lecture Series: Landscape Design and its Relation to the Modern Highway.* New Jersey Roadside Council/Rutgers University.

Edmund Bacon, 1974. *Design of Cities.* Penguin Books.

Jonathan Barnett and Nory Miller, 1983. Edmund Bacon: a retrospective. *Planning,* Dec.

John F. Bauman, 1983. Visions of a post-War city: a perspective on urban planning in Philadelphia and the Nation, 1942–1945. In: *Introduction to Planning History in the United States.* Rutgers University Press.

Edwin Bronner, 1962. *William Penn's "Holy Experiments."* Temple University Press.

David Clow, 1989. *House Divided: Philadelphia's Controversial Crosstown Expressway.* Society for American City and Regional Planning History.

Jack P. Green, 1993. *The Intellectual Construction of America: Exceptionalism and Identity from 1492–1800.* University of North Carolina Press.

Constance M. Greiff, 1987. *Independence: The Creation of a National Park.* University of Pennsylvania Press.

Samuel Hazard (ed.), 1850. William Penn's Instructions to Commissioners. In: *Annals of Pennsylvania from the Discovery of the Delaware* 1609–1682. Hazard and Mitchell.

Franz Kafka. *The Castle.*

Amy E. Menzer, 1999. Exhibiting Philadelphia's "Vital Center:" negotiating environmental and civic reform in a popular post-War planning vision. *Radical History Review*, 74.

Albert C. Meyers (ed.), 1912. Letter from William Penn to the Committee of The Free Society of Traders, 1683: A Short Advertisement of the City of Philadelphia and the Ensuing Plat-form thereof, by the Surveyor General. In: *Narratives of Early Pennsylvania, West New Jersey and Delaware 1630–1707.* Charles Scribner & Sons.

Lewis Mumford, 1957. The skyline: Philadelphia – II. *New Yorker*, 9 Feb.

National Park Service, 1994. *Cultural Landscape Report: Independence Mall, Independence National Historic Park.* US Dept of the Interior.

Philadelphia plans again. *Architectural Forum*, 1947.

John W. Reps, 1965. *The Making of Urban America: A History of City Planning in the United States.* Princeton University Press.

Arthur Schlesinger, 1949. *The Vital Center: The Politics of Freedom.* Houghton Mifflin Co.

Neil Smith, 1996. *The New Urban Frontier: Gentrification and the Revanchist City.* Routledge.

Sam Bass Warner, 1987. *The Private City: Philadelphia in Three Periods of its Growth*, 2nd edn.

Chapter 10 Asian megacities

Asia Development Bank, 1997. The Asia Development Bank on Asia's megacities. *Population and Development Review*, 23(2).

R. Banham, 2001. *Los Angeles: The Architecture of Four Ecologies.* University of California Press.

Demographia, 2001. http://www.demographia.com/db-world-metro2000.htm, accessed January 24, 2002.

A. Duany, Plater-Zyberk, E. and Speck, J., 2000, *Suburban Nation – The rise of Sprawl and the Decline of the American Dream.* North Point Press.

D. Forbes, 1999. Globalization, postcolonialism and new representations of the Pacific Asian metropolis. In: *Globalization and the Asia-Pacific* (K. Olds *et al.*, eds), pp. 238–254. Routledge.

D. Forbes and Thrift, N., 1987. Regional integration, internationalisation and the new geographies of the Pacific Rim. In: *Asia Pacific: New Geographies of the Pacific Rim* (R. Watters and T. McGee, eds). C. Hurst.

J. Friedmann, 1986. The world city hypothesis. *Development and Change*, 17(1), 69–84.

N. Ginsburg, Koppel, B. and McGee, T. (eds), 1991. *The Extended Metropolis: Settlement Transition in Asia.* University of Hawaii Press.

P. Hall, 1998. Cities in Civilization: Culture, Innovation and Urban Order. Weidenfeld and Nicolson.

Jakarta Post, 1996. Integrate a "green GDP" into development: scholar. 26 December.

Rem Koolhaas, 1977. "Life in the Metropolis" or "The culture of congestion." Architectural Design 47, no. 5. In: *Architectural Theory Since 1968* (M. Hays, ed.). MIT Press.

Rem Koolhaas, 1978. *Delirious New York: A Retroactive Manifesto for Manhattan.* Oxford University Press.

H. Lefebvre, 1996. *Writings on Cities.* Blackwell Press.

G. C. S. Lin, 1994. Changing theoretical perspectives on urbanization in Asian developing countries. *Third World Planning Review* 16(1).

F. C. Lo and Yeung, Y. M. (eds), 1996. *Emerging World Cities in Pacific Asia.* United Nations University Press.

S. Macleod and McGee, T., 1996. The Singapore–Johore–Riau growth triangle: an emerging metropolitan region. In: *Emerging World Cities in Pacific Asia* (F. C. Lo and Y. M. Yeung, eds). United Nations University Press.

T. McGee and Robinson, I. (eds), 1995. *The Mega-Urban Regions of Southeast Asia.* University of British Columbia Press.

R. Marshall, 2002. *Emerging Urbanity – Global Urban Projects in the Asia Pacific Rim.* Spon Press.

M. Perry, 1998. The Singapore growth triangle in the global and local economy. In: *The Naga Awakens: Growth and Change in Southeast Asia* (V. R. Savage, L. Kong and W. Neville, eds), pp. 87–112. Times Academic Press.

P. Rowe, 2001. A difference of degree or a difference in kind: hyperdensity in Hong Kong. In: *Hong Kong: Defining the Edge* (J. Brown, E. Mossop and R. Marshall, eds), pp. 14–39. Harvard University Graduate School of Design.

D. Sudjik, 1993. Bangkok's instant city. *Blueprint,* 99, 19.

United Nations Department of Economics and Social Affairs, 1998. *World Urbanization Prospects: The 1996 Revision.* United Nations.

Paul Virilio, 1986. *The Overexposed City,* from *L'espace critique* in *ZONE 1–2,* 1986. In: K. Michael Hays (ed.) 1998. *Architecture Theory Since 1968.* MIT Press.

World Bank, 1993. *The East Asian Miracle: Economic Growth and Public Policy.* Oxford University Press.

Chapter 11 New urbanism

Bengt Anderson, 2001. Making territory in urban America: New Urbanism and Kentlands. In: *Hovedfagsstudentenes Årbok.* Årbokredaksjonen.

Zymnut Bauman, 1999. *In Search of Politics.* Stanford University Press.

Thomas Bender, 1982. *Community and Social Change in America.* Johns Hopkins University Press.

Stephanie Bothwell, 2000. Six. In: *Charter of the New Urbanism.* McGraw-Hill.

Peter Calthorpe, 2000. One. In: *Charter of the New Urbanism.* McGraw-Hill.

Robert Cervero, 1996. *Subcentering and Commuting: Evidence from the San Francisco Bay Area, 1980–1990.* University of California Transportation Center.

Charter of the New Urbanism, 2000. McGraw-Hill.

John Chase, Margaret Crawford and John Kaliski, eds, 1999. Monacelli Press.

Gordon Cullen, 1968. *Townscape.* Reinhold.

James Donald, 1997. Imagining the modern city. In: *Imagining Cities: Scripts, Signs, Memory* (Sallie Westwood and John Williams, eds). Routledge.

Andres Duany, 1997. Quoted in: Urban or suburban: a discussion at the GSD. *Harvard Design Magazine.*

Andres Duany and Elizabeth Plater-Zybek, 1992. The second coming of the American small town. *The Wilson Quarterly,* 16(1).

Andres Duany and Elizabeth Plater-Zybek, 1994. The neighborhood, the district and the corridor. In: *The New Urbanism* (Peter Katz, ed.), pp. xvii–xx. McGraw-Hill.

Andres Duany and Emily Talen, 2002. Transect planning. APA Journal, Summer, 68 (3).

John A. Dutton, 2000. *New American Urbanism: Re-forming the Suburban Metropolis.* Abbeville Pub. Group/Thames & Hudson.

Frederich Engels, 1967. *Engels: Selected Writings.* Penguin Books.

Gerald Frug, 1997. Urban or Suburban? A Discussion. Harvard Design Magazine, Winter/Spring.

Patrick Geddes, 1968 [1915]. *Cities in Evolution.* Ernest Benn.

Miles Glendinning and Stefan Muthesius, 1994. *Tower Block: Modern Public Housing in England, Scotland, Wales and Northern Ireland.* Yale University Press.

Peter Hall, 1988. *Cities of Tomorrow.* Basil Blackwell.

David Harvey, 1996. *Justice, Nature and the Geography of Difference.* Oxford University Press.

David Harvey, 2000. *Spaces of Hope.* University of California Press.

Werner Hegemann and Elbert Peets, 1992. *The American Vitruvius: an Architects' Handbook of Civic Art.* The Architectural Book Publishing Co.

Ebenezar Howard, 1898. *Garden Cities of Tomorrow.* Faber.

Jane Jacob, 1961. *The Death and Life of Great American Cities.* Random House.

Samuel Kingsley, 1880. *Sanitary and Social Lectures and Essays.*

Alex Krieger, 1991. Since (and before) seaside. In: *Towns and Town-Making Principles* (A. Duany and E. Palter-Zybek, eds). Rizzoli

Leon Krier, 1991. Afterword. In: *Towns and Town-Making Principles* (A. Duany and E. Palter-Zybek, eds). Rizzoli.

James Kunstler, 1993. *The Geography of Nowhere.* Simon & Schuster.

William Lennertz , 1991. Town-making principles. In: *Towns and Town-Making Principles* (A. Duany and E. Palter-Zybek, eds). Rizzoli.

Dean MacCannell, 1999, "New Urbanism" and Its Discontents. In: *Giving Ground: The Politics of Propinquity* (J. Copjec and M. Sorkin, eds). Verso.

John O. Norquist, 1999. *The Wealth of Cities: Revitalizing the Centers of American Life.* Addison Wesley.

Clarence Arthur Perry, 1929. The neighborhood unit: a scheme of arrangement for the family-life community. *Neighborhood and Community Planning, Monograph One.* New York Regional Plan Association.

Edward Robbins, 1997. The New Urbanism, unkept promise. *Harvard Design Magazine,* Winter/Spring.

Edward Robbins, 1998. The New Urbanism and the fallacy of singularity. *Urban Design International,* 3(1).

Edward Robbins, 2000. Can/should designers foster community? *Designer/Builder,* March.

Vincent Scully, 1994. Architecture of community. In: *The New Urbanism* (P. Katz, ed.), pp. 221–230. McGraw-Hill.

José Luís Sert, 1933. The Town Planning Charter, Fourth CIMA Congress, Athens, 1933. *Can Our Cities Survive.* Harvard University Press.

Daniel Solomon, 2000. Nineteen. In: *Charter of the New Urbanism.* McGraw-Hill.

Michael Southworth, 1997. *Streets and the Shaping of Towns and Cities.* McGraw-Hill.

Raymond Unwin, 1909. *Town Planning in Practice* (reprinted 1994). Princeton Architectural Press.

Urban Land Institute, 1985. *Shopping Center Development Handbook.*

Robert Venturi and Denise Scott Brown, 1977. *Learning from Las Vegas: the Forgotten Symbolism of Architectural Form.* MIT Press.

Anthony Vidler, 1978. The scenes from the street: transformations of ideal and reality, 1750–1871. In: *On Streets* (S. Anderson, ed.), pp. 29–112. MIT Press.

Gwendolyn Wright, 1981. *Building the Dream: A Social History of Housing in America.* Pantheon.

Chapter 12 The Imaginary Real World of CyberCities

Mark Anderson. "Katka and New York: Notes on a traveling narrative," in *Modernity and the Text.*

William Bechtel and Adele Abrahamsen, 1991. *Connectionism and the Mind: An Introduction to Parallel Processing in Networks.* Basil Blackwell.

Michael Benedikt (ed), 1992. *Cyberspace: First Steps* MIT Press.

Homi K. Bhaba, 1990. "DissemiNation," in *Nation and Narration,* Homi K. Bhaba (ed.), Routledge.

Homi K. Bhaba, 1991. "Race", time and the revision of modernity. *The Oxford Literary Review,* 13(1–2).

Brian Boigon and Sanford Kwinter, 1991. Manual for 5 Appliances in the Alphabetical City: A Pedagogical Text. *Assemblage* 15.

M. Christine Boyer, 1983. *Dreaming the Rational City: The Myth of American City Planning 1893–1945.* MIT Press.

Italo Calvino, 1972. *Invisible Cities* (trans. William Weaver). Harcourt Brace Jovanovich.

James Clifford, 1986. "On ethnographic allegory," in *Writing Culture,* James Clifford (ed.), University of Wisconsin Press.

Vincent Crapanzano, 1992. *Hermes' Dilemma and Hamlet's Desire.* Harvard University Press.

Sean Cubitt, 1991. *Timeshift: On Video Culture.* Routledge.

Francesco Dal Co., 1990. *Figures of Architecture and Thought.* Rizzoli.

Gilles Deleuze, 1992. Postscript on societies of control. *October, 59.*

Celia W. Dugger, 1991. A Neighborhood struggles with despair, *New York Times,* 5 November, A1, B2.

François Ewald, 1992. A power without an exterior. In: *Michel Foucault Philosopher.* Routledge.

Michael Foucault, 1978. *The History of Sexuality,* vol. 1. *An Introduction,* Pantheon Books.

William Gibson, 1984. *Neuromancer.* Ace Books.

A. Keith Goshorn, 1992. "Jean baudrillard's Radical Enigma," in *Jean Baudrillard: The Disappearance of Art and Politics.* ((William Strearns and William Chaloupka, eds). St. Martin's Press.

Donna Haraway, 1991. "A Cyborg Manifesto," in *Simians, Cyborgs, and Women,* Routledge.

David Harvey, 1989. *The Condition of Postmodernity.* Basil Blackwell.

Charles W. Haxthausen, 1990. A New Beauty: Ernst Ludwig Kirchner's images of Berlin. In: *Berlin Culture and Metropolis.* Charles W. Haxthausen and Heidrun Suhr, eds).University of Minnesota Press.

Michael Heim, The erotic ontology of cyberspace. *Cyberspace.*

Michael Heim. The erotic ontology of cyberspace. In: *Cyberspace: First Steps* (M. Benedikt, ed.) MIT Press.

Andreas Huyssen and David Bathrick, 1989. Modernism and the experience of modernism," in *Modernity and the Text: Revisions of German Modernism* Andreas Huyssen and David Bathrick (eds) Columbia University Press.

Fredric Jameson, 1991. *Postmodernism, or, The Cultural Logic of Late Capitalism.* Duke University Press.

Manuel de Landa, 1991. *War in the Age of Intelligent Machines.* Zone Books.

Alan Liu, 1990. Local transcendence: cultural criticism, postmodernism, and the romanticism of detail. *Representations, 32.*

Karen Lucie, 1991. *Charles Sheeler and the Cult of the Machine.* Harvard University Press.

Thomas J. Lueek, 1991. Times for a change in builder incentives?" *New York Times,* 8 December.

Jean-François Lyotard, 1984. *The Postmodern Condition: A Report on Knowledge.* University of Minnesota Press.

Paul Mann, 1991. *The Theory-Death of the Avant-Garde,* Indiana University Press.

Alison Mitchell, 1992. "Euphoria is scarce as Dinkins loosens fiscal belt," *New York Times,* 26 April.

Alan Oser, 1991. "Banding together for local betterment," *New York Times,* 10 February.

Marjorie Perloff, 1991. *Radical Artifice: Writing Poetry in the Age of Media.* University of Chicago Press.

David Robbins, (ed.) 1990. *The Independent Group: Postwar Britain and the Aesthetics of Plenty.* MIT Press.

Naomi Schor, 1987. *Reading in detail: Aesthetics and the Feminine.* Methuen.

Edward Soja, 1989. *Postmodern Geographies: The Reassertion of Space in Critical Social Theory.* Verso Press.

Quoted in Jon Stratton, 1990. *Writing Sites.* University of Michigan Press.

Richard Terdiman, 1991. "On the dialectics of postdialectical thinking." in *Community at Loose Ends.* Miami Theory Collective (ed.) University of Minnesota Press.

Stephen Tyler, 1987. *The Unspeakable Discourse, Dialogue, and Rhetoric in the Postmodern World.* University of Wisconsin Press.

Raymond Williams, 1989. "Metropolitan perceptions and the emergence of modernism," in *The Politics of Modernism.* Verso Press.

Sharon Willis, 1989. Seductive spaces. In *Seduction and Theory: Readings of Gender, Representation, and Rhetoric.* (Diane Hunter ed., University of Illinois Press.

Index

Note: page numbers in *italics* denote illustrations